The five societies

Face Values

Face Values

Some anthropological themes

by Anne Sutherland

with contributions from

Jeremy Boissevain
Patricia Caplan
Anthony Forge
Jean La Fontaine
Terence Turner

Edited by Anne Sutherland

with a Preface by HRH The Prince of Wales
Patron of the Royal Anthropological Institute

British Broadcasting Corporation

This book accompanies the BBC Television series *Face Values*, first broadcast on BBC 1 at 10.10 p.m. starting Thursday 13 April 1978

Published to accompany a series of programmes prepared in consultation with the BBC Further Education Advisory Council by the British Broadcasting Corporation
35 Marylebone High Street, London W1M 4AA
ISBN 0 563 16102 7
First published 1978

Printed in England by Jolly & Barber Ltd, Rugby and bound by Webb Son and Co. Ltd.
This book is set in Monotype 11/13 pt Baskerville.

This book, like the Television series to which it is linked, has been produced as part of a collaborative project between the BBC and the Royal Anthropological Institute. The aim of both is to explore the nature and meaning of human differences.

Various anthropological films have been shown on television, but these have mainly been 'descriptive ethnographies' focusing on one particular society. This BBC/RAI project has sought to build on this experience by introducing a new, and perhaps more difficult method, that of comparison. Taking as our starting point some ideas suggested by E. R. Leach, we have gathered film material from five contrasting societies, and have, in the programmes, compared some of the symbols that all peoples think of as 'natural', but which in fact communicate social meaning. 'Natural' symbols such as space, gender, or the human body, express different social ideas for different peoples, in ritual as well as everyday life. This book develops the ideas of the series more systematically, and provides more detailed accounts of these societies by the anthropologists who studied and filmed them.

The series is produced by David Cordingley, working in collaboration with the RAI consultant Jean La Fontaine. Anne Sutherland, the book editor, also worked on the production of the series, and the other anthropologists who have contributed to the book also gave advice on the societies they have studied.

Contents

Preface

by HRH The Prince of Wales

This book on anthropology is really the result of a rash statement I made at a dinner I attended in 1973 upon assuming office as Patron of the Royal Anthropological Institute. I remember at the time there was considerable anxiety about the future of the Institute and I was keen to see its continuation as a learned body, the preservation of its library and the dissemination of its ideas and knowledge to a much wider audience. With supreme disregard for the dictates of caution and diplomacy I urged that a great deal of good could be achieved by well-made films, primarily in order to explain to people living in this country the reasons for our behaviour and to show the similarities that exist even in the apparent differences between ourselves and other races. My belief rested on the feeling that if only more people could have the advantage of information and knowledge about other people's social behaviour, customs, religion and so forth, then perhaps *some* of the prejudice against immigrant groups in this country might be slowly reduced.

To my amazement, the BBC took me up on this basic and rash remark, offering to make a series of anthropological films for television which would attempt, as it were, to popularise anthropology to the extent that it could be shown how the study of man has very definite advantages for us all and that we stand to gain something if we begin to try and understand the meaning of our behaviour patterns and the origins of our social system. The best way to do this, of course, is to have a look at the way people from other societies react to life and how similar their responses are, despite the apparent differences caused by a variation in emphasis on such things as morality or religion.

This book has been written as a result of the television series and is designed to give further information that cannot be fitted into the films. I do sincerely hope that it will help to show the infinite variety of ways of being human and that *some* greater understanding and tolerance of one another's attitudes, responses and beliefs will eventually be forthcoming.

Introduction

by Jean La Fontaine

Man is a self-conscious animal. The mental world of all human beings includes beliefs and theories about how they are different from other living creatures. Ever since the Greeks, and probably before them, although we have few records from those early times, people have thought about themselves and speculated on what is the essence of humanity. So anthropology is part of an intellectual tradition that is nearly as old and as widespread as mankind itself. It includes history, human biology, theology and the more specialised modern subjects like sociology and political science. All these branches of knowledge have common origins; each is founded on the investigation of one strand of a complex phenomenon: the varieties of human modes of life. Each subject approaches the study of man from a different angle and uses different methods. Anthropology, like sociology, is concerned with social life; unlike sociology however, it concerns itself with all varieties of social arrangements. Its characteristic method is comparison; the systematic investigation of different societies in order to discover what common features lie behind the bewildering variety of ideas and behaviour to be found all over the world.

The basis for what is generally called anthropology, but should properly be called social anthropology, is its concern with the social nature of human beings. The fundamental assumption is that human nature is determined by the fact that we are social beings whose survival has depended on the permanent existence of groups rather than individual members of the species. Of course there are social animals as well: gazelles, lions, apes and monkeys are some of these and their social life, when we know more about it, may provide us with a sharpened awareness of how human and animal social life resemble each other or differ. However, human social life is embedded in language rather than being closely tied to instinctual behaviour. All peoples, whatever the particular characteristics of their society, teach their young the language, ideas and behaviour they will need to function as adult members of the group. Thus social life can be equated with a body of knowledge, with language and tradition and so distinguished from man's physical being. The human infant must develop both physically and socially; babies must be socialized as they mature. Much of this process is not a matter of conscious teaching but of the development of ways of behaving which seem natural, since they are not a matter of conscious choice.

The fact that our social life is second nature to us, presents anthropology with one of its major problems. In order to live in a society, the individual members of it acquire ideas of what social life is; they have conceptions of what order is, what different social relations should be, how individuals in certain positions should behave and numerous deep-seated beliefs about how they, as a group, differ from others. Just as we are not conscious of a language's structure when we speak it, so we are not aware of the underlying structure of the social life we live, even though in both cases part of the pattern, the grammar so to speak, is explicit and can be expressed as rules. The rest of the pattern is implicit, embedded in how we view the world and in what we see as human nature.

Every one of us, then, is, in one sense, an anthropologist. We have a view of social life constructed from basic assumptions and knowledge that we have acquired by living a social life. But the social life of one community is not social life in general, merely a particular form of it. We know, not society but *a* society or a part of one society, and our everyday views of what social life is are entirely coloured by our experience of one form of it. All peoples have deep convictions that the way they live is natural and proper and that others are in some sense unnatural or peculiar. Such ideas predispose us to see the world in a distorting mirror, the distortions being produced by the very characteristics we are trying to study, the fact that we are deeply social.

One of the central problems of anthropology becomes just this quest for objectivity. How can we understand other societies if our ideas, the tools of our trade, are shaped by one society? The problem can be compared with the problem of translating ideas from one language into another, although it goes deeper than that. The structure and vocabulary of a language cuts up the world in a particular way, making distinctions and classifications which are not identical to the divisions made by another language. In order to translate French into English it may be necessary to use several words where French uses one; an exact equivalent may be hard to find, for the vocabulary of one language represents divisions into separate ideas which may not be the same in other languages. The French – *marcher* and *aller à pied* – can both be translated 'to walk'; but the former refers to the physical action, the latter contrasts the means of going with, say, going by car. The English phrase 'to go on foot' has slightly different connotations although it is a literal translation of *aller à pied*, just as the French *se promener* has the connotation of a stroll in public while the English 'to go for a walk' implies healthy exercise. There are words and phrases in French which seem to be virtually untranslatable, for they refer to ideas which are quite foreign to English. Languages are often enriched by adopting untranslatable words from each other; thus we have gained 'chic' while the French speak of 'le weekend' (though not without some disapproval from the purists of the Académie Française).

We translate one language into another on the assumption that there are some fundamental similarities in all languages, that they reflect thought processes that are broadly similar. If they were not, then not only would languages be untranslatable, but no communication between speakers of different languages would ever be possible. This sometimes seems to be the case where members of different societies confront each other, for the social attitudes with which we are imbued are often diffuse, not easily expressed in words and so rarely made explicit that they are not easily recognised as such. There is a good example of the difficulties involved if we consider a fundamental institution of social life, the family.

In Britain, most people consider that the family of mother, father and children is a natural group established by the biological ties between parents and their offspring. The special terms we use emphasise this for they mark off certain relations as unique. We also think that wider family ties are just the result of successive generations of children being born, growing up and establishing their own families. The ties between them are seen as 'natural'. This makes it difficult to understand other people whose ideas on this subject are rather different. Yet all societies believe that relatedness is the result of marriage and birth, of biology. Human biology and physiology is the same everywhere but the way people regard family relations varies so that biology cannot be the determining factor. These relationships are social, not natural.

The Gisu people I worked among found it strange that in English there is only one word, uncle, for father's brother and mother's brother. 'Can't you see' I was told 'they are quite different? The father's brother is much closer than the mother's brother because hs shares the same blood with you'. This man was saying that biology, as the Gisu see it, determines such relations. He clearly thought the English very ignorant about the facts of life.

But, it might be said, we are scientific; so if our ideas of family relationships fit with scientific ideas they must be right. However, historical research has shown that our ideas about family relations existed long before science demonstrated the mechanisms of reproduction. So our ideas on this matter are no more scientific than those of the Gisu. Indeed we use 'uncle' to refer to men who are quite unrelated by blood; the husbands of our parents' sisters. This English term mixes up blood-kin and in-laws in a way that other peoples would consider extraordinary.

This discussion shows how the ideas our own society endows us with, colour our view of what the world is like. It is a discussion which teachers of anthropology regularly have with students in order to show them how they derive their ideas from the society they live in. It also shows that the anthropologists views are rather different from the views held by other members of their own societies.

To some extent then, anthropologists are professional outsiders. They are committed to an attempt to disengage their ideas from the social bias they know they must have. The stages of anthropology's development can be seen as the progressive abandonment of ideas that were crudely shaped by the social setting of their time. Indeed, the history of anthropology can in some ways be seen as a struggle to reach an objective answer to the question: What is Man? The development of anthropology, which has, until recently, taken place in Western Europe has accompanied Europe's progressively greater involvement with the rest of the world. Today we live in one world, involved inextricably with one another and the expansion which has brought this about has resulted both in the accumulation of knowledge of other ways of life and a deepening interest in the similarities and differences among peoples. Some people would claim that anthropology is merely the reflection of the political and economic expansion of western Europe and America, that it is an intellectual prop of imperialism. While it is true that the theories of anthropologists, like those of others, have often appeared to confirm the prejudices which assert the superiority of a particular society or type of society, I believe this is too simple a view. Anthropology has developed through the conflict of ideas as much as through the simple matching of hypotheses against the available evidence and every epoch has produced competing interpretations of the evidence. Having said that, I am going to discuss the development of anthropological ideas as though there were, indeed, a dominant idea characteristic of each broad historical phase. The reader should bear in mind though, that I am only discussing dominant ideas and ideas which still have some importance today.

Although I have claimed a much more ancient origin for the study of man, it is convenient to begin about two hundred years ago with the

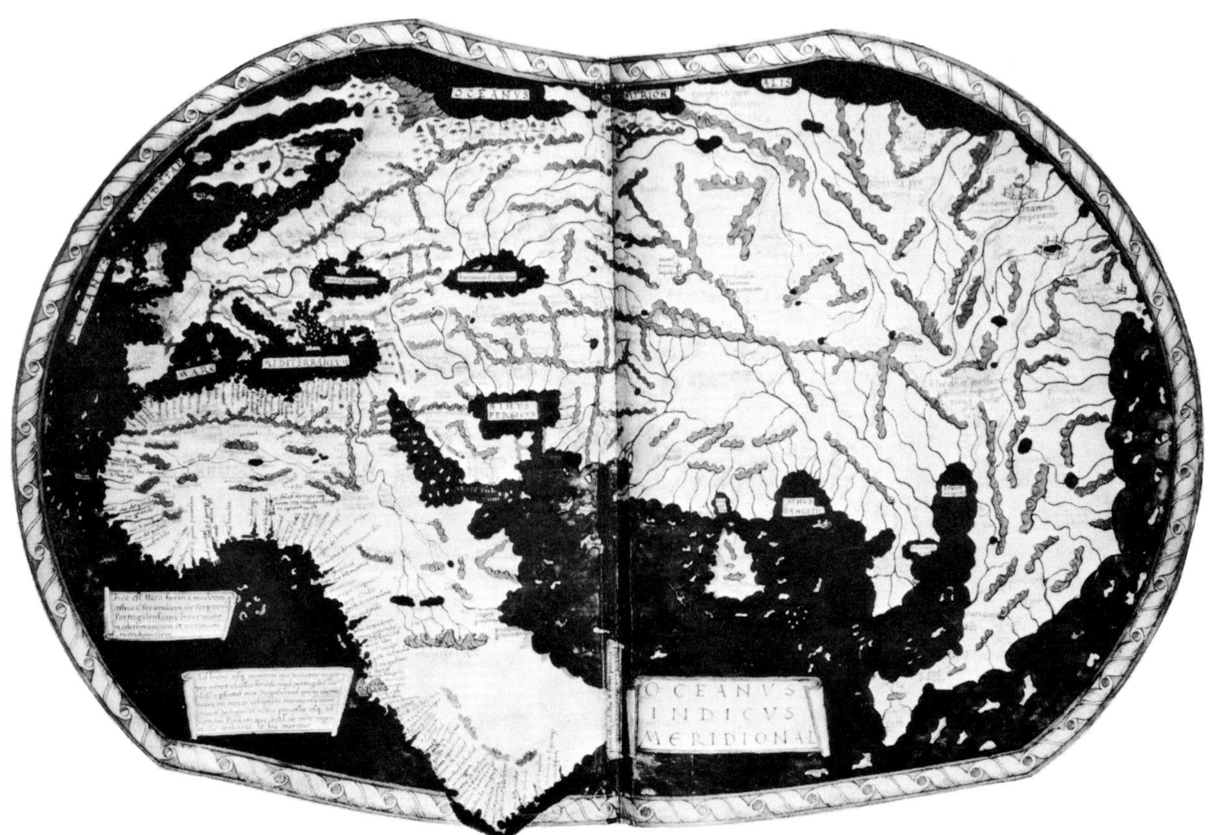

This map, dated 1489 shows what was then known as the whole world. It does not include the Continents of America, Australia and the two Poles, and the knowledge of Africa, India and Asia is clearly rather limited.

ideas of the Age of Enlightenment, because it established, in a recognisably modern manner, some of the fundamentals of what has become anthropology. It began with the aim of applying to the study of man the principles of reasoning which had yielded such substantial developments in knowledge about nature. This method was empiricist, arguing from the detailed evidence to general conclusions about natural laws. It was an essential part of the method to compare diverse forms in order to establish common features and to test conclusions against further data. Thus, in the early eighteenth century, writers compared the Indians of North America or the Chinese with the early Hebrews or with Greek or Roman society. Implicitly it established a classification into civilised (Us) and savage (Them) which was justified by the other assumption underlying this work, that of the accumulation of knowledge and the progress of man's understanding. Thus ancient Greek, Roman or Jewish society were taken as simple forms from which the complexity of the writer's own civilisation had developed. The metaphor used was an old one: the analogy with the birth, growth and death of the human being. Civilisation was seen as the accumulation of knowledge, as age brings more experience to the maturing adult. Ancient society was viewed as the childish origin of complex modern nations. By equating the more exotic peoples of the world with ancient times, these writers were preparing the way for the evolutionary theories of the nineteenth century.

The distinction between savage and civilised was made explicit in Linnaeus' classification of mankind into homo sapiens among whom he recognised five sub-classes and homo monstrosus with six sub-classes. Other writers were less concerned with the minutiae of fine classification but in general they proceeded on the assumption that 'the savage', however defined, was a more simple version of the civilised and therefore could more clearly represent the essential nature of man unmodified by later developments. Two quite opposed pictures were built up, reflections of which are with us still. In one the state of nature which is depicted is rough, full of dangerous conflict pitting all against all; the development of society is thus seen as the imposition of law and order, the establishment of peace and the accumulation of wealth and knowledge made possible by such peace. This is essentially Hobbe's view and one which was similar to that of other writers, in France and in Scotland, whose work had great influence on the thought of the second half of the eighteenth century.

It was a Frenchman, Jean Jacques Rousseau, who provided the basis for the opposing view of human nature. He too saw a progressive development of society but to the detriment of humanity. For Rousseau, as for many others since, 'simple' society seemed to show a harmony, lack of conflict and admirable simplicity, since the social ideas which drove men into conflict had not appeared. For him, inequality, injustice and conflict were not natural but the result of the development of complex social forms. Rousseau's attack on contemporary society was avowedly revolutionary and his ideas undoubtedly influenced the political leaders of the French Revolution. The concept of 'the Noble Savage', which is a cruder version of Rousseau's concept of natural man,

The picture shows a young Hottentot, brought up by the Dutch Governor of the Cape of Good Hope, giving back his European clothes to the Governor before returning to his people clad in a traditional sheepskin. Rousseau entitles the picture: *He returns to the Egalitarians*, and uses the story to show how shocked the young man was at the inequalities and conflict of the white Christian way of life.

Il retourne chez ses Egaux.

still survives in the sentimental views of those who attribute all evils to modern society, to the extreme development of technology and an ever-increasing production of material goods. For modern holders of this view, as for Rousseau, the myth of the noble savage (for it is a myth) serves to underline a distinction between our society and others. Dissatisfaction with one's own society is still a motive for admiring simple societies and links the twentieth century to the eighteenth, although in other respects our ideas and knowledge about the rest of the world have changed dramatically.

If the Noble Savage does and did not exist, nor did the Brutish Savage. The contrast made by Hobbes and others, who saw the history of mankind as a progressive improvement, served equally to demonstrate an attitude to contemporary society, stressing improvements in material welfare and in prosperity, security and stability of government, rather than the wars of former times. It was optimistic, implying a vast potential for human good as yet unrealised; as such it was a powerful influence on the theories of the nineteenth century. However, both it and the myth of the Noble Savage depend on similar thinking, on a conviction that reason and observation rather than divine revelation or introspection are the means to finding out about man's nature. It is this approach rather than particular conclusions which have been perpetuated in modern anthropology, for today it is clear that different peoples cannot be classified in this way. All men share capacities for peace and war, co-operation and conflict, greed and altruism.

I shall return to this later. Here it is important to note what was new in eighteenth century thinking. All the Enlightenment writers on man whom I have been discussing followed Descartes in their rejection of the Church's authority to pronounce the answer to the questions they posed. Moreover they adopted inductive reasoning, testing their generalisations against experience rather than the writings of the established Schools of Philosophy. Moreover they declared a faith in the possibility of a natural history of man, by which they meant that the differences among men were to be explained in terms of the inherent laws of development of man, now seen as a social being. It was Montesquieu's achievement to establish that these laws could only be discovered by comparing different forms of social life, as the botanist compared plants. The idea of progress as a fulfilment of inherent features, present in simple forms and only fully developed in the course of history, was the eighteenth-century's contribution to what would become the science of man.

Although the nineteenth century is often described as the cradle of anthropology, in fact it merely developed and systematised ideas that were influential much earlier. There were some new elements, notably considerable improvements in techniques of investigation, more information with which scholars could work and the development of ideas about the mechanisms which brought about the evolution of social forms. The impetus for this development came from a number of related disciplines and coincided with the Industrial Revolution which inaugurated a period of far-reaching changes in social life. The nineteenth century scholar's view of the history of mankind is

An engraving of the archaeological site of Mycenae showing the pits dug by Schliemann to identify the different layers of occupation of the city. It shows Dr and Mrs Schliemann viewing the Royal Tombs in the Grave Circle

now part of the popular wisdom of today, although within the established discipline of anthropology most of the conclusions drawn by the writers of that time have been rejected.

Anthropology in the nineteenth century included within it both archaeology and physical anthropology. Its task, most writers agreed, was to trace the origins of social life back to their earliest beginnings, beyond the most ancient writings then known. In this it continued the attack which had begun in the Age of Reason, on the religious dogma of the founding of the world. Specifically, the geological and archaeological research of the nineteenth century made undeniable a much longer chronology of man's development than was at all compatible with the biblical account of the founding of the universe, which was still believed by many to be historically accurate as well as true in a religious sense. In biology, Darwin's *The Origin of Species* set out a theoretical framework which was so closely paralleled in anthropological writings that it has sometimes been thought, wrongly, to have inspired them. In fact it was the geologists' method of dating rock forms by their place in the successive layers of rock and the archaeologists' discovery of layers of occupation at important sites that provided stimulus for both. Archaeologists were able to show a sequence of material objects showing development from simple to complex that also demonstrated conclusively that the simplest form was the oldest. This seemed to confirm to the eighteenth century view of the develop-

An early engraving of representatives of North American Indian peoples. Morgan studied the Iraquois, represented here by the man on the extreme left.

ment of social forms and encouraged these writers in the next century to develop their theory of mankind's evolution.

Nineteenth century anthropology discarded the crude pictures of natural or savage men, which had served earlier writers, for a more empirical approach. Some of them, like Maine or Morgan, had first-hand knowledge of societies very different from their own. Others drew on the ever-increasing numbers of accounts by travellers, missionaries and traders for their information. Their methods depended on two basic assumptions: first that simple societies were archaic. Contemporary peoples like the Australian Aborigines, Bushmen in South Africa, or Eskimos, were taken to be peoples who had somehow ceased to evolve, who were frozen as it were at an early stage of development. Thus where records of social evolution were lacking, as they usually were, it was thought legitimate to arrange peoples separated by geographical and cultural differences along a spectrum which turned these differences into historical stages. Why evolution had ceased to operate in some societies was never explained, as it should have been, given the general idea of progress operating generally in social life. Further, the anthropologists differed from Darwin in their view of evolution because they assumed no development in some social entities while Darwin postulated that each contemporary form had evolved over time, thus accounting for greater divergences in later than earlier forms.

The other necessary assumption which was emphasised was the axiom of the psychic unity of mankind. Less pompously phrased, this meant the assumption that people everywhere are much the same which underlies the idea that there can be translation from one language into another. No Victorian scholar expected to find societies representing the very earliest stages of human development, for they assumed a pre-human ancestor for mankind. However, given the psychic unity of humanity, the scholars felt that they might justifiably speculate as to what might have preceded those societies which they identified as the most primitive. Or alternatively it was believed that the most widespread belief was the earliest so that one might speculate as to what was the origin of very general features of social life. Thus Tylor could plausibly argue that the origin of religion lay in the experience of death or dreams. Morgan claimed that the first form of society must have been without the institution of marriage, basing this claim on his own reasoning from rather limited data. He discovered that in certain societies, the term for father is used, not for individuals but for a class of men. He argued that therefore the members of such a society were unable to tell who the fathers of children were because there was no permanent association between men and women. This argument seems very naive to us today for it was based on complete ignorance of what life was actually like in any of these communities. It was not thought necessary for the scholar to collect his data himself. It is said that when someone once asked the great Sir James Fraser, author of the twelve

A 19th century model of an Indian Kutchery or Court House from Hyderabad. Sir Henry Maine, a lawyer, served as a legal member of council in India from 1862 to 1868. His book *Primitive Law* published in 1861 was a comparison of different systems of law, and his later work: *Village Communities of East and West* published in 1871, drew directly on his Indian experiences.

Mask from New Ireland in the British Museum. The human face and the birds on the side-pieces have been stylised into sophisticated design motifs in a manner characteristic of this area.

volumes of the Golden Bough, if he had ever seen a savage, he said: 'My dear fellow, God forbid'.

While modern anthropology uses comparison and assumes the fundamental similarity of all human beings, it interprets these ideas in a rather different manner, as we shall see later. However the nineteenth century can be claimed to have freed itself from some subjective ideas. While the image of the Noble Savage could be said to be the last faint reflection of the religious doctrine of the Fall, science and reason were generally believed to be superseding religion as anthropology was superseding the Bible as an explanation of the origins of peoples. Faith was the lingering survival of an earlier stage of development just as magic could be detected here and there among societies which had passed into the religious stage. Hence the study of man was to be a science: founded on observation and information, not created as the mirror image of some view of one's own society.

Dürer's picture of the Fall of Man shows Adam and Eve as beautiful innocents in the Garden of Eden. Notice how the cat benignly regards the mouse which is so close to it; even the animals are gentle.

However, let there be no misunderstanding: the attempts of the anthropology of the nineteenth century to account for the diversity of peoples in terms of evolutionary stages, were mistaken. In spite of the label 'stone age' which is even now applied to peoples who lack modern technology, there is no evidence to support the idea that all mankind progresses through stages of development which are represented by living peoples of the modern world. Studies of social change show that it is a far more complex series of events than a rather simple progression from one stage to the next. There is no easy way of characterising societies as more or less simple, although the terms are still used, but with caution. Peoples like the Highlanders of New Guinea had a simple technology but a highly developed art and symbolic system; the complexities of Australian aboriginal marriage systems have resisted definitive analysis for nearly a hundred years. It has taken the great French anthropologist Lévi-Strauss four scholarly volumes to elucidate one part of the mythology of the South American peoples. The West is not the latest product of evolution and therefore superior to others who may be placed on lower rungs of the same ladder.

Nevertheless the nineteenth century saw the establishment of anthropology as a distinct subject of study with a set of problems of its own. As the gathering of data became the responsibility of the analysts themselves and the idea of universal stages of evolution came under attack at the end of the century, so the writing of anthropologists became more accurate. The careful tracing of movements of peoples and their detailed interrelations was seen as a necessary preliminary to any large scale theory. Ethnology, the description of particular societies and the investigation of their origins, became the dominant strand of anthropology in America, where it remained linked with archaeology and physical anthropology. In this respect modern cultural anthropology in America is still much closer in approach, though not in aims or methods, to the nineteenth century than is social anthropology in Britain.

It was the influence of the developing discipline of sociology which made a distinctive difference to British anthropology and turned it into social anthropology, sometimes acknowledged as a branch of comparative sociology. The beginning of the twentieth century saw the rejection of the search for origins in favour of a comparison of contemporary forms of social life. Whereas formerly the emphasis on the search for origins had encouraged speculative hypotheses from fragmentary data, sociology sought to establish its own strict canons of proof based on empirical research. The world of human variation was to serve as the laboratory of the new science; thus Weber, in order to demonstrate the role of religious ideas in the development of capitalism compared a number of societies with similar economies but different religions and Durkheim, studying the causes of suicide, compared statistics on the suicide rates of different nations, and different categories of people within nations. The nature and interrelation of different social institutions and patterns (which Montesquieu had noted and which the nineteenth century writers had paid scant attention to) became a central concern.

More than this, the sociological influence turned anthropology from the study of different traditions into the analysis of the constitution of

ALBERT9
DVRER
NORICVS
FACIEBAT
1504

societies. The focus became not the beliefs and practices which constituted a people's distinctive way of life (their *culture*) but a study of how those beliefs and the rules of behaviour connected to them, served to define the relations between individuals and integrate them into social groups. The same sort of data was required but it was used to determine the constitution of groups and the nature of rules of social behaviour and so to depict the social framework (the *social structure*) within which particular individuals lived their lives. In addition, it was shown in a number of different ways, how to a large extent the characteristic behaviour of individuals was moulded by social life. Instead of the nature of individuals, noble or brutish, phlegmatic or excitable, determining social life, these very characteristics could be shown to derive from society. Hence it is useless to try and explain the varieties of social life by reference to individual behaviour, even behaviour which is so common in a particular society that it appears to epitomise it. English society cannot be explained by reference to British humour, British love of dogs and eccentrics, nor the 'stiff upper lip', though humourists have sometimes half-persuaded us to the contrary.

In addition, anthropologists, particularly in Britain, began the tradition of research known as participant observation, for which they are now well known. At first it was dissatisfaction with the piecemeal information provided by others, which persuaded anthropologists either to send out questionnaires for traders and missionaries to fill in, or to go collecting data themselves. As anthropologists themselves experienced life among different societies, they became aware of how much there was to know about them. The tradition of living and participating in events with the people studied, learning their language and finding out what their ideas really are (instead of guessing) was well-established by the thirties, and has remained the characteristic method of social anthropology since. In effect the anthropologist uses himself as a research instrument, learning the meaning of words as he learns to speak the language, watching how people behave and coming to understand their reactions. It is a fascinating experience during which one learns almost as much about one's own unexamined assumptions as one does about those of others. The good field-worker comes back, not only with files of records, pictures, maps – the raw material of analysis – but with what can only be described as a 'feel' for another way of life, which is hard to put into words but which guides subsequent interpretation. There is, of course, the danger that too great an emphasis on one field experience may lead one to see all other societies through the eyes of this one, but in my view the advantage of the deep understanding gained by immersing oneself in another society far outweighs such a risk.

The foundation of social anthropology is the thorough description of other societies; the rules, ways of enforcing them or avoiding them, beliefs, attitudes, aims and problems, in order to show the different social structures through which individuals must order themselves and their lives. This description is ethnography, the recording of material. Normally ethnographic description concentrates on one society, informed of course by general theoretical principles but rich in descriptive detail. There are now

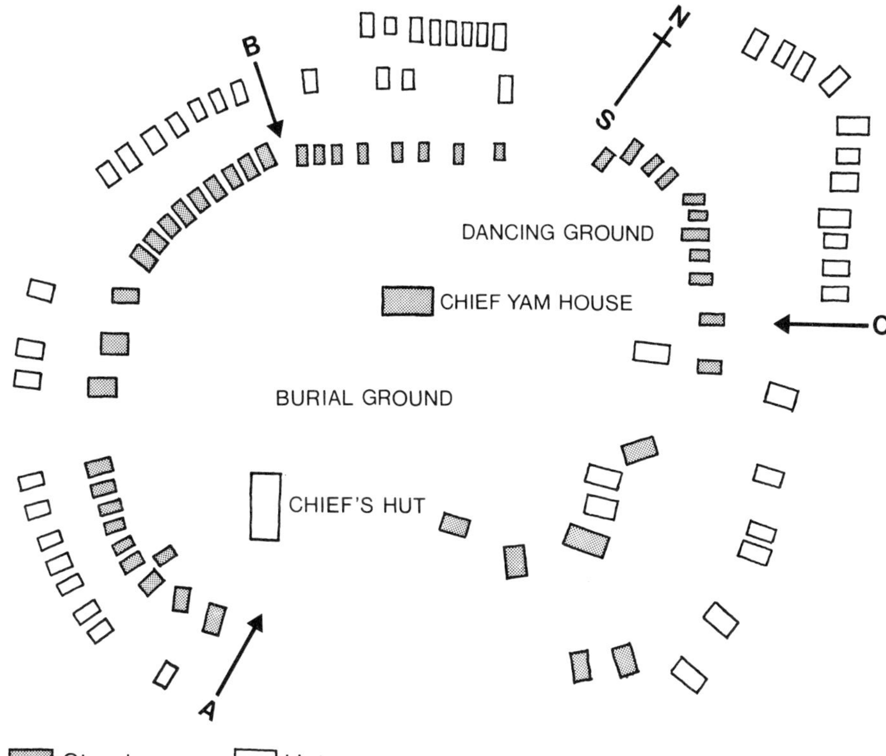

Plan of Omatakana from B Malinowski's *Sexual life of Savages*.
A village plan enables the anthropologist to spot the significant social divisions which appear in the layout of buildings. In this plan the Chief's wives occupy a whole segment of the village, commoners are grouped together and the public buildings, including the Chief's hut are in the centre. A circular plan with the major social focus in the centre is a very common way of arranging a village.
Huts A to B are occupied by the chief's wives, the area A to C is occupied by the chief's maternal kinsmen. The area B to C is occupied by commoners who are not related to the chief either as kinsmen or as children.

ethnographic films as well, which portray a particular people in some important aspects of their life.

As modern social anthropology has developed, and it has made great strides in the last fifty or so years, ethnographic detail has become richer until it is rare to find the whole life of a single people covered in one book. The writer must select a particular aspect of life or important argument around which to construct a description. Description has always included some selection of course; it would be naive to assume that there is 'pure' description where the facts are assembled without interpretation. The perception of what *are* facts, the choice of details, are influenced by pre-existing ideas. The training of research workers in anthropology is designed to help them relate what they observe to the more abstract propositions of general theory.

Nevertheless one can distinguish ethnography, where the description of a society illustrates or even illuminates general principles, from more abstract theoretical writing in which society, not *a* society is the theme. Theory in social anthropology is based on comparison, but a comparison which no longer looks for the 'natural man' behind his social mask, nor seeks to construct an evolutionary ladder which all societies must ascend to a pinnacle represented by ourselves. Moreover, elements of society are now the normal units of comparison, not whole societies. For example, a social anthropologist might compare ancestor worship in different societies in order to determine the relation between such beliefs, the nature of the authority of elders and the organisation of descent groups or clans. In the interpretation of particular ethnography, comparisons will also be made to strengthen the theoretical conclusions and drive the argument home. But however comparison features in anthropological writing it derives from the axiom that no society can be evaluated against any other in moral terms – as higher or lower, better or worse, for there are no neutral standards against which to judge.

Social anthropology today displays no single unified body of theory, although perhaps in a hundred years the major themes will seem clear to historians of anthropological ideas as the preoccupations of the nineteenth century seem clear to us. There are some shared basic assumptions: that the search for the origins of social life cannot be based on speculation about the nature of man stripped of his social attributes; that there is no single necessary evolutionary path followed by all peoples for all of them have had a long history of development; that a community or society cannot be explained by the ideas or behaviour of its constituent members but must be approached as a distinct object of enquiry. These ideas represent the rejection of earlier theories which have been found untenable. There is also an agreement that explanation must follow observation and depend on the careful collection of detailed information, that is, on an examination of the evidence. The accumulation of data has been strikingly rapid during the twentieth century and still continues. Paradoxically though, the more we learn about ourselves and others, the more we realise how much more we need to know before we can reach the goal of understanding social life in all its variations.

As anthropology has become more and more specialised it has developed a distinctive vocabulary. This has been necessary (although some writers have been guilty of much jargon-loaded and unnecessarily obscurantist writing) because of the dilemma I have already referred to: that our social ideas are moulded by the society we live in. Hence the very words of our language carry a load of meaning which prevents them being culturally neutral. Anthropologists have had to define their terms, or use unusual words in order to try and achieve a language which is more nearly objective than common speech. Thus the term culture in anthropological writing refers to technology, language and social rules, and never to the artistic and intellectual activities of the 'cultivated' section of a modern society. The word means more than it does in common speech. In other cases anthropologists limit the meaning of words: for example they distinguish between social *group* – an organised collectivity with specific criteria for membership and for relations within it – and social *category* – a class of people who have some things in common but who are not organised in any way. This distinction indicates a difference in the social significance between, for example, a football club and football players generally, the former are a group, the latter members of a category who do not all have specific social relations with one another.

Some of the terms used in this book show the difference between common usage and the technical meanings which anthropologists have assigned to words: '*status*' according to the Oxford English Dictionary has several meanings which refer to the condition of things or persons and also as 'position and standing in society'. These meanings are too many and too vague for technical use. Anthropologists use *status* to refer to a socially defined position such as 'teacher' or 'mother'. The word indicates the attributes of such a position and the terms 'rank' or 'prestige' are used to indicate the value a society may place on such a position and 'power' or 'authority' to indicate the influence such a position confers. The terms status then refers, not to an individual, for an individual may occupy many different statuses, but to the social attributes of a position. All members of society learn, as they grow up, what the statuses established in their society are and how to recognise them. Often a status is recognisable from behaviour; most people would think that the woman holding a child's hand in the street is likely to be the child's mother or, if older, grandmother for such care constitutes part of these social roles. This latter term derives from the notion of acting a part which is appropriate, for role implies, not spontaneous individual activity, but the expected activities which derive from a particular status. Thus the role of mother includes behaviour which most mothers will exhibit; if they do not they are classed as 'bad' mothers, or 'unnatural' mothers. It should be clear by now that behaviour which is not appropriate to a particular role is not unnatural but unsocial, that is, going against common ideas of what such behaviour should be.

Common assumptions and a specialised vocabulary define the common ground of anthropology but do not impose agreement about what conclusions may be drawn. There are a number of competing theories but it is possible to distinguish between two types of approach to the problem of explaining social behaviour. One sees the material facts of existence: the environment, level of technology and means of organising the production of food and other necessities of life, as the fundamental force which determines social forms. In this view customary behaviour, the relations between individuals and groups together with ideas and beliefs, are reflections of patterns established by the pattern of distribution of resources or of power. Different versions of such materialist theories stress different factors as dominant and assert differing relationships linking material forces to the form of society that is shaped by them.

The second type of theory is based on the opposite view: that social experience moulds perceptions of the world to such an extent that the differences between peoples are to be explained less by their material circumstances than by their distinctive views of the world, their cultures. Cultures are built up from a complex web of fundamental convictions, assumptions and axioms which cannot be identified with the conscious mental activity of an individual but which form a cast of mind implicit in the attitudes and behaviour of all members of one society. There are concerns which are common to all humanity: the natural and social environment, the human body and its workings, the life-cycle of procreation, birth maturation and death. The particular ways in which these common themes are expressed must, in this view, be related to the varieties of human behaviour we can observe.

This book is designed to accompany a series of television programmes which are based, broadly speaking, on the second type of theory.

The programmes take common themes in order to show both the recurrent similarities and the variable treatment given to common themes, by several different societies. The book aims to set the programmes in a broader context. It is divided into two parts. The first half, of which this introduction is part, is concerned with anthropology in general. In this section I have aimed to give some account of the development of anthropological ideas and to set anthropology in the context of other disciplines which seek an answer to the philosophical question: 'What is Man? Thus theology is concerned with the soul and man's metaphysical beliefs, human biology and physical anthropology studies human beings as a natural species and the social sciences, including anthropology, take the collectivity as their subject.

The next section of this book takes up the general themes which form the basis of the television programmes and discusses them in a wider context. The aim is to develop the general statement that peoples are much the same everywhere, in that they show common pre-occupations. Fundamental cultural symbols turn on remarkably few themes, given the dispersal of human populations all over the world, in a variety of environments and physical conditions. Such differences often appear as variations on common themes. Particular forms are deep-rooted in the different cultures, not easily given up. Culture is not a suit of clothes that can be changed at will. Moreover, all peoples feel that they alone know the proper way to behave; those who think differently are only rarely regarded with tolerance. Normally such differences are interpreted as showing the gap between civilised and savage, good and bad.

The final section of the book concerns the five societies filmed to provide material for the television programmes. It provides the reader with more general information on villages in Malta, Bali, Chole Island off the coast of Tanzania, American Gypsies and a village of Indians in the Brazilian jungle. Each people is described by the anthropologist who studied them and who helped in the filming. The chapters can be read separately to follow up an interest in a particular people but they also refer to the middle section by showing how particular symbols are significant in each society. Inevitably there is much that is omitted, but there are references to other works which give fuller accounts.

The book goes from the most general account of anthropology to the details of life in particular places. It does not aim to cover all anthropology nor all the many kinds of human social life that anthropologists know about. Its aim is to communicate an essential anthropological attitude: interest in the varieties of human being.

Part One

An Anthropological Perspective

by Anne Sutherland

Chapter One Ourselves and Others

When we are first faced with an unfamiliar society, it appears to be complex, jumbled and incomprehensible. What is happening in any given situation may not be apparent so that the behaviour of people may be extremely confusing. Such a situation faces the traveller or the social anthropologist who encounters an unfamiliar society. But while the traveller overcomes the strangeness by moving on, the task of the social anthropologist is to become incorporated as much as possible into the society in order to understand why people are doing what they do, to make sense of the apparent confusion, and to translate the 'logic' of their actions into terms that we, in our society, can understand.

But if we wish to gain insight into unfamiliar societies and groups, how do we go about doing this? Initially, we must start from some common ground, that is, some position that all societies share. There are certain basic distinctions that people in all societies make. One is that 'we are human beings and not animals'. Different societies have different ways of explaining this distinction.

In our society there are several views of what is essentially human. Those who prefer a religious explanation may point to the existence of the human soul which is felt to be unique to humans. Some people prefer biological explanations and thus have changed their definition of the human in contrast to the animal as more is learned about both. Use of tools, highly developed language, size of the brain, greater adaptability to the environment and flexibility of social organisation are some of the criteria used. Some people would claim that these biological distinctions between animals and humans are more a matter of degree than of essential differences in nature, but by far the most common view is that we humans are intrinsically different from and superior to animals.

In some societies, other distinctions are singled out as important. The Kayapó Indians of Central Brazil, for example, emphasise in their myths that humans cook food whereas animals do not, and it was only when humans took fire from animals and began to cook that they became truly human. The Balinese emphasise differences in eating as well, but they are most of all concerned to appear different from animals. To them humans should be

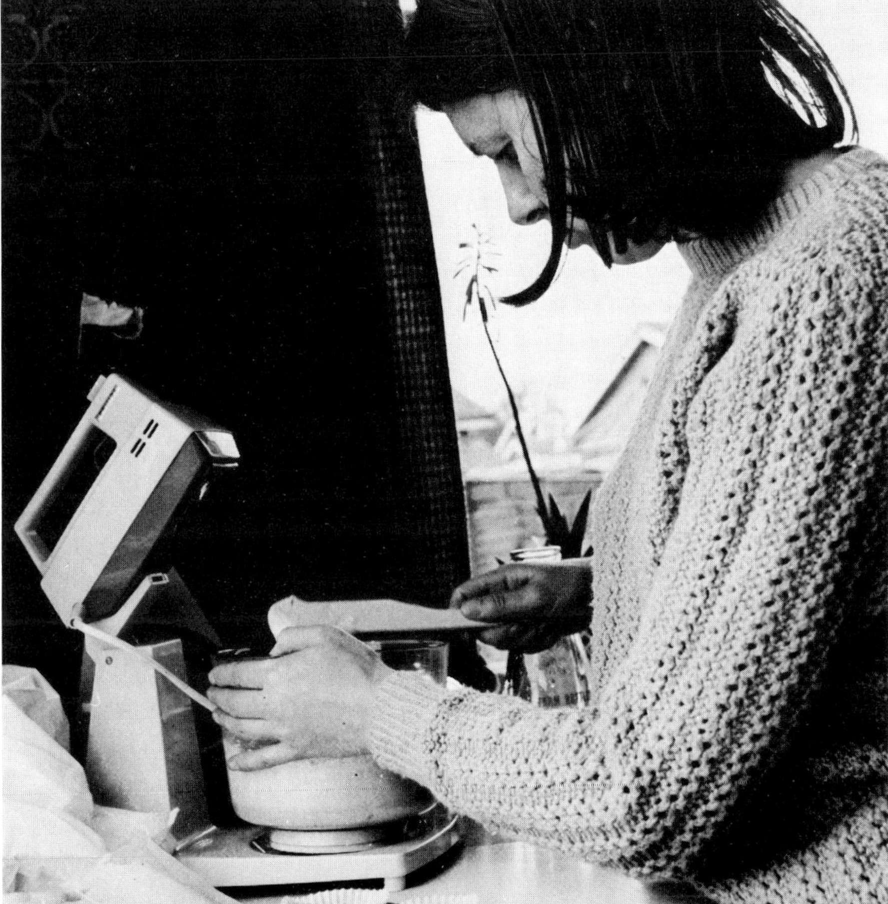

To a person used to a British Kitchen, cooking on Chole Island seems very different. Though, in many societies, the act of cooking is seen as the most important distinguishing characteristic between animals and humans.

hairless, smooth-skinned bipeds with flat teeth in contrast to animals which are hairy, coarse, have fangs and walk on all fours. Because this contrast is so important, the Balinese do not allow their babies to crawl and have their teeth filed flat.

A second distinction that all societies make is between themselves and others. Every society is saying 'we as a group are different in some way from any other group'. Any society or group must be aware of itself as a discrete unit. For whatever reason, members of a group must *see* themselves as sharing some common identity in contrast to other groups and must be recognised by others as a group. Of course membership, from the point of view of the individual, is overlapping. Most people belong to more than one group, which may include nations, ethnic groups, tribes, families or households.

When people differentiate themselves from others, they also make, by implication at least, a value judgement of superiority. They are saying 'we as a group are superior to other groups'. This attitude, which is found in all societies, anthropologists call *ethnocentricity*. Being ethnocentric may take many 'positive' forms, such as patriotic pride in the achievements or history of your nation or people, loyalty to a social movement or class, feelings of solidarity to a group, etc. But it may also take a very 'negative' form such as stereotyping, without any attempt to understand, other nationals or people as inferior or wrong. For us derogatory words such as 'krauts', 'coons', 'yanks' and 'pakies' imply inferiority because such people are different in some way or simply are 'not British'.

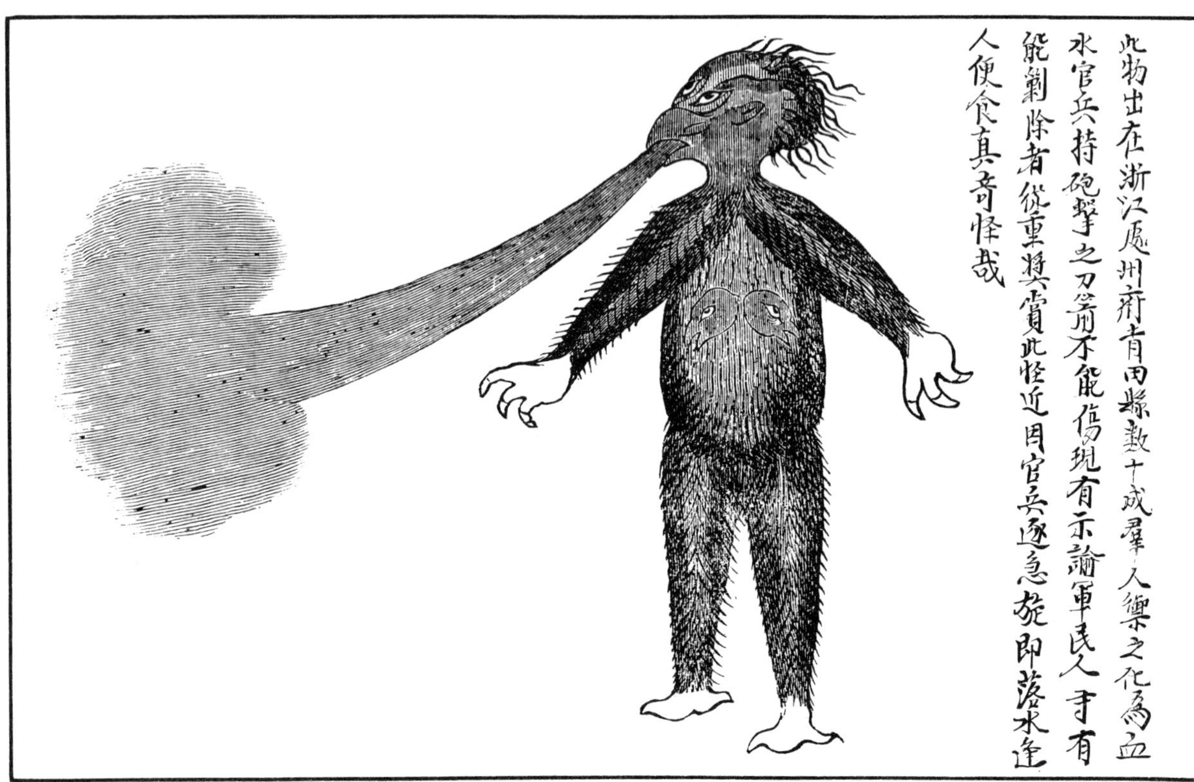

Chinese caricature depicting an English sailor in much the same style as the mythological monsters of old China. The smoke from the mouth is probably meant for fumes of tobacco. The text says:'This creature appears in the Tsing-teen-heen district of Choo-chow-foo, of the capital of Che-keang. Several troops of men surrounding it, it then changed into blood and water. Soldiers should shoot it with firearms, for bows and arrows are unable to injure it. When it appears, the people and troops should be informed that whoever is able to destroy or ward it off will be most amply rewarded. If the monster finds itself surrounded by soldiers, it turns and falls into water. When it meets anyone it forewith eats him. It is truly a wonderful monster.'

A copy of Governor Davy's proclamation to the Tasmanian Aboriginals in 1816 which was intended to show that equal justice would apply to blacks and whites.

Ethnocentric behaviour can range from mild abuse or joking to extreme forms which result in drawing such a strong moral boundary between ourselves and others that behaviour prohibited in our own society is condoned in another. Ethnocentricity, taken to an extreme, can become a statement that 'we as a group are so different from any other group that only we are *real* human beings'.

This is not as far-fetched as it seems. In the 19th century Tasmanians were hunted like game animals by British gentry on horseback.

When the Spanish occupied the Carib Islands, the Carib Indians were mistakenly thought to be cannibals and were systematically killed or exiled. On the other hand, Captain Cook was so taken with the noble bearing of the Maoris that he refused to believe they were cannibals (until some of his own sailors were eaten).

Hierarchical distinctions

Boundaries that are drawn between groups within a society are very similar to those between societies. Hierarchical distinctions based on inequalities in wealth and political power can become the basis for we-they distinctions, for example, when class-based consciousness or ethnic group solidarity develops.

Europeans seem to find the idea of cannibalism particularly horrifying. Captain Cook's first contacts with the New Zealand Maori in 1769 provide a nice contrast with Columbus' treatment of the Caribs. The Maori were actually cannibals, but Cook was so favourably impressed by their intelligence, technical ingenuity and general nobility that he refused to believe that this could be so until one of his own sailors suffered the indignity of being cooked and eaten.

When Columbus first landed in the West Indies in 1492 he was at first pleasantly surprised to discover that the local inhabitants were human beings and not monsters. Then, having noticed that they were very generous and hospitable, he reflected upon how easy it would be to reduce them to slavery. In the course of the next century the native Carib inhabitants of the West Indies were almost entirely exterminated by the Spaniards. The Spaniards justified their brutality by reporting home that the Caribs were cannibals. Our word cannibal comes from the Spanish word for Carib – Caribales – but it is unlikely that Columbus ever encountered a genuine cannibal.

In American society wealth is one of the main prerequisites of rank. American Blacks have for centuries suffered both an economic and social disadvantage. Unemployment is always higher among Blacks than white Americans, and many Blacks are faced with a social dead end.

Sometimes the existence of such hierarchies is not recognised. In the United States of America, for example, most people believe in the ideal of equality. This ideal has been formally declared in the preamble to the constitution and in constitutional amendments guaranteeing equality under the law and equal opportunities in education, employment, and governmental representation. Yet even the most superficial glance at American society indicates that, in a society where wealth is one of the main prerequisites of rank access to wealth is highly differentiated by race and sex and that a class system based on economic inequality is an integral part of American society.

In some societies the disparity between cherished values and the realities of social life is greater than in others. It has often been said that when this gap becomes too large some change must take place, either in the ideal or the real. But social anthropologists have found that most societies have a long-lasting ability to 'carry' contradiction in the system. In fact, such contradictions and inconsistencies are a fundamental part of every system.

Unlike Americans, almost everyone in Britain recognises that here there are class distinctions. Class analyses in the social sciences are very complicated and full of heated arguments, and I shall not attempt to enter into this debate. I want to focus on an aspect of class that is less publicised but where anthropology has a special contribution to offer; the ways that class membership or background are recognised. Most people in Britain know how to recognise the class of an individual in most cases even if they have never heard of or read theories of class. This common body of knowledge about class has been described humorously by Nancy Mitford. She provides a lengthy list of attitudes, dress, food, accents, vocabulary and so on, that are 'U' or 'non-U'. Though now perhaps somewhat out of date, one of the interesting things about this book is the reluctance to use the *word* 'class'. Euphemisms such as 'U' and 'non-U' take its place.

In some middle class circles in particular, the very mention of class is considered impolite. During my student days, I was reprimanded most severely by a very middle class lady for even mentioning the existence of class distinctions. This same lady, who says she never 'thinks about' class, divides her world into people who 'have no accent' and those who do, people who have 'good taste' and those who don't. But most important of all, she determines class by what people eat, how they eat it and where they go to eat. She herself would 'never eat fish and chips because the fat is rancid' nor, she warned me, should I go to a restaurant with a sauce bottle on the table. Although she uses common symbols of class to distinguish people, she will not use the word 'class'.

Food and eating reflect differences. Food preferences are established in childhood and are influenced by changes in class status later in life. Caviar and Champagne, lamb chop and peas, or bangers and mash all have class associations.

Symbols of differentiation

An important way that people recognise 'we-they' distinctions is through symbols of differentiation. Symbols, by their very nature, are capable of many meanings and are often very emotive. Symbols condense ideas, objects, categories, etc, uniting them into a single whole. Symbols such as the cross, the swastika and the Queen are powerful precisely because they bring together many meanings for many different people into one representation or person. Non-verbal symbols such as these are potent because they are simple in form and complex in meaning.

Words may also be seen as symbols. For example, the foods that are peculiar to a group of people often may be taken to represent the whole nation. 'Frog', which refers to one particular culinary custom of the French, is used to represent all the differences between the French and English, and some of the contempt that goes with it. In the same way, Americans use 'Limey' to refer to the British because British sailors ate limes to avoid scurvy, a custom that apparently struck Americans as strange.

A place may come to symbolise a whole institution. Fleet Street is used to mean 'the Press', Harley Street for 'private medicine' and Downing Street for 'the government'. Parts of the body may also refer to essential differences in groups. The short hair of the Roundheads became a kind of symbolic shorthand for all their political and religious differences with the Cavaliers. In India, left- and right-hand sides of the body in some contexts represent the essential nature of males and females.

A symbol such as the cross is powerful because it brings together many meanings for many different people.

A place may come to symbolise a whole institution. Downing St. comes to mean 'the government'.

Differentiation in ritual

A ritual is a series of events in time that express meaning. Both the sequence of events and the meaning expressed are usually established by tradition. The meaning is not always religious, though rituals with religious meaning are very important ones. Ritual could be, for example, the preparation of a meal. Setting the table and eating in a certain 'proper' way exemplify these aspects of ritual. First, in laying the table there are different cultural patterns. For example, in Britain, the fork and knife always go on certain sides of the plate. Second, these acts involve more than the purely technical problem of getting food into the body. For example, 'meat and two veg' is a 'proper' meal. But the British idea of a 'proper' meal is quite different from that of the Chinese, and the meal 'tea' has one meaning for working class people and another for middle class people. Thus the form and meaning of a meal varies from one class to another and from one society to another.

Laying the table is a ritual that indicates the culture and social class of a group of people.

Both secular and religious rituals express important values, the system of classification, and the conflicts of a particular group that may not otherwise be verbally expressed. In other words, ritual has a high concentration of symbolic meaning for the society. Because of this, ritual has an important emotional aspects. Furthermore, public ritual is also theatre. People

National rituals such as the Queen's Jubilee celebrations, may be more elaborate and on a larger scale than preparing a meal, but both express important values in the society.

are playing a part, decorating themselves, going on stage and expressing themselves. The anthropologist Monica Wilson claimed that –

'Rituals reveal values at their deepest level ... men express in ritual what moves them most, and since the form of expression is conventionalised and obligatory, it is the values of the group that are revealed. I see in the study of rituals the key to an understanding of the essential constitution of human societies.'
(Wilson, 1954: 241)

'Ritual and religious beliefs are gradually coming to be seen by social scientists as decisive keys to the understanding of how people think and feel about economic, political and social relationships and about the natural and social environment in which they operate.'
(Turner, Victor, 1969:6.)

Though we do not often recognise it, our lives are permeated by ritual. Washing ourselves regularly, preparing and eating a meal, celebrating a birthday or wedding, and drinking in the pub are all rituals of everyday life. National rituals, such as the Queen's Jubilee celebrations, may be more elaborate and on a larger scale than preparing a meal, but each of these expresses something about the important values in a society, how they have developed and why they change. For example the Good Friday procession in Malta, as well as expressing in ritual the Christian belief that Jesus Christ was

Good Friday, when Jesus Christ was crucified to save the world, is an important event in the Christian calendar. In Malta the Good Friday procession has also become an event with some secular importance as an expression of Maltese patriotism.

crucified to save the world from sin, has taken on an added significance. Today the Good Friday procession expresses not only religious sentiment, but also a renewed patriotism. Thus, in spite of increasing secularisation in Malta, the Good Friday procession each year is becoming a more and more elaborate event.

Ritual has another very important function that of marking changes in the life cycle of an individual from birth to death. Edmund Leach has remarked that:

'most ritual occasions are concerned with movement across social boundaries from one social status to another, living man to dead ancestor, maiden to wife, sick and contaminated to healthy and clean, etc. The ceremonies concerned have the double function of proclaiming the change of status and of magically bringing it about. From another point of view they are the interval markers in the progression of social time.'
(Leach, 1976:77).

Rituals are concerned with movement and change, and for the individual these transitions mark the changes that an individual must go through in a lifetime from birth to puberty to marriage and death. Although time and age are continuous processes (we all age every moment of every day), the continuous flow of age from conception to death is marked in every society into periods of differing importance.

In our own society we too differentiate phases in the life of an individual by arbitrary markers of social time. The churching of women after childbirth used to mark their entrance back into normal life. Among some

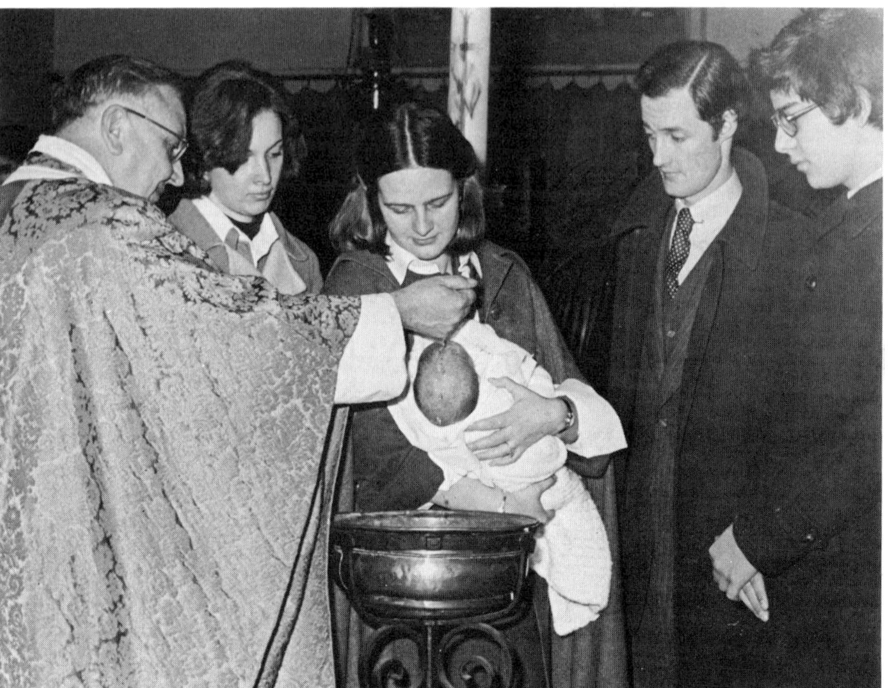

At some Christian baptisms, the child is absolved of original sin with a symbolic 'washing' and initiated into the Christian community of the church.

Even though the voting age has been reduced to eighteen and many people marry before their twenty-first birthday, in Britain it is still considered a significant point in the move from dependency on parents to full adulthood.

British people at the 21-year-old birthday, parents give their children a symbolic key (on a card) as well as a real key to the house in recognition of the attainment of social maturity and adult responsibility. Marriage, as in most societies, changes the status of the individuals to be married and gives them new rights, obligations and legal status. The wedding ceremony is the ritual that expresses formally this transition from single to married status and the establishment of new kinship bonds between two families.

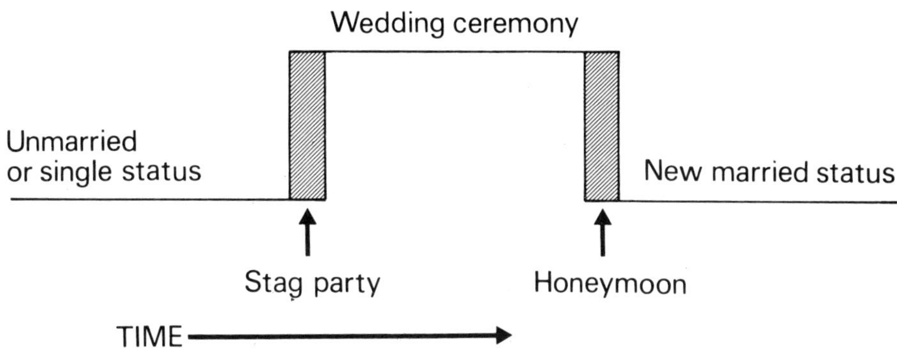

Marriage in Britain

As in most rituals of individual transition, the first step is to set the individual apart from his or her usual activities. Immediately before the wedding, the bride and groom are separated. The groom is taken out by male friends to indulge in ribaldry, excessive drinking and sexual joking before the wedding. The bride is not allowed to see the groom (it would be 'bad luck') on the

The bride in white (symbolic of purity and virginity) is symbolically 'given away' by her father to her husband. This ritual expresses the dependent status of the woman in both the unmarried and married state.

wedding day until she actually arrives at the church. At the wedding ceremony, the relatives and friends of the bride are seated on one side of the church (usually the left side facing the altar) and the relatives and friends of the groom are seated on the opposite side, in a symbolic spatial statement of the relationship between the two families. The bride in white (symbolic of purity and virginity) is traditionally brought in and 'given away' by her father or some male relative. The symbolism of the marriage ceremony itself is very rich and has changed significantly in the last few years. For instance, women's attitudes towards the relationship of wife to husband have changed so that fewer brides nowadays promise to 'love, honour *and obey*'.

Finally, the couple must be incorporated into 'normal' life again in their new married status. In contrast to being set apart from each other, now the couple as one unit are set apart from other people during their honeymoon. At this time they must 'go away' (even if only to a hotel) and are expected to be in a special state of mind and to behave in a way that is inappropriate for 'normal' married couples (e.g. gaze into each other's eyes, have frequent sexual intercourse, etc). At the end of the honeymoon the groom traditionally carries the bride over the threshold of their new home, and the ritual is completed.

Social boundaries

In this book, we are dealing mainly with the symbolism of social life, that is, what people perceive their society to be, the way they represent it symbolically and in ritual and the consequences this perception has for their everyday behaviour. All societies differentiate and mark out social boundaries – boundaries between themselves and others, between people within the society, boundaries in space and time, etc. The variety of ways of doing this is very great. Furthermore, societies have a very rich repertoire of natural and socially invented symbols on which to anchor these divisions. Some symbols, for example, are associated with a particular culture. The polar bear is not likely to be a symbol used by the Bedouin Arabs, though a camel might be. On the other hand, animal symbolism is common to a great many cultures. So we very often find that societies draw upon the same fundamental and universal representations to express symbolically their important categories of thought and social differences. The natural terrain and other divisions of space, the parts of the body, and the perceived sexual differences are some of the 'natural' symbols that we find again and again in society and that will become the focus of this book. Thus, although much of this book is concerned with ways of expressing differences in society and between societies, it is also concerned with the fundamental unity of people in that these natural themes express very basic concerns common to all.

To achieve this end, we have chosen five societies that we will try to understand in terms of the basic themes. Examples from British society are also used when relevant, though there is no attempt to present a systematic view of British society. The five societies, the Kayapó of Central Brazil, the Maltese, the Gypsies of America, the Balinese, and the Swahili of Chole Island, Tanzania are not typical of any *type* of society; they do not represent any 'stage' of social evolution, nor are they *typical* of any degree of technological development. They are simply five different societies in widely separate parts of the world.

Among the five societies we find represented three world religions – Christianity, Hinduism, and Islam – and two societies with unique religions. There is a wide range of racial types as well as several levels of technological complexity. Each society has its own particular and unique social organisation, but none of them live in isolation, removed from the events of the wider nation of which they form a part. Furthermore in each society, a social anthropologist has undertaken an intensive analysis of the social organisation of the people and lived for a period of time as one of them.

Chapter Two Social Space

Inside the house, in the street, behind the counter, in church: each of these locations has its own particular social meaning to us, and our confusion when confronted with an unfamiliar society stems partially from the unfamiliar way space in that society is organised. One task of the social anthropologist is to understand the spatial order or boundaries created by a society because space is one of the ways in which society is experienced.

Boundaries of space appear in many contexts. They may be tangible, physical boundaries such as a wall between two rooms, or they may

In this Housing development in Camden, the boundaries between houses are carefully constructed to give each family a very private area.

be intangible spatial boundaries such as the amount of space people leave between themselves when passing each other on the street. We are, all the time, dividing up space into bounded areas. We draw boundaries between our private living area and areas of public activity, between religious activities and secular situations, between people we can be physically close to and those from whom we keep a correct distance. In all of these cases, both the way the space is cut up and the behaviour appropriate for a particular piece of space, is determined by the social context.

Both the society we are part of and the natural physical environment influence our perception of space. So whether you live in the Saharan desert or the Amazon jungle will have an effect on the way you perceive, for example, distance. When we try to understand how societies use space, how they divide it up both conceptually and physically, we are looking at a combination of their form of social organisation and their perception of the physical environment. Both of these elements, the social as well as the physical, will form a single interacting whole in which no one element can be said to determine the other. For example, ancient building sites in Britain were placed very much according to the lie of the land. Durham Cathedral and York Minster are so situated that they can be seen from any direction for miles. Nowadays, this criterion has become virtually irrelevant, and other features of the social environment, such as the location of industries, influence the choice of building sites.

The towers of Durham Cathedral, located on a rise in the middle of a peninsula in the River Wear, dominate the landscape for miles in each direction.

Traditionally in Britain the bridegroom carries his bride across the threshold of their new home. The threshold represents their entrance into a new life.

Physical space is also often used as a way of representing social relationships. This is most easily seen when there is a change in social status or in the public recognition of a social relationship because such a change may be accompanied by a move from one determined space to another. So in Britain, traditionally when a man and woman get married, they move from their parent's home to their own home, and the bridegroom carries his bride across the threshold of the house in a symbolic gesture that she is crossing the boundary from unmarried to married status. When Gypsies in California get married, the bride is said to be taken through the 'gate' – that is, she is symbolically handed over in the marriage hall from a representative of her relatives to a representative of her husband's relatives, sometimes with violent verbal exchanges. This is a metaphorical way of stating that she passes from one status to another and from one kin group to another.

However space in society is divided up, it is always conceived in relative terms. Earth is relative to sky, close to distant, east to west, public to private etc. Boundaries are, therefore, not absolute. How do we know where the boundary to one kind of space ends and the other begins? Isn't a boundary itself a piece of space? In the space between A and B, where does the boundary belong? In practice what happens is:

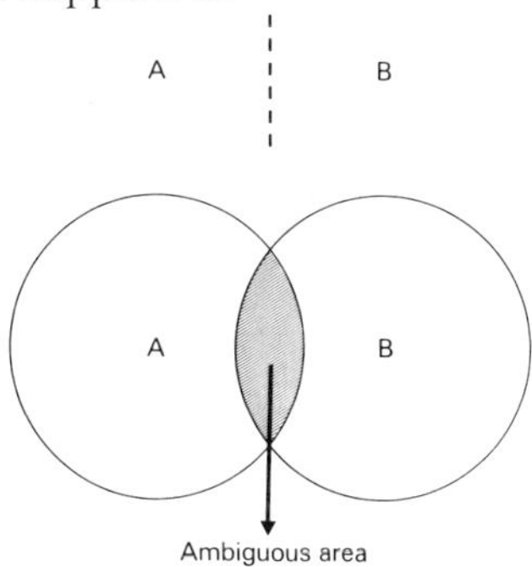

To use a familiar example, boundaries between nations usually contain a hazy 'no man's land'. Property boundaries are also classic sources of ambiguity. Good fences may make good neighbours, but they also create the problem of who actually owns the fence and is responsible for its upkeep.

The crossing of physical boundaries, whether they be frontiers or thresholds, is always accompanied by ritual just as is the transition from one social status to another. When people enter your house certain formalised

Boundaries between nations usually contain a hazy 'no man's land'. The Berlin Wall is an example of a rigid boundary constructed for political purposes, but even here there is a desolate and deserted no man's land.

Good fences may make good neighbours but who actually owns the fence?

Boundaries between domestic and public contexts

actions are expected of you, such as greeting them, offering them a seat or something to drink or eat. These actions depend on factors such as the closeness of their relationship to you, the purpose of the visit, and their relative social standing. The appropriate action towards people crossing the threshold seems so 'natural' to us, we hardly need to think about it.

A familiar boundary is the threshold. Although the crossing of the threshold is a move from a public area to a domestic (but not always private) area, societies give it different meanings, and deal with it in different ways.

In Malta, for example, all villages are arranged with a large church in the centre and a public square around it. Most people live in villages where they are known by everyone. On the streets and in the public square, their actions are subject to public scrutiny. Their home, on the other hand, is a private domestic area that is protected from public scrutiny. The house is open for public view on two notable occasions: the annual festa and the baptismal party. On both occasions the house is decorated, the windows are thrown open, and the front rooms are occupied and lighted. Many people who normally do not cross the threshold are invited in, and others can look in.

In Naxxar village in Malta, the square around the church is both the physical as well as the social centre of the village.

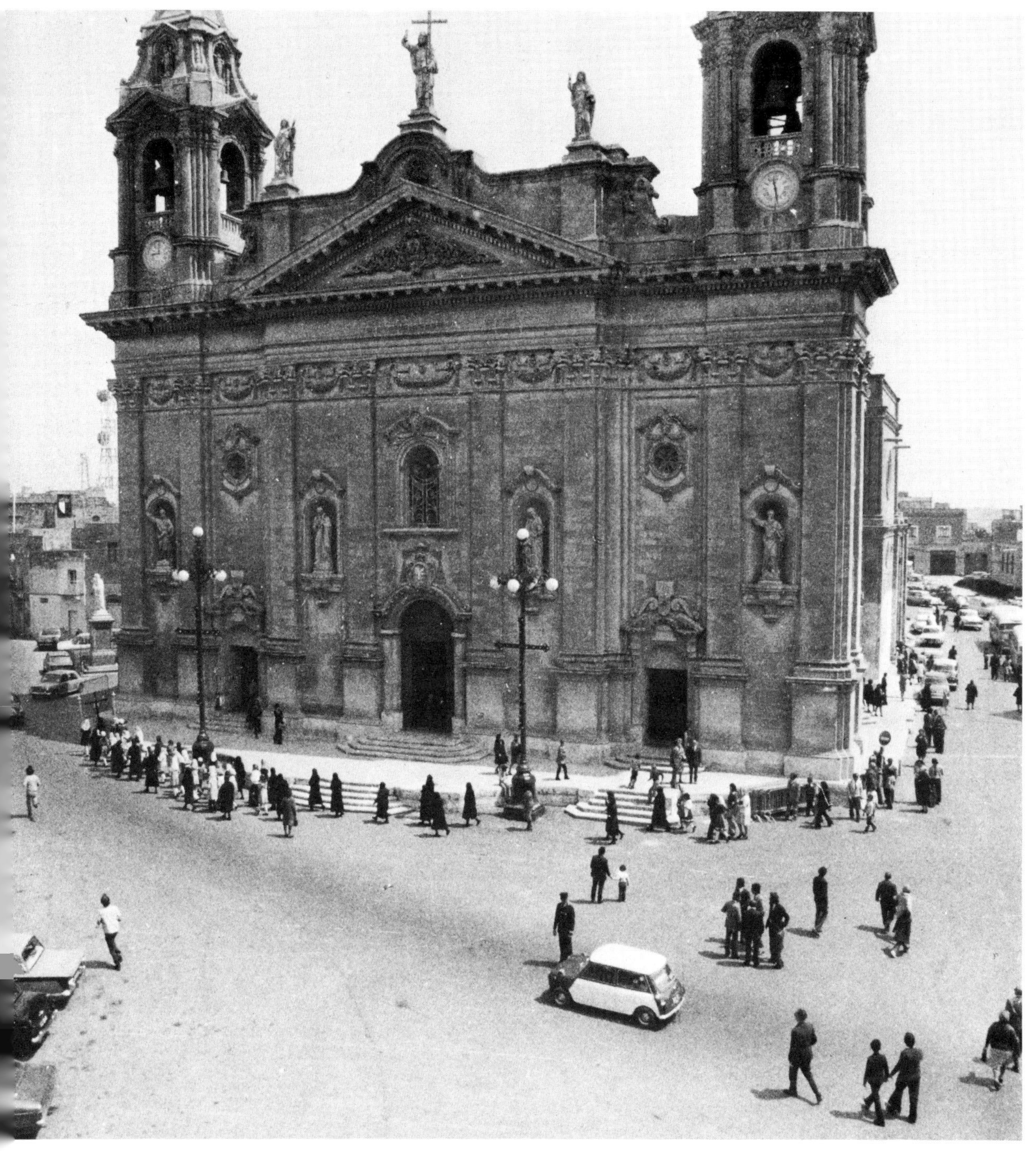

Maltese houses look inward to an inner courtyard where relatives and good friends are received and strangers are not allowed to penetrate.

Maltese houses look inward to an inner courtyard where only relatives and good friends are allowed. The front rooms, usually separated off, are for receiving formal guests. But it is in the entrance to the house, the ambiguous area between public and domestic domains, that danger lies. The Maltese attribute the evil eye to certain strangers and outsiders, all non-relatives. One Maltese woman explained what the evil eye is:

'Well, somebody looks at you in such a way that he wants some evil to happen to you – some harm to happen, and it's like witchcraft. It's mentioned in the religious books you know. We used to believe in it – that people who mean harm can wish you something very bad. It was believed that if you burned olive leaves you would keep the evil eye out of your house. I remember mother burning some olive branches, and she would scatter them around the house or near a dying cat and immediately the cat would be well again. When the priest came to bless our house we used to be given one of these branches.'

In Malta danger from the evil eye is only apparent when these outsiders come into your own home, i.e. cross the threshold. Thus the entrance to each house, the boundary between public and domestic space, is

protected by certain objects with the power to counter the evil eye. Usually there is a mirror that meets the eye from the door, in the hope that if a person with the evil eye looks in, the evil will be reflected out again. Horns, of a goat or bull, and blessed olive branches generally used throughout the Mediterranean area to ward off the evil eye, are placed somewhere in the entrance to the house. The hope is that by the time a person has passed through these magical devices, the effects will be countered. Horseshoes on doors and rowan trees in the front garden in Britain serve the same protective purpose.

In Chole the compound at the back of the house is the woman's area and is separated from the public area of men in front of the house by a wall of thatch. At Muslim festivals the compound is filled with the women of the village who cook the feast and have their own ceremonies behind the fence.

In Kanga village, on Chole Island, on the other hand, the front of a house is a public area where men sit and talk to visitors on the veranda. The courtyard at the back of the house is an area designated for women, and here they cook and chat with each other. Compounds of houses, therefore, have a male area in front and a female area at the back. The boundary between male and female areas is usually marked by a fence, and during some rituals, when many women gather in the back to pound rice, this fence may be extended to accommodate the increased numbers.

On Chole Island, there is a strong emphasis on individual privacy. This is expressed, in household terms, in the desire for each married couple or single adult to have his or her own house. Old people, barely able to care for themselves, will still insist on their own house and even young boys approaching manhood will leave their natal home, and construct their own house. A widowed or divorced woman will live in her own house rather than join the household of a relative.

The Gypsies in California, on the other hand, enjoy living in communal caravans or houses in groups of large extended families, sometimes spanning 3 or 4 generations. When they occupy a house, they immediately knock down as many walls as possible to create one large living space. Outsiders who happen to enter their house, such as policemen or social workers, cross the threshold into the exclusive world of the Gypsies. Gypsy hospitality requires that they offer food or drink to anyone that enters this house, so the Gypsies maintain their distance from outsiders by allocating one chair and one set of dishes for outsiders that are not then used by other Gypsies. This action avoids danger of contamination from non-Gypsy pollution and at the same time is a symbolic act of reinforcing their own separateness. For similar reasons, some middle class people in Britain keep a special mug for workmen's tea.

On Chole Island, boys who are approaching manhood leave their home and build a small hut of their own, next to their parents' house. This move to their own house is part of the transition from childhood into manhood. Here a youth and his younger brother are putting up a wattle frame prior to filling it in with mud.

The streets in Naxxar radiate out from the church square away from the area where the wealthiest and most influential people live.

Sacred and secular space

In many societies, there are areas that are designated as special, abnormal or sacred in some way. Sacred, in anthropological usage, refers to some thing, place, person or object that is *set apart*, for whatever reason, from ordinary persons, activity or objects. Sacredness is best understood when seen in opposition to the secular; a person in a sacred, abnormal state may be expected to behave in a different or opposite manner to his normal behaviour. For example, a person in trance may become so still that death is simulated or may become possessed with wild erratic movements. In sacred states or ritual situations, a person sometimes takes on a role that is the reverse of their usual role. For example, in Malta on Maundy Thursday the priest washes the feet of twelve men in a gesture of humility, just as Christ washed the feet of his 12 disciples at the Last Supper.

Sacred space is, similarly, set apart from space where normal, everyday activities take place. In Malta the spatial organisation of the village parish reflects the central role of the church. The church stands out in the centre of the village and is easily the most dominant building there. The structure of the village can be seen as a series of concentric circles with the church at the centre moving out to the secular outer edge of the village. Around the central church live the most influential people in the village who are also the most influential church members. On the main streets stretching out from the village square live those who enjoy wealth and high prestige and who because of their position in the community, participate in religious associations. Next come the devout rank and file, and on the outskirts of the village are the least active parishioners. Persons of lowest status, that is persons who have some 'shameful' past and are virtually outsiders in parish activities, often live in outlying farmhouses. Moreover, farmers who, because of their occupation, are obliged to live in outlying farm areas, and therefore are geographically and socially isolated from important activities taking place in the village, have low status, partially because of their isolation. The scale of religious prestige corresponds with the scale of secular prestige, wealth and political influence.

This rather simple presentation of social and spatial structure from sacred core to secular periphery has been modified, in recent years in particular, by the increase in the number of tourists living in Malta. Tourists have built villas on the outside of the village, and some influential Maltese have also started doing the same. Recently, then, the village has opened up considerably, and many people now look outside the parish for entertainment and work. Furthermore the presence of the Labour Party club, historically in opposition to the church, in the central square, has also challenged the authority of the church in the parish.

Religion in Malta is always evident, and for the Maltese there is not always a strict separation of 'sacred' and 'secular'. Priests live at home, and people sometimes read the newspaper in church. The church is the centre of sacred activities and from this core, sacredness radiates out into the village in many ways. Shrines on every corner and street are like arms of the church reaching out into the village.

The best spatial representation of the presence of the church is a procession. Processions start in the church and move with sacred objects, statues and banners, to the village streets, on to the edge of the village, and return in a circle back to the church. Not only the route of the procession but the order of the participants is significant. For example, in Our Lady of Sorrows procession, one of the most important religious processions in Malta, the following order was observed:

The order of Our Lady of Sorrows procession.

In Maltese villages shrines on every corner and street are like arms of the church reaching out to the periphery of the village.

All processions and funerals follow this same order; the most sacred position is at the end of the formal part of the procession. Here the statues carried by villagers mark the transition between the sacred and secular sections of the procession.

Social and natural space

Most of us live in an environment where nature in an untouched and 'wild' state is not easily visible. Most of our visible space is changed and moulded by

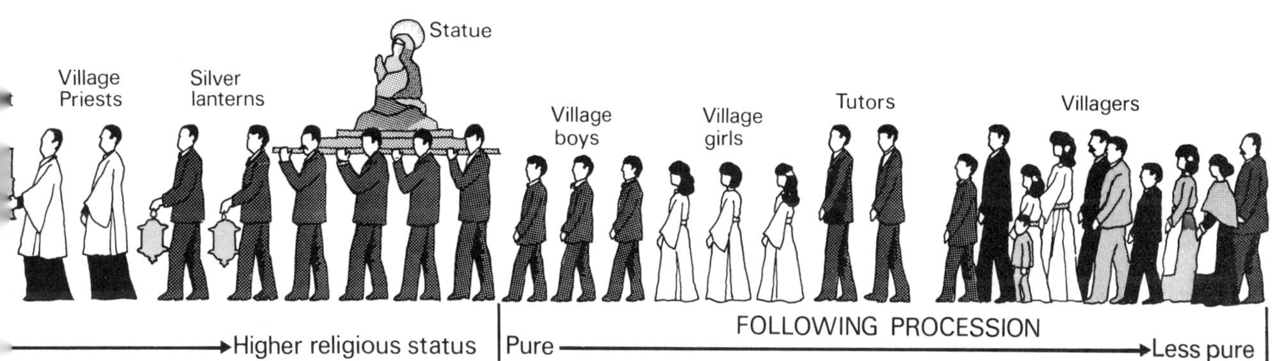

For the Kayapó Indians, most of their environment consists of untouched rain forest and natural waterways that appear as a jumble of random curves.

our society. For some societies, however, 'pure' nature seems a jumble of random curves. It contains no straight lines and few geometrical shapes of any kind. This contrasts with the man-made world where regular, geometrical shapes – straight lines, rectangles, triangles, circles and so on – are predominant. As we might expect, in such places the contrast between 'nature' and 'culture' may take on an important physical and spatial meaning.

The Kayapó of Central Brazil draw a map of their village that looks like this:

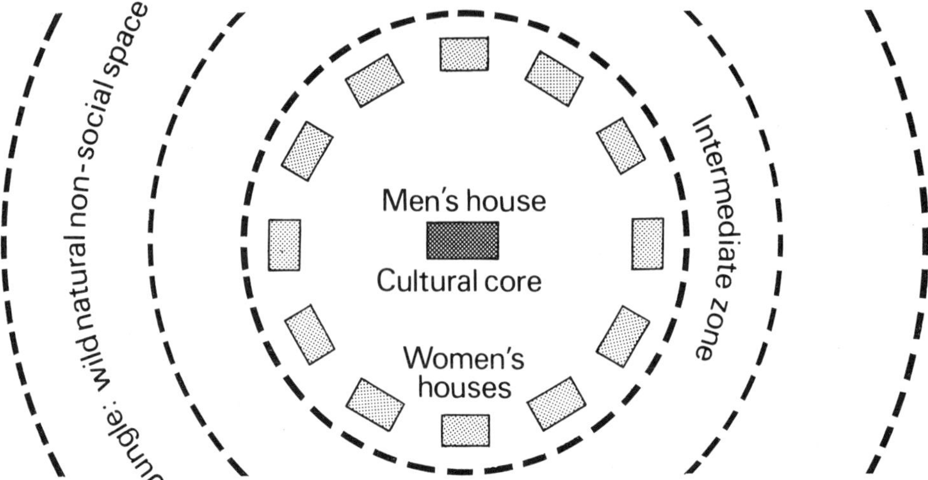

An actual village may not be arranged exactly as shown; however the Kayapó perceive the ideal order of a village in this way. The centre of the village is not only the physical centre, it represents the cultural or social core of the village – human activity at its most communal level as in Malta. Appropriately, as we move outward we move towards the less communal. Women's households are the centre of extended family life, but not the focus of more general community activities. Outside the village is non-social, natural space.

In the intermediate zone between the social world of the Kayapó village and the natural world of the forest, many rituals of transition take place. Young boys and men regularly chop down the encroaching forest.

The intermediate zone is one of transition from natural to social. The activities, which are mainly ritual ones, that take place here are those of transition from one social condition or social state to another. The graveyard, where the Kayapó bury those who move from this life to an after life, is located there. And young boys who go into seclusion for initiation into manhood are secluded in the intermediate zone. Terry Turner explains how the significance of this spatial map is highlighted in ritual:

'Dances are dramatic performances with choral singing, coordinated dance gestures and steps, and spectacular feather ornaments. The dance proceeds in a circle around the periphery of the village plaza, then the dancers make a sally into the 'bush' outside the village, returning after penetrating a short distance into the 'natural' (a-social) space surrounding the social space of the village. All ceremonial songs and dances are thought to come from animals or ghosts – in short, the 'natural' world outside of society. Dancing out of the village into 'natural' space and back symbolises this idea that the ritual consists of the transformation of something natural into something social.'
(unpublished communication)

Kayapó dances take place in the centre of the village where communal activities are usual, though sometimes they dance out into the bush into the world of animals and ghosts and then return to the village. For the Kayapó, the village is an area of social activity in contrast to the 'natural' world of the forest.

For the Balinese the mountains are holy and the abodes of the Gods in contrast to the sea which is unholy and filthy.

For the Kayapó, nature is clearly distinguished from the village, which represents social or cultural life. The main concern in ritual is in transforming the natural into the social – the natural self through body painting into a social person and the natural animals and spirits into the social core of the village. This nature-culture contrast, so evident in the spatial map of the Kayapó environment, must not, however, be seen only in such literal terms. Many societies make a distinction between nature and culture in a broader, more metaphorical sense. It might be easier to appreciate this if we think of 'nature' or of the 'wild' as anything outside the social, and moral boundary of a society, however it may be defined. The contrast may often be generalised to one between the 'known' and the 'unknown'. All that is outside one's own society is treated as an unknown and therefore because it is not part of the accepted order of one's own society, it is the 'wild'.

Bali: cosmological orientation and hierarchical space

So far the kinds of contrasts we have been examining – public and domestic, sacred and secular, nature and culture – have been relatively simple. But there are societies where spatial orientations are more complex and take on a more permanent significance.

The island of Bali, in Indonesia, is such a case. It is a natural volcanic island surrounded by the sea. The mountains, in the centre of Bali are conceived of as the abode of the Gods and are the highest and most holy place. The sea, by contrast, is the lowest place; it is unholy, and all that is filthy must be cast there or into the rivers that carry filth to the sea. The Balinese are never unconscious of their position in space on two dimensions; first, all orientation is either *kaja*, towards the mountain, or *klod*, towards the sea. This means that in South Bali, *kaja* is north and in North Bali it is south. East and West remain the same on all parts of the island. The Balinese are very careful always to know in which direction lies the mountain, and when people discuss directions they say, for example, 'the person on the east', or 'the temple to the north of me'. To be lost in Bali, is not to know where *kaja* or, the mountain, is. A person is 'lost' when he has lost a sense of his own position in relation to the cosmological directions. Jane Belo describes a case of being 'lost':

'We once sent a small boy of eight to a distant village where he was to learn to dance, living in the house of his teacher. Riding in the car, the child lost his sense of direction. When we visited him three days later, he had not begun his lessons, for he was still *paling* (lost). "How can I tell him to turn to the East, to advance towards the North, when he is *paling*?" said the teacher. The boy was returned to his village, where once on familiar ground, he found himself. After several days he went back to the house of the teacher, intently watching every curve of the winding road. But it was no good – he was again *paling*. He grew anxious and was unable to eat and sleep. Then someone thought of taking him out into the fields, where he could see the high cone of the Gunung Agung, the highest mountain, rising to the North. He was cured of his trouble on the spot, and had no recurrence of it during the six weeks of his stay in the village. He seemed happy there and made great progress with his dancing'.
(Jane Belo, 1935:127)

As well as keeping a sense of North-South directions, a person should also keep a sense of balance in relation to the ground. There are three ways for a Balinese to be: standing, seated (sitting or squatting) and lying down. Lying down is only correct when sleeping or ill. To fall down is considered an unlucky sign, and even children never stand on their heads or turn somersaults. There is felt to be something wrong about the inverted position, with the head where the feet ought to be. One of the best known demons is pictured standing on his hands and is known as the 'Upside Down Demon' (Belo, 125). Balance and correct orientation are considered essential in every moment of life, and this is very evident to the outsider observing the Balinese walking down the road or working. The absolute poise and balance of bearing is noticeable in posture, walk and the slightest gesture. People move slowly and with considerable grace; clumsiness and poor posture are almost never seen.

The Balinese are always conscious of their position above the ground which should not be higher than that of their social superior. The Balinese have a modified form of the Indian caste system with three higher

Balance and poise are important in Bali and are particularly developed in dancers.

castes, the Brahmana, Wesia and Ksatriya and the low caste, the Sudras. In spatial terms, this caste system is expressed in the ideal of higher castes sitting above lower castes, men above women and adults above children. In private family groups, seating arrangements in a hierarchical fashion may not be observed, but on public occasions, politeness requires it.

The most prestigious priest in Bali, the *pedanda*, is habitually seated on a platform or a high place. When a *pedanda* makes holy water, which he does daily as part of his own personal worship as well as for rituals, he washes his feet before sitting on his platform, thus symbolically removing all relationship with the ground before entering into communication with the gods. Therefore, he is seen as suspended in space between earth and sky and thus in a correct sacred position for inviting the gods down to him.

Both of these dimensions, hierarchy and cosmological orientations, can be seen in the way a Balinese courtyard, for example in South Bali, is organised. At the north-eastern corner of the courtyard, on a raised platform

The *Pedanda istri* (female priest) sits on a platform to make holy water helped by several attendants and surrounded by all the accoutrements of the task.

is the household shrine or *Sanggah* where offerings to the gods are placed. If a courtyard has a temple it will be in the northeast corner which is the most sacred direction, combining the abode of the sun with that of the mountain. Living quarters will be in the centre between north and south; the kitchen is always a separate building and is located generally to the south of living quarters because this is the area where food, brought in from outside, is

A family shrine, or Sanngah, is in the north east corner of a courtyard.

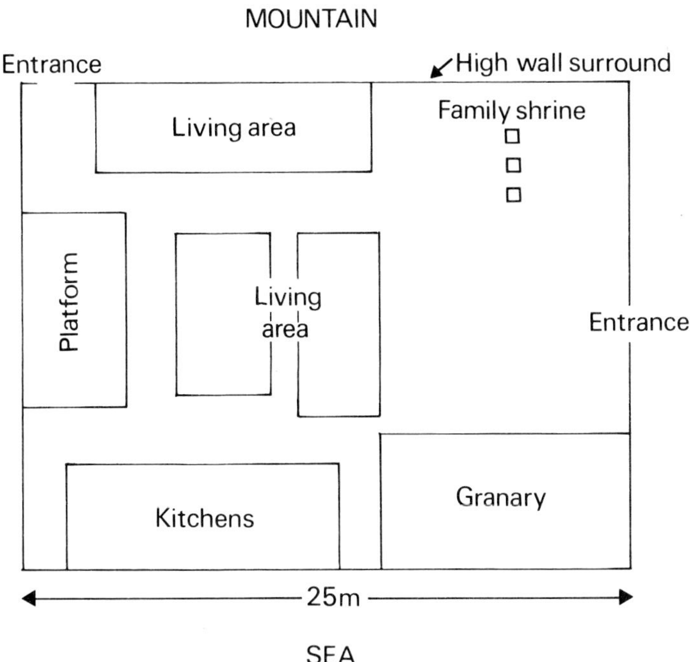

The courtyard is arranged according to Balinese spatial concepts, so that the holiest place, the Sanngah with the household gods, faces the mountain and the most unclean items, such as a mother and newborn baby, are on the side facing the sea.

transformed into something which is acceptable to the 'inside'. The granaries, where things from outside are stored, are in the southernmost corner of the courtyard, and it is here too that a mother with her new baby will stay until she is allowed back into normal society. Inside the courtyard, there is usually a pavilion or raised platform used both as a sitting area as well as for the performance of personal rituals. This platform is also important for displaying the corpse when a death occurs, for it must be kept high off the ground.

There is also in Bali a concept of completeness or wholeness that is expressed in many ways. For example, no person is complete without marriage because the complete person is the harmony of male and female joined together. God images in Bali tend to come in pairs, but they share one name. They are so alike it is very difficult to identify the male or female, since they are merely male and female aspects of a single entity. It is in the nature of Gods to be complete, to combine maleness and femaleness and to share one name and one fundamental identity.

A spatial manifestation of completeness in Bali is the idea of the 'centre'. The centre is the seat of power because it combines the virtues of all the directions surrounding it. The symbol of the centre, as the unity of the surrounding directions, is nowhere more apparent, in spatial terms, than in the 'twin purifying ceremony'.

In Bali, the birth of different sex twins to a member of the three upper castes is a good omen, but the same event in a Sudra family is considered a disaster, and as a result the whole village is polluted. The Balinese assume that indecent intimacy (i.e. incest) has taken place between brother and sister in the womb, and whereas among the Gods, and even the upper castes, such a situation is acceptable, for the Sudras who come from the 'ground', it is a

God images in Bali come in male and female pairs that share the same name and look almost identical. The Balinese concept of completeness requires the joining of male and female.

highly polluting state of affairs. No ritual can take place in the community – no one can be married or cremated – until it has been purified, and the people live in a state of anxiety and ill omen during the period of pollution.

Since the birth of dissimilar twins occurred when we went to film in Bali, there was a purification ceremony affecting a community or ritual area of four villages. This purification ceremony is representative of Balinese ritual in that it contrasts high and low and the four main directions. Cleansing consists of taking the pollution down to the sea, then transferring it to intermediate objects (from the twins to offerings), attracting the spirits who benefit from pollution and throwing the offerings into the sea. Offerings to the Gods are kept high, and the high offerings are carried back into the village. Offerings to the spirits, who benefit from pollution, are put on the ground, and these are thrown into the sea or allowed to be eaten by dogs. The sea itself is not so much polluting as the means by which pollution is removed. Sea water is the antithesis of holy water. The pollution is removed by a combination of, negative and positive acts: transforming pollution to offerings that are discarded into sea water, and washing with and drinking Holy water which contributes to the well-being of the family and community.

When the twins were born the first move was to isolate them and their parents from the rest of the village for six weeks. In former times the house of the family would have been dismantled and moved to the graveyard outside the village where all sorts of demons, witches, and horrors, such as disembodied limbs, reside. Because of the physically difficult conditions for the mother and children, usually one or both of the twins died. Nowadays the family are merely isolated in their own courtyard. Finally, on an auspicious day, at the end of the 6 weeks, the villagers go down to the beach carrying all of their Gods and offerings. The Gods must be carried to the sea where all pollution will be cast off though it would be polluting for the God figures themselves to be put into the sea. Instead the pollution is transferred to offerings symbolising the god figures and these are then thrown into the sea.

These objects and offerings are made in the village and carried down to the beach where they are laid out on the sand in the four directions, North, South, East and West. The composition of each offering is extremely complex and only known by certain Brahmana women who are specialists in such matters. Nevertheless, there are certain offerings for each direction. For example, certain colours are associated with the four directions: North with black, South with red, East with white, and West with yellow. In the twin purification ceremony, a chicken skin with feathers of each colour is laid out in the correct direction, and a chicken with multicoloured feathers is placed in the centre. The centre brings together all colours, as it is the unity of all directions.

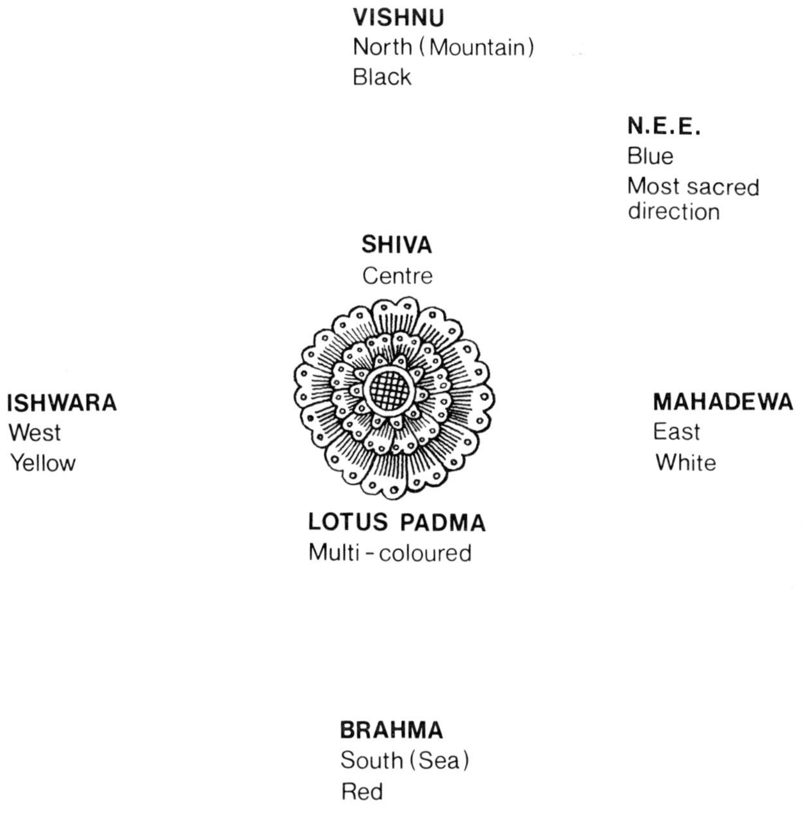

VISHNU
North (Mountain)
Black

N.E.E.
Blue
Most sacred direction

SHIVA
Centre

ISHWARA
West
Yellow

MAHADEWA
East
White

LOTUS PADMA
Multi-coloured

BRAHMA
South (Sea)
Red

The trinity of Vishnu, Shiva, and Brahma, part of the Hindu Pantheon of Gods, are on the North-South axis.

During the ceremony, the *pedanda*, or Brahmana priest, climbed onto a raised platform facing East and went through the usual ritual procedure for making holy water. Offerings for the Gods were also placed on the raised platform. Finally, the twins and their parents sat facing the priest in order to be sprinkled with holy water three times. After being sprinkled with holy water they turned to face the offerings laid on the ground. A woman, standing on the South side, by the sea, wafted the essence of the ground offerings out to sea and another woman on the East side wafted the essence of the offerings on the raised platform upwards towards the mountain. Then a woman took a twig broom and circled around the offering three times, sweeping and symbolically cleaning the ground. Bamboo klackers made noises to attract the evil spirits to their offerings, and when the ground had been cleaned and raked three times everything was gathered up and thrown into the sea where the dogs, who are earthly representations of evil spirits, immediately ate them up. Finally the representatives of the Gods that were kept on the platform at all times were carried back to the village.

Boundaries

Spatial orientations in Bali are complex and multi-dimensional and illustrate some of the ways that social ideas of cosmological directions and hierarchy can have a deep significance. The Balinese example also demonstrates two principles important in understanding the use of space to symbolise aspects of culture. First, spatial organisation depends on and expresses the social organisation. In other words, societies use physical space as a metaphor for social space. Secondly, no space is a unit in itself, it is always in relation to some contrast. Up has meaning in relation to below, East to West, sky to earth, mountain to sea, and so on. The notion of boundary is very important because to set bounds around a place or a person is both to relate it to something else and to set it apart.

The Human Frame

Chapter Three

All human beings use their bodies to communicate with other human beings. Charles Darwin first recognised the importance of communication through the medium of the body, but he concluded wrongly in his book, *The Expression of the Emotions in Man and Animals* (1872) that 'all the chief expressions exhibited by man are the same throughout the world'. (359) He based this on the assumption that bodily expression is universal because it is transmitted genetically.

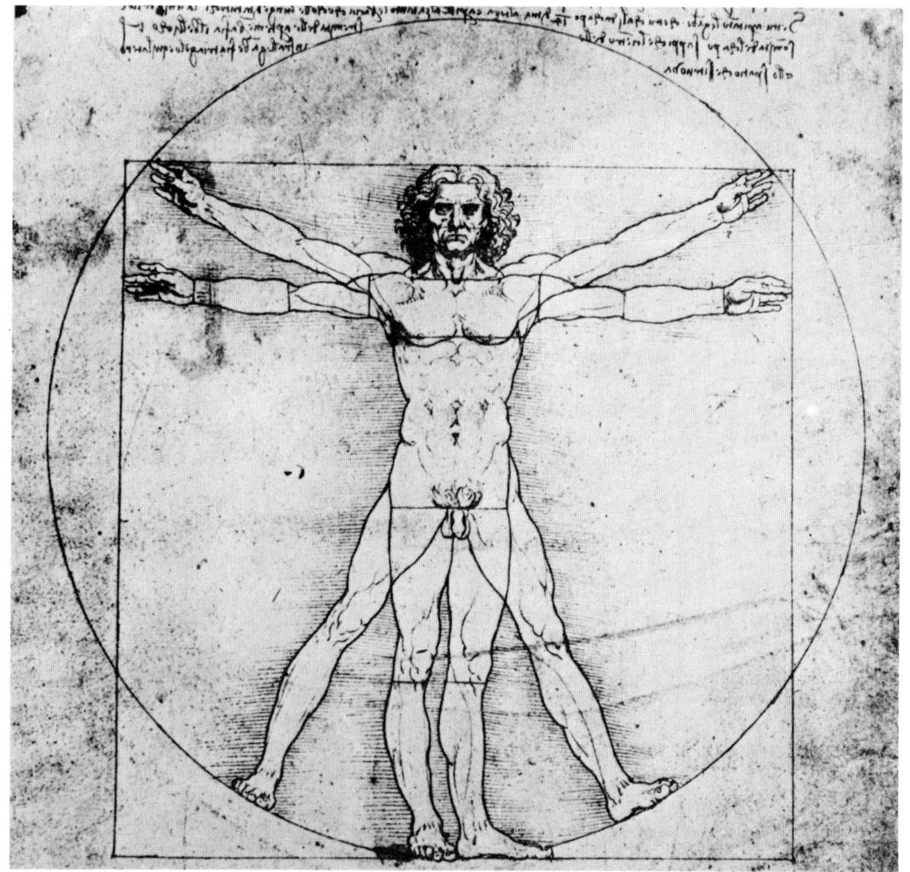

Drawing (by Leonardo da Vinci) showing the symmetry of the body.

Plate from 'The Expression of the Emotions in Man and Animals' by Charles Darwin 1892 edition titled 'Laughter'.

The first evidence that contradicted this conclusion came from studies of bodily expression in particular societies. It was found in these societies that body movement, gestures, facial expressions and so on not only varied considerably from Western society, but they were consistent with the society's particular form of social organisation. Bateson and Mead, for example, in a photographic study of Balinese parents and children, showed how the parents trained or elicited, though not necessarily consciously, the correct bodily expression in the child. A child of four or five years, for example, had already learnt the very Balinese ability to 'disassociate' or switch off when faced with a situation of stress or conflict.

By five years old, a Balinese child has learned to disassociate when faced with something fearful such as being photographed by a foreigner.

There is now a considerable corpus of evidence on bodily expressions. It is clear that although certain facial expressions which occur in situations of instinctual response (such as fright, extreme anger etc) may be universal, a very large number of expressions are culturally variable. What is interesting is why does this variability occur, and how is it learnt? One answer given by many scholars is that bodily expressions are like words in that they are merely arbitrary signs of a particular meaning, in the same way that the word DOG is purely an arbitrary *sign* for a canine animal. But a more satisfactory view is that bodily communication like any communication, though partly arbitrary, also depends on a social context to be meaningful. We can only understand the message to be communicated and the signal used to communicate it (i.e. the body in this case) if we understand the social or cultural context within which it operates. It is here that we will find the answers to the question of variability.

Human bodies are universal elements in any society, but the way people conceive of their bodies varies considerably and is reflected in the way they order their society.

Social perceptions of the body

We know that the members of a particular society share certain basic attitudes towards the human body. In any society there will be a communally shared knowledge of how a 'healthy', or a 'beautiful', or an 'erotic' body is defined. This means that the 'social body' has an influence on the way the physical body is perceived. In other words, the physical body as we perceive it is a part of our 'social construction of reality'.

In our society we tend to think that our bodies merely express our own individuality. It is true that, in the most obvious sense, bodies are a visible, external package for the personality of the individual. In all societies, people can demonstrate their own individual personality through their facial

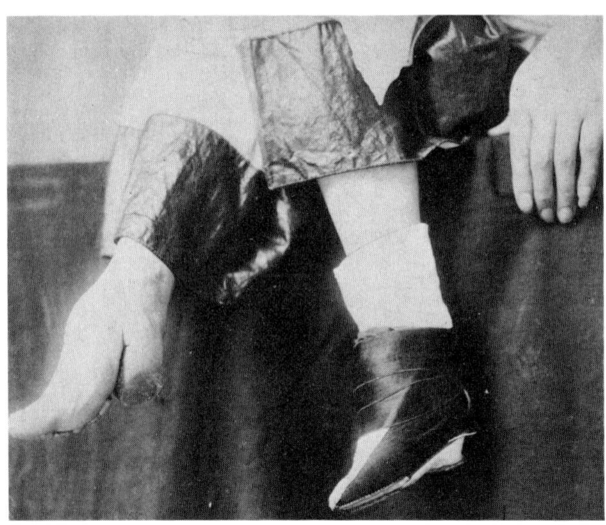

Above and centre left
The high status bride of an Indian Prince is covered from head to toe, lower status village women are far less completely covered.

Above
Public display of the body by Raquel Welch.

Below left
The foot of this Chinese woman is completely deformed by binding. Her toes have been folded under to produce a 'dainty' point.

expressions, gestures, postures, clothing, body paint, etc. We learn about an individual partly from understanding these external messages. But if the cultural context is unfamiliar, then expressions of individuality are lost on the observer. We have all experienced the impression that people of a different culture or 'race' all 'look alike'. People of other races also feel the same about us. This is because individual differences are only meaningful to the observer within a particular cultural context. Without knowing the context, perception of a number of faces is often based on too little information to sort out subtle differences. So we only understand the 'messages' when we understand the cultural context within which they are expressed.

It follows then that the external appearance of people carries cultural information. By studying dress, hair, decorations and facial expressions, gestures, and postures, we can glean information of a particular society's ideas of beauty, gender (masculinity and femininity), eroticism and health. What's more, we even find that hair, feet, nails etc., are often altered, in some cases drastically, to fit with the culture's ideas of the correct, healthy, beautiful or sexy body.

Western women, for example, wear special apparel to produce, upturned breasts, and the absence of a bra may be perceived as slatternly, immoral or defiantly Women's Lib. Some of the more wealthy women go so far as to pump silicone into their breasts and have ribs removed, faces 'lifted' and noses shrunk. Higher status Western women expect to be 'on

The Kayapó cover their bodies with paint both because it is beautiful and as a way of identifying age set status.

display' and seen publicly. In contrast, higher status Indian women are displayed less, and their bodies more covered and veiled, whilst women in Indian villages of lower status cover themselves less. Aristocratic Chinese women used to bind their feet so they became atrophied, and therefore took 'dainty' steps.

Kayapó men, to enhance their beauty, wear lip discs – wooden discs that fit into a hole in the bottom lip which is distended gradually. The Kayapó pluck their facial hair, including eyebrows and eyelashes, and paint their bodies partly because they believe it to enhance beauty and attractiveness. The patterns of body paint also vary according to which 'age grade' an individual Kayapó belongs to and therefore acts as a way of identifying status as well.

The Balinese, on the other hand, have a horror of appearing animal-like – such as being hairy, having pointed teeth like fangs or crawling on all fours. In art, Balinese demons are pictured with fangs covering their faces and drawings of animals exaggerate the fangs, adding them to the face and head as well. The Balinese, at puberty or marriage, but at least before cremation (which is necessary for reincarnation) have their teeth filed flat to emphasise the quality of being essentially human. A Balinese who fails to have his or her teeth filed, never having been really human, cannot expect to be reincarnated.

The Balinese make a strong distinction between animals and humans. Demons in Bali are humans with animal-like fangs, hairy bodies and gross snouts on the face.

One of the strangest cultural conceptions of the body is found among the 'Nacirema', who live between Canada and Mexico, and have been described by Horace Miner in his article 'Body Ritual Among the 'Nacirema':

'The fundamental belief underlying the whole system appears to be that the human body is ugly and that its natural tendency is to debility and disease. Incarcerated in such a body, a man's only hope is to avert these characteristics through the use of the powerful influences of ritual and ceremony. Every household has one or more shrines devoted to this purpose. The more powerful individuals in the society have several shrines in their houses, and, in fact, the opulence of a house is often referred to in terms of the number of such ritual centres it possesses. The focal point of the shrine is a box or chest which is built into the wall. In this chest are kept the many charms and magical potions without which no native believes he could live.

The charm is not disposed of after it has served its purpose, but is placed in the charm box of the household shrine. As these magical packets are specific for certain ills, and the real or imagined maladies of the people are many, the charm-box is usually full to over-flowing. The magical packets are so numerous that people forget what their purposes were and fear to use them again. While the natives are very vague on this point, we can only assume that the idea in retaining all the old magical materials is that their presence in the charm-box, before which the body rituals are conducted, will in some way protect the worshipper.

Beneath the charm-box is a small font. Each day every member of the family, in succession, enters the shrine room, bows his head before the charm-box, mingles different sorts of holy water on the font, and proceeds with a brief rite of ablution. The holy waters are secured from the Water Temple of the community, where the priests conduct elaborate ceremonies to make the liquid ritually pure. The daily body ritual performed by everyone includes a mouth-rite. Despite the fact that these people are so punctilious about the care of the mouth, this rite involves a practice which strikes the uninitiated stranger as revolting. It was reported to me that the ritual consists of inserting a small bundle of hog hairs into the mouth, along with certain magical powders, and then moving the bundle in a highly formalized series of gestures.'

(Miner 1956)

These practices are also shared by the 'Hsitirb' who live on the Islands North of the English Channel and serves to show that one society's 'hygiene' is another society's ritual.

Bodily emissions and mutilations

There is frequently an idea of ritual efficacy or dangerous powers associated with the body or areas of the body. The emissions of the body in particular – blood, urine, faeces, menstrual blood, semen, vomit, saliva, sweat, etc – are all by-products that may be considered purifying or polluting, natural or unnatural, powerfully good or powerfully evil.

The Gypsies, for example, consider all emissions from the top half of the body to be clean and curative and all emissions from the lower half to be polluting and inauspicious. Saliva, for example, is a health-giving curative substance that can counter the evil-eye. Vomit, from a certain spirit called *Mamioro* ('little grandmother') is the most valuable Gypsy cure and is used for all serious diseases as well as to conquer fear. Contact with menstrual blood, urine, faeces and semen, on the other hand, can cause illness and result in social exile.

On the other hand, among some South American Indians, faeces are considered the 'natural' by-product of food whereas vomit is the 'unnatural' waste. During ritual occasions when many kinds of normal behaviour are reversed, the normal processing of food is also reversed, and emetics are given so that extensive vomiting will take place.

It is very common to find that all bodily emissions are considered polluting. They are, once discarded from the body, both dangerous and defiling. Furthermore, parts of the body that may be removed – such as the foreskin in circumcision or hair which is shaved off – are also often seen as polluting and the rite of removal is seen as one of purification. Why should this be so? Edmund Leach suggests that:

'When we draw a social distinction between an infant and an adult the boundary is artificial; there is no biological point of discontinuity so we must make one. The act of violence, the physical mutilation of the body, marks a break point, a threshold, a point of entry. It then becomes logical to declare that whatever has been thus removed from the body is "matter out of place", it is dirty. By its removal, the purity of our social categories has been preserved, the mutilated body has been cleansed.

The opposition clean/dirty has deep psychological roots. Every individual child, as it develops a consciousness of identity, necessarily becomes concerned with the question "What am I?" "Where is the boundary of myself?" The exuviae of the human body present particular difficulty. "Are my faeces, my urine, my semen, my sweat, a part of me?" By analogy with what I have just said, the orifices of the human body constitute gateways and all exuviae are "matter out of place", like the by-products of ritual mutilation. They should logically therefore become a focus of taboo. And indeed they do. In most societies, as in our own, body products such as I have listed are the prototype of "dirt".'
(Leach 1976:62)

But Leach goes on to add that power resides in the ambiguous area of boundaries. The paradox is that the perfectly 'clean' individuals would have no potency because 'power is located in dirt'.

For example, one of the most potent sources of body symbolism in a large number of cultures is hair. It has been suggested that the hair of the head is seen as the inverse or mirror image of pubic hair on the genitals, and thus often provokes powerful emotions. It is often found that long hair is associated with unrestrained sexuality, short or bound hair with restricted

Contrasting hair styles and life styles. A lawyer, with short hair and 'clean'-shaven explains an eviction order to a 'hairy' squatter.

In Britain, long hair in men is often associated with 'lack of control'.

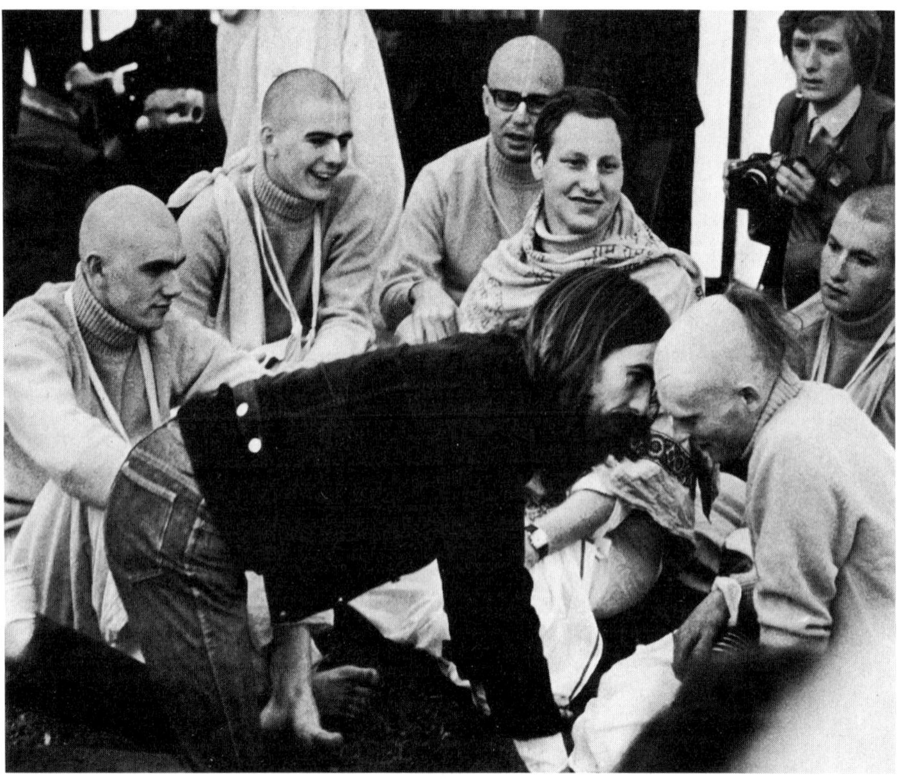

Members of The International Society of Krishna Consciousness and Beatle George Harrison.

sexuality, and shaven heads with celibacy. But the important point about hair is that whatever length of hair is considered acceptable for one social situation, for another social context a contrasting hair style will be considered correct. For example, the correct length of hair for men is likely to be the opposite of the right length for women.

In Britain, short hair is associated with masculine control and discipline whereas very long hair is associated with feminine sexuality or, in men, lack of control. But in other societies, the masculine and feminine associations of hair may be the reverse. Samson, for example, had potency, strength and power only while he kept his long locks.

The removal of hair denotes a change in the social state of an individual. Monks, and in some cases widows, shave their heads when they have entered a new state of celibacy. For a widow, the period of mourning often ends when her hair grows back again. In Bali, an infant has a ritual hair-cutting 210 days after birth, and this marks a major introduction into society and a stage in the recognition of the child as a socialised human being.

A change in the way hair is controlled or bound may have the same effect. A Gypsy bride, during the transfer from her family of birth to the family of her husband at marriage, has her hair unbound by her new sisters-in-law and is taken by her new brothers-in-law to dance in a winding, snaking line with her hair flowing freely. Once the marriage has been consummated, her new mother-in-law ceremonially binds her hair and adds the *diklo*, or marriage scarf to symbolise her married status.

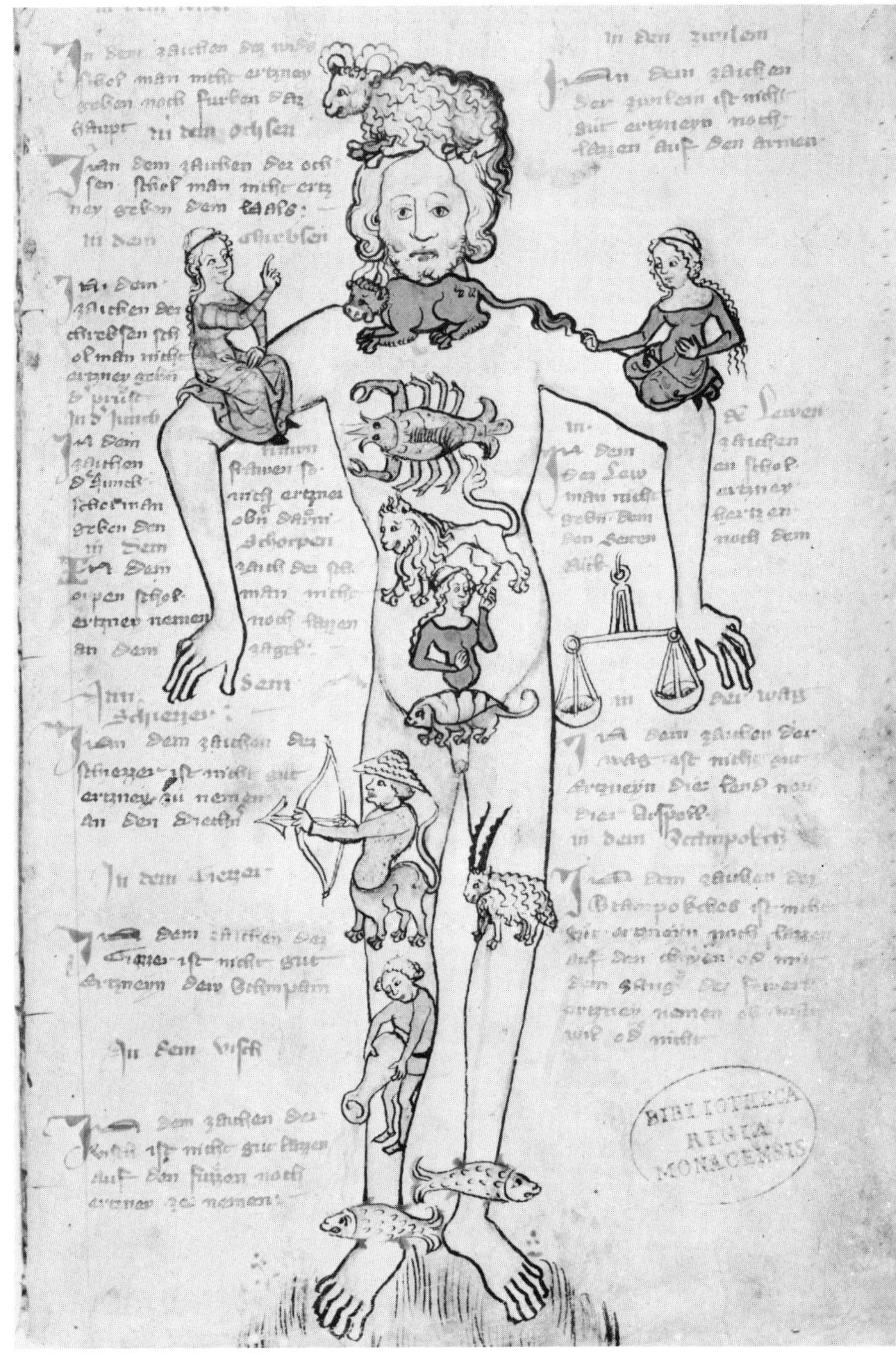

The body often acts as a 'natural' symbol for expressing ideas about social order. The Zodiac cosmology is placed on parts of the body.

Not only hair, but all changes in the body frequently mark, in an easily visible way, changes in an individual's social status. Cutting hair, painting the body, or changing clothes are reversable visual changes. So in Malta, for example, when entering a church, that is when moving from a secular to a sacred context, women cover their heads and men uncover them. Bodily mutilations, in contrast, are irreversible and are more likely to mark permanent changes. For example, in many societies the uncircumcised male is a social infant; the circumcised male is a social adult. In the same way, the binding of the feet of Chinese women created a permanent disability, and the filing of Balinese teeth is a permanent symbolic movement towards becoming truly human.

The body as a natural symbol

When we speak of the social perception of the body, we mean much more than merely the social meaning of the body's appearance. We must also look at the significance of the body as a 'natural' symbol for expressing ideas about social order. Mary Douglas suggests that far from being just like any other segment of socially perceived reality, the body occupies an especially important place since:

'the physical experience of the body, always modified by the social categories through which it is known, sustains a particular view of society. There is a continual exchange of meanings between the two kinds of bodily experience so that each reinforces the categories of the other.'
(Douglas, 1970:65)

If she is correct that 'the human body is always treated as an image of society' (70), then it follows that by examining a people's attitudes to the human body, and their definition of its boundaries, we should gain some understanding of the informant's society. The body is often a home-made image of society.

The particular perceived relationship between the human body and the social body may be extended, in a society, to a general interrelationship between nature and society. The boundary between the human social world and the non-human natural world is often an area of ambiguity and danger. In Western Europe, witches were (or are) humans who consorted with the animal world in an irregular fashion. Werewolves and vampires are

A Werewolf of Eschenbach 1685. Werewolves are humans who transform themselves into animals and terrorise other people.

Title page of a German book on Witchcraft, Leipzig 1668 giving a graphic illustration of witches consorting with animals, a demon defecating into a pot and general sexual licence.

'people' who crossed the dangerous threshold between the social and animal domains, and their behaviour is consistently anti-social. In Central America there is a widespread belief that a person may have an animal guardian spirit, called a *Nagual*. Each person's destiny and being is linked to a particular animal, and the result may be that if he kills that animal, he too will die. Or if he is evil, his 'soul' may enter the body of that animal and attack his enemies by causing them to sicken and die.

A contrast between the human and animal worlds is not the only form this boundary may take. It can also take the form of a contrast between self and society. It was Freud's opinion that the skin, which gives

Above
Eve, considered the weaker sex in Christian mythology, was created from the *left* rib of Adam.

Above right
In pictures of the last judgement, it is the right hand which points to heaven, the left hand to the jaws of hell.

warning of pain and senses invitations to pleasure, was the original organ of the Ego or the consciousness. There is something to be said for this notion because the skin acts as a mirror of psychological states. It blushes and turns pale from fright. It also reacts to physiological changes as with psoriasis, leprosy and chicken pox. The Gypsies in California regard the skin as a good indication of the inner state of cleanliness or moral worth of a person, and skin diseases, in their opinion, are the visible signs of moral unworthiness and the public exposure of the impurity of private thoughts and actions. In Britain too, it is popularly and mistakenly believed that many skin complaints are the result of dirt and neglect of the body, whereas the medical view is that these are infections. Thus skin diseases also may carry the moral stigma of poverty.

The Kayapó, in applying a 'covering' of social decoration, that is painting the body, give an indication of social status as we do with clothes. Terry Turner describes their body painting as a sort of social 'skin' on top of the natural skin. But he adds, they are not only marking and changing their bodies, they are also creating the 'self' in a social image by transforming the inner 'natural' energy of the body into an outward social form. Thus, among the Kayapó, the most elaborate body painting, that requires the most time and involves the most intricate designs, is for young children. Children, who are the least socialised members of the Kayapó society, and the least defined in terms of the 'self', require the most attention in body painting.

There is a second important way that the body may become an image of society. The natural pre-eminence of right-handedness in the human, for example, often becomes a symbol of positive attributes – auspiciousness, moral up*right*ness, rectitude, dexterity, superiority, maleness and physical strength. Left-handedness, on the other hand, may be associated with the sinister, gaucherie, clumsiness, inferiority, impurity and femaleness. Right- and left-handedness in many societies also become symbols of the opposition between the sacred and the profane. For example, in pictures of the Last Judgement, it is the Lord's raised right hand that indicates heaven to the elect, while his lowered left hand shows the damned the 'gaping jaws of Hell ready to swallow them' (Hertz: 1960:13). Furthermore, Eve, considered the weaker sex in Christian mythology, was created from the left rib of Adam.

What is striking is that 'left' and 'right' as symbols of the opposition between sacred and profane, male and female, pure and impure, good and evil, etc. are extremely common oppositions found in India, Africa, South America, Indonesia, Ancient Greece and the Middle East. There are exceptions, as with the *Zuni* who personify left and right as brother gods with the left being the elder and wiser. But that an arbitrary set of symbols, such as the left and right of the body, should have such a degree of consistency in their actual contextual meaning is in itself indicative of the importance of body symbolism and the way that a slight asymmetry in the body can take on a rich meaning.

In India, for example, the left hand is considered polluted and inferior to the right. Left and right sides of the body are also clearly identified with female and male. The clearest statement of this association of the two sides with sexuality is the frequent representation of the God Shiva as male and female joined in one body, with the right side of the body male and the left female. The male or 'right-sided' sex is generally considered superior in India.

In Hindu and Muslim societies, as on Chole Island, the left hand is polluted because it is used for cleaning the body after defecation, even though it is always thoroughly washed. The right hand is kept clean and is used for eating, greeting friends, etc. The proscription against left-handedness is so strong in the Arab countries that less than one per cent of the population persist in being left-handed, compared to approximately ten per cent in Britain.

The body is a natural symbol for expressing ideas about the social order. Left and right are, of course, not the only division of the human body that are metaphors for the 'social' body. Logically, the body can be divided into four divisions:

Left/right
Up/down
Front/back
Inside/outside

Any one or all of these 'sections' of the body may take on a social significance. Left and right are probably the most common, but inside and outside are also very frequently symbols of other attributes. We have already seen how the Kayapó interpret the boundary between the inside (private, individual self) of the body and the outside (public, social self) by focusing on the 'social' skin.

The Gypsies in England also put great emphasis on the distinction between the inside and outside of the body. The inside symbolises the private 'Gypsy'self and is pure in contrast to the outside which symbolises the impure, public body – the part of the body that has defiling contact with non-Gypsy society. Consistent with this notion of the body, is their emphasis on the purity of food, which enters the body. It follows that the washing of items that come into contact with food, such as dishes and tea towels, must be kept separate from items that touch the outside of the body, such as clothes. English Gypsies often judge one another's worth according to how strictly 'clean they are about their tea towels'. One visible way of estimating this is by observing the washing hanging on the line; tea towels are always separated from other clothes.

Unlike right and left in India, the top and bottom halves of the body, do not have, for the American Gypsies, hierarchical connotation of superiority and inferiority, but they are related to ideas of purity and impurity. The purity of the body is maintained by keeping separate, as much as possible, the upper and lower halves of the body. The purity of an individual is related to his or her ability to keep the body clean, in the sense of separate from pollution. This in turn reflects on a person's own health and personal luck. A person who keeps 'clean' will enjoy good health and an auspicious life, in other words, have lots of children and become very wealthy. Being 'clean' is also dependent on the age of an individual. The 'dirt' of the lower body is most dangerous when the individual is sexually potent or active, during puberty and adulthood. Children and sexually inactive old people are in less danger of pollution, whereas adults must take many precautions to prevent polluting themselves and others.

Conclusion

There are two main ideas about the body that have anthropological importance. First, the body is perceived through the ideas our society imbues in us. This includes perceptions of differences between humans and animals, clean and unclean parts of the body, classifications of bodily emissions, ideas about what a beautiful, healthy, or sexually attractive body looks like, etc. The body may be altered to fit these ideas either through dress or bodily mutilation. The body may also be decorated by paint or dress to express ideas of social status.

Second, the society's perception of the body itself may become a symbol for expressing ideas about social order, social boundaries or social change. Thus, for example, left- and right-hand sides of the body or upper and lower halves of the body may act as a 'natural' metaphor for such ideas as good and evil, pure and impure, or male and female.

Women and Men

Chapter Four

Difference between the sexes

We all tend to think of 'maleness' and 'femaleness' as naturally endowed attributes, even if we may disagree about exactly which attributes they might be. However, the evidence from a large number of societies demonstrates quite clearly that male and female roles, behaviour, tasks and essential characteristics differ from society to society. What is considered a 'natural' task for women in one society, such as carrying heavy loads, is considered a natural task for men in another. What is 'feminine' behaviour in one society, such as adorning oneself, is 'masculine' behaviour elsewhere. Not only do such characteristics differ cross-culturally, but they differ within one society from one period to another. Today the frilly garments of 18th century men may seem effeminate.

What was 'masculine' dress for men in the 18th century, by today's standards looks very 'feminine.' Even the body stance of Louis XIV and fellow Billiards players would strike us as distinctly unmasculine.

A young Indian girl carries a rock on her head. In many societies women are expected to carry heavy loads regularly.

There are also differences between ranked 'categories' (see glossary) or classes. Whereas, for example, for 19th century middle class women to be idle and even sickly was considered feminine, working class women were expected to undertake strenuous, back-breaking labour.

If one simply compares the five societies we are looking at in this book, one finds an extraordinary diversity of sex roles and behaviour. Although industrialists often maintain that women are better at sewing because women are dextrous and are good at detailed, meticulous work with their hands (they don't often point out that they can pay women less), on Chole Island men give the same reasons for doing the sewing themselves. Furthermore, it is usual for men and women each to wash their own clothes. One man

For Nineteenth century middle class women to be weak and sickly was considered feminine, but working class women were expected to undertake strenuous back-breaking labour.

remarked: 'Well, I generally wash my own clothes as well as those of the children and of my wife. Sometimes I just wash my clothes and the children's, and my wife washes her own. But women usually don't wash men's clothes'.

In Britain, more and more women are working both before and after having children, but it is still generally true that the man's job is considered more important than the woman's. With Gypsies it is the reverse. As soon as they are able, a Gypsy family in California will invest in the wife's job and move where she can set up her own fortune-telling office. Shrecha, a formidable old lady explained: 'You never seen a gypsy man work did you . . . Have you ever seen one? They never work. All women tell fortunes, some good, some bad, some of them do it and some don't do it no more. But they're supposed to earn the money'. The ideal wife and the successful man are those who can expect a large income from the wife's work. There is, however, no stigma on men for working, and when a family is in need, the whole family, men, women and children, help to gain support. Nevertheless, the moral responsibility for support of the family is still felt to be the woman's.

In Bali, men and women are perceived as equal and complementary halves of a whole, though in practice there are more differences in behaviour than are admitted. Nevertheless men and women dress and behave in strikingly similar ways, do the same jobs, hold the same offices, and perform

Balinese men and women doing the same labour in rice fields.

the same ritual and religious duties to their ancestors. Men and women work equally hard on road gangs, carrying heavy loads of rock and sand, the only difference being that women carry these loads on their heads, whereas men carry them on their shoulders. They work in the rice fields doing the same jobs in equal and full membership in the co-operatives. One of the few exclusively male activities is cock-fighting, and there is a close identification between a man and his cock (there is the same pun in Balinese as in English). Caring for children, on the other hand, is not an exclusively female task, and in fact, men often spend more time holding and attending to their babies than the women who, after feeding them, hand them to someone else to look after them. The main exclusively female activity is selling and running the markets, and here, like men at a cock-pit, women abandon their normally reserved and poised behaviour and become, for them, very aggressive and boisterous.

This simple point, that male and female roles vary dramatically from society to society, was put across forcefully by Margaret Mead in her book, *Sex and Temperament in Three Primitive Societies*. In 1931 she set out to study sex differences and found three societies no more than 100 miles apart. 'In one, both men and women act as we expect women to act – in a mild parental responsive way; in the second both act as we expect men to act – in a fierce initiating fashion; and in the third, the men act according to our stereotype for

One of the few exclusively male activities in Bali is cock-fighting, when men can indulge in boisterous, aggressive behaviour unlike their normal refined behaviour. Men often develop an anti-social passion for cock-fighting and neglect their families in order to bet on their cocks.

women – are catty, wear curls and go shopping, while women are energetic, managerial, unadorned partners'. Although this passage shows that Margaret Mead is seeing these societies through the American view of male and female stereotypes, she did point out that male and female are cultural roles. Since her work, the ethnographic evidence is far greater, and of better quality, so that today no anthropologist can doubt that there is a great variety in sex roles. We now know that it is no longer possible to assume that any social activity such as child care, hard physical labour, or in fact any kind of behaviour or personality is *exclusively* male or female.

Even though roles, tasks and behaviour differ greatly as to whether they will be considered appropriate for males or females, the fact that women bear children is of course a constant. Furthermore, until recent times, with alternative forms of feeding for infants, most infants relied on their mother's breast milk for survival. Child bearing, and, until now, early feeding thus have been exclusively female activities.

This has meant that women, during their child-bearing years, have tended to be confined to the domestic sphere of activity. Child care, for other than very young infants, does vary from society to society, but in most societies it is the task mainly of women. This does not necessarily mean the task of child care falls on the biological mother. Very rarely is it the biological mother on her own who is responsible for child care. In some societies child care is shared by men and women, but in no society that I know of, is it the exclusive domain of men, though in a few, such as Bali, men take a major responsibility for children. So a large part of women's lives has, particularly in the past, been devoted to the bearing and raising of children, and their lives have tended to centre around the household.

Among the Kayapó, the Gypsies of California and the Swahili of Chole Island, where the domestic, household sphere and the public sphere of work, leadership and ritual activities are very closely tied together, women's activities tend to be highly valued. In societies such as ours, where work and home, public life and family life are very separate spheres of activity, women's activities tend to be devalued by society, and the greatest recognition is given to the separate public male world of authority and power. Particularly in technologically specialised, industrial societies where a person's worth and prestige are calculated largely in terms of how much money is earned, women's work, which either is low-wage earning or non-wage earning, has low value. In societies where cash transactions are either non-existent (eg Kayapó) or only account for a small proportion of the production of goods (eg Chole Island) – that is, societies where work and home are not rigidly separated – women's work in child-care, food production and preparation achieves more social recognition and reward.

In every society, the overwhelming majority of women and men do some work, but the social value that is placed on a particular piece of work varies considerably. In our society, the value that is given a particular job depends at least partly on how much people are paid combined with the status and amount of power they have. We know, for example, that medical doctors

Women and children working in cotton fields. In most societies women are involved in economic production as well as childcare.

are highly valued in our society because they are well paid, because the government invests considerable amounts in hospitals and medical research and because of the high degree of control that members of the medical profession have over a very important aspect of our lives, our health care. But in other societies, such as Malta, Chole Island, and among the Kayapó, it may be the production of food, the reproduction of children, or the control of ritual and ritual symbolism that is highly regarded.

> Despite the variation in male and female roles from society to society, it has been found that whatever is highly valued in a society tends to be in the hands of men. If we define male dominance as a situation in which men have highly preferential access, though not always exclusive rights, to those activities to which society accords the greatest value, and the exercise of which permits a measure of control over others, then the anthropological evidence is that a degree of male dominance exists in all known societies. (Friedl, 1975:7)

The comparative study in anthropology of the relative status of women and men in society, past and present, is, oddly enough, very recent. Consequently, this subject is underdeveloped compared with the progress anthropology has made in other areas. There are several reasons for this: first, it was generally men who became ethnographers, and therefore they tended to talk with men from other societies. Thus information on women was collected from men and by men rather than women, and this inevitably resulted in some distortions. Secondly, even when women went to study a society, they often failed to question their own society's general assumption that men's activities are more socially significant than women's activities. Women anthropologists who resisted this position, such as Margaret Mead and Audrey Richards, were rare exceptions. In most anthropological theory, exclusively female activities, such as childbirth, were given little consideration. We now know this to be an ethnocentric bias that has produced some strange distortions. For example an economist named Marshall went to Rossel Island in the Pacific to study their unique and complex monetary system, and although he recorded and analysed 22 kinds of money used by men, he only mentions in a footnote to his work that there were also 22 kinds of money used by women for their economic exchanges.

A third problem with the data is that many ethnographers have found that women who are generally less active in public, formal activities in the society, have tended not to give a formalistic bounded view of society of the kind that attracts anthropologists. Ethnographers have a predeliction for seeking order (within an apparently confused mass of data) and thus have sought as informants those people most likely to generalise about their own society, often people in positions of authority. Such people are very often men. Women, who are less prevalent in the public sphere, have generalised about their own sphere of activities, but these either have not been sought or else considered unimportant.

The position of women in society.

In spite of all these problems with the ethnographic data, our understanding of the nature of the relationship of women to society is improving. First of all, there is always a contrast made between 'male' and 'female'. This contrast is one of the *idea* of maleness and femaleness, and societies have very different ways of defining the essential attributes of each. Often they are seen as opposites. For example, in Britain, male is seen as 'aggressive' and female as 'passive'. But, there are other ways of making the contrast. *Yin* and *Yang*, the male and female principles, are part of a complementary whole, represented as:–

Here the emphasis is on union and completeness. Female and male are together necessary to achieve unity.

Second, the status of men and women will be both different and unequal. Their roles, both economic and social, will be related to their status. Thus women usually have less publicly recognised power and authority than men. Even so, there are societies where women have considerable recognition and informal power (much more so than in our society), and in many societies this power has previously been unrecognised by the ethnographer studying it. Most studies of society are being re-evaluated, or need to be re-evaluated, in the light of this. As this is happening, we are finding more and more evidence that women play an important though often unrecognised political role.

A good example of the deceptiveness of looking only at the formal position of women in society is presented in the case of Swahili women on Chole Island. In one sense, women on Chole appear to be in a clearly subordinate position to men. Women are generally kept separated from men, cannot sit on the village council or hold office in the mosque, and have unequal rights in certain areas of law (for example, men can divorce women more easily, and have rights to a larger percentage of the family inheritance). But, if we look more deeply into the actual conditions of their lives, we find that the situation for women is not as onerous as it might appear.

The teacher of the Koran school in his formal Islamic clothes.

Chole Island women sitting at back of house plaiting strips to make mats which they sell for cash.

To begin with, women have equal access to cultivable land. They obtain a cash income from mat-making; they remain members of their natal kin group from whom they get support, for example, if a woman's husband treats her badly. Women are active in non-Islamic ritual and have a great deal of informal political power, for example, through singing of songs at rituals which extemporise on current social issues. Women on Chole also share child-care with each other so that the burden is not necessarily on the biological mother. Thus women do have considerable informal power and influence, are not dependent on men either economically or for their rank in society, and they share with men responsibility for domestic duties. In general, women are treated as independent individuals rather than as appendages of men.

Some anthropologists argue that there are, or have been in the past, societies that are truly egalitarian for men and women. Many societies, for example, have myths which indicate that the origins of the society and of all power came from women. These 'myths of matriarchy', however, usually highlight women's failure as rulers and therefore serve to legitimate the social order dominated by men. Myths are fascinating documents for understanding important beliefs in a society, but they are unreliable as straight-forward history. Our own Biblical story of the fall of Adam and Eve from the grace of God due to the temptation of Eve by the Devil may tell us something about the way we view women in our society, but it is an act of faith to accept this as an historical account. In the same way, we must be cautious about accepting people's mythical accounts of a former matriarchy as accurate history. So if we must reject myths of matriarchy as reliable descriptions of former societies and view them, at least partly, as statements about the present lower status of women, we still need to explain why women are generally excluded from the most publicly recognised forms of power.

One answer that has long been popular is that female subordination is somehow natural or biologically ordained. Let us look at this explanation briefly. No one can question that the sexes differ biologically. The most important biological difference in terms of the social consequences for a large number of societies is that women bear children and produce milk whereas men do not. There are of course other differences: in their reproductive physiology, in aspects of hormonal endowments, and probably in size and potential physical strength. Finally, there is the fact that women live longer than men.

As we saw when we looked at social perceptions of the body and of space, physical differences alone do not tell us very much about society. We know that people will create order in the space around them and may use the natural environment for spatial orientations, but this tells us nothing about the value they will place on, for example, volcano and sea, East and West, inside and outside. Similarly, the fact that males seem to be stronger in some ways than females and that females rather than males bear children, will not explain what value is placed on these activities or how they will be perceived in the overall society.

Amazon women were believed to be huge, fierce warriors who ran their own society.

Moreover, we also know that culture can influence biology. Modes of dress, decoration and body mutilations can alter the shape as well as the appearance of the human body. Human hormones are highly sensitive to changes in the social and psychological environment. For example, in studies of women who were close friends living in dormitories in universities, it has been found that their menstrual cycles, controlled by hormones, will begin to occur simultaneously. It is now accepted that there is a close and complex interaction between our biological make-up and social activities. What this means for the sexes is that the behavioural possibilities are extremely variable and flexible and are constantly adapting to new environments.

Another argument put forward, related to the biological argument, is based on evolution. An assumption of this argument is that the most significant part of the evolution of *homo sapiens* took place when man was a primitive hunter, and that current hunting and gathering societies (with no or only incipient agriculture) give us a view into our own past. It is argued that hunting large animals demands cooperation between several individuals, and because it often involves danger and extensive travel, women, who must produce and feed children, are too constrained in their movements to participate. Women, therefore, become responsible for gathering berries and fruit. Hunting, a specifically male activity, is therefore credited with providing the bases for the first forms of social cooperation and the first use of tools. This advantage provided a basis for the dominance of men over women, by giving men access to and control of the 'creative' and 'intellectual' aspects of society.

There are several problems with this thesis. One is that small game hunting (which is nutritionally more important in most hunting and gathering societies than large game hunting) can be done individually and without cooperation. Furthermore, the argument ignores the economic importance of gathering which is done by women and which produces the bulk of the food supply. Furthermore, it could equally be argued that gathering, food processing, and the socialisation of children also require cooperation and the use of tools, and in both these roles, women predominate.

But the main problem with all evolutionary arguments is that they are speculative, and we simply do not know and may never know how cooperation and the first use of tools evolved. Furthermore, evolutionary arguments cannot answer two important questions:

1 If our world today is so different from that of our ancestors, in other words, if hunting and gathering have for so long been irrelevant, why is it that social groups which have changed radically through time, continue to produce and reproduce a social order where women are regarded as 'the second sex'.

2 If our evolutionary past is the same (hunting and gathering), why do we find such an extraordinary diversity of sex-linked roles in our own and other societies? A satisfactory explanation of relations between women and men must be able to explain this apparent contradiction. Such an explanation will not be based on a single, necessary cause, but it should indicate a variety of different factors including biological, psychological, social and economic aspects of human life.

Domestic and Public Oppositions

Michelle Rosaldo (1974) suggests that we must look at the social consequences of women's role in child care to answer these questions. She takes this as the basis for a distinction between 'domestic' and 'public' spheres of activity.

'Women become absorbed primarily in domestic activities because of their role as mothers. Their economic and political activities are constrained by the responsibilities of child care. . . . This orientation (towards children and home) is contrasted to the extra-domestic, political and military spheres of activity and interest primarily associated with men. Put quite simply, men have no single commitment as enduring, time-consuming, and emotionally compelling – as close to seeming necessary and natural – as the relation of a woman to her infant child; and so men are free to form those broader associations that we call "society" . . .'

(Rosaldo, 1974: 24)

This of course, is highly simplified and applies to society generally rather than to specific individuals or societies. However, Rosaldo argues that this simple distinction between domestic and public spheres has several far-reaching consequences. First of all, she suggests that it affects the social and personal development of both boys and girls. In most societies a girl learns what womanhood means through her personal relationship with her mother. She is integrated into the adult world of work through ties with older female kin so there is a sense of continuity between her emergence into adulthood and her particular personal ties (though at marriage often women experience a break with their natal kin group). In this sense, a woman's status comes 'naturally'. In contrast, boys in childhood are not generally expected to work. They frequently form close attachments to peer groups and learn to play in a competitive spirit. As they grow into adulthood, they must break

Kayapó boys play in groups hunting small birds and practising skills of manhood. They leave their mothers and enter the men's hut at eight years of age.

away from their mother and kinsmen, with whom they have interacted less frequently and learn what it is to become a man. Boys tend to learn manhood as an abstract set of rights and duties. They learn to act in terms of formal roles while women tend to grow 'naturally' into motherhood without leaving the domestic sphere. The success or failure of boys is often judged in terms of male hierarchies, whereas most women, as wives, mothers or sisters, gain respect, power, or prestige through their personal relations with men.

The Kayapó provide a good example of this contrast. The women's sphere of activity centres around the domestic households on the periphery of the village, and indeed these are said to belong to the women. Women grow up in a household and never leave it. In contrast, men when they marry, move into the wife's household in a very subordinate status to their father – and mother-in-law. Only the older men and women in a household exercise a measure of authority over younger men through the young wives. Boys and girls alike grow up in the household of their parents, but unlike the girls who begin to help their mother in female tasks, such as preparing food and caring for young babies, as soon as they are able, boys roam freely with their peers and practice shooting with bows and arrows or play games. At around eight years of age, a boy is taken from the household by a substitute father and mother and enters into the exclusively male world of the men's hut. The man is therefore, separated dramatically from his home of childhood and initiated

Kayapó women 'own' their houses and never leave the house of birth whereas men move to the men's hut at puberty and their wife's house at marriage.

into manhood away from women and under the instruction of older men. It is through this separation that he gains access to the most communal forms of organisation that dominate the more restricted sphere of extended family households.

Thus a girl becomes a woman often with a great deal of continuity, through her personal relationship with her mother, whereas there is more frequently a break in a man's experience. For a boy to become an adult, he must prove his masculinity among his peers, and he must be taught to understand the public, male world of authority. Thus we find, that in many, though not all, societies, women tend to be associated with naturally endowed *ascribed* status and men with socially *achieved* status. Women 'naturally' become mothers and adults; men must 'learn' to become men.

In most societies it is rare to find women who are recognised as legitimate leaders. Most women are given a social role by virtue of their age (the menopause often brings with it a certain amount of power) or of their relationship to men. Whereas men achieve rank as a result of explicit achievement, women's roles are usually thought of as the product of personal characteristics, such as personality, temperament, or appearance.

Because of these patterns of socialisation and ranking, men are frequently seen to be the creators of culture in contrast to women whose lives appear to be the result of their 'natural' sexual endowment. Women's rank is often derived from their particular stage in the life cycle, from their biological functions, and, very frequently, from their sexual and biological ties to particular men. What is more, women in many societies are more often involved in the grubby and dangerous (but powerful) stuff of social existence – giving birth and mourning death, feeding, cooking, and disposing of faeces. So we find in many cultural systems a recurrent opposition between man, associated with symbols that stand for culture and order, and woman, who (defined through symbols that stress her biological and sexual functions) stands for nature and often for disorder and 'anti-structure'.

Women, in many societies, are thus often seen as threatening to culture, disorderly, anomalous or dangerous. Cultural notions of the female gravitate around her sexual and biological functions, and these are often seen as polluting or dangerous to men in the same way that disorder is dangerous to society. In societies where women are viewed as anomalous and dangerous, they often turn this threatening aspect of their beings to their own advantage and use it to defy the ideals of the male order. Because they are considered dangerous, they exercise all sorts of informal power, often illegitimate and covert, through influencing the men, who in the final analysis they tend to outlive anyway.

The Gypsies of California are a good example of a group where women are endowed with this anomalous, dangerous role. Gypsy women are seen as more polluting than men, but while the onus is on the woman to keep men pure, they can use their innate pollution to their own advantage. Old women, in particular, no longer under the authority of an older male, and having acquired considerable knowledge of ghosts and spirits, medicines and

The Indian goddess Kali is the goddess of death and destruction.

This old Gypsy woman is feared because of her knowledge of the supernatural and her ability to bring bad luck through cursing.

curses, become shrewd and feared forces in the politics of the extended family and territorial control of economic resources.

There are societies where women have achieved prestige, where they can gain considerable authority as legitimate leaders, though usually through a husband, father or son (eg Indira Gandhi, Eva Peron, Mrs Bandaranaike). But as Rosaldo points out, what is striking is how 'the wives of herders, agriculturalists and businessmen lead lives that are conceptualised in remarkably similar terms. Women who are characterised everywhere as 'the other', are often seen by missionaries and colonists as the easiest people to interact with, convert or educate: the hispanisation of the New World, for example, seems to have depended in large part upon the colonist's use of native women as lovers and domestics, and therefore as mediators between the two worlds. The fact that sisters can be married off to foreigners (whether in the New Guinea Highlands or the crowned courts of Europe), that women can be 'exchanged', corresponds to the fact that cultural conceptions of women's roles are universally very similar; much of what women do in any one society may be seen to have immediately available equivalents in any other'. (Rosaldo, 1974:29)

If this universal opposition between public and domestic spheres leads to a symbolic opposition between women as 'natural' and men as 'cultural', then how do we relate this to woman's position in society? Rosaldo suggests that women's status will be lowest in those societies where there is a strong distinction between domestic and public spheres of activity and where women are isolated from one another and placed under a single man's authority in the home. A good example of such a situation is the position of women in Malta. In Malta, as in many Mediterranean societies, women are viewed as unequal in capacity to men and have a legal status similar to minors and the insane. A woman's proper role, according to the Catholic church, the government and social opinion in general, is as wife and mother in the confines of the home. The husband is the legal head of the family so, for example, married women may not fully administer their own property, may not hold government jobs, nor do they hold any administrative offices in the church.

Furthermore, women's position is raised when they can challenge those claims to authority either by taking on men's roles or by creating a sense of rank, order and value in a world in which women prevail. Therefore, there are two possibilities for women who wish greater autonomy:

(a) to enter the men's world (which is the alternative chosen by many women in our Western society given the very strong separation of domestic and public spheres), or

(b) to create a public world of their own (which in Western society has been attempted by the women's movement of the 70s).

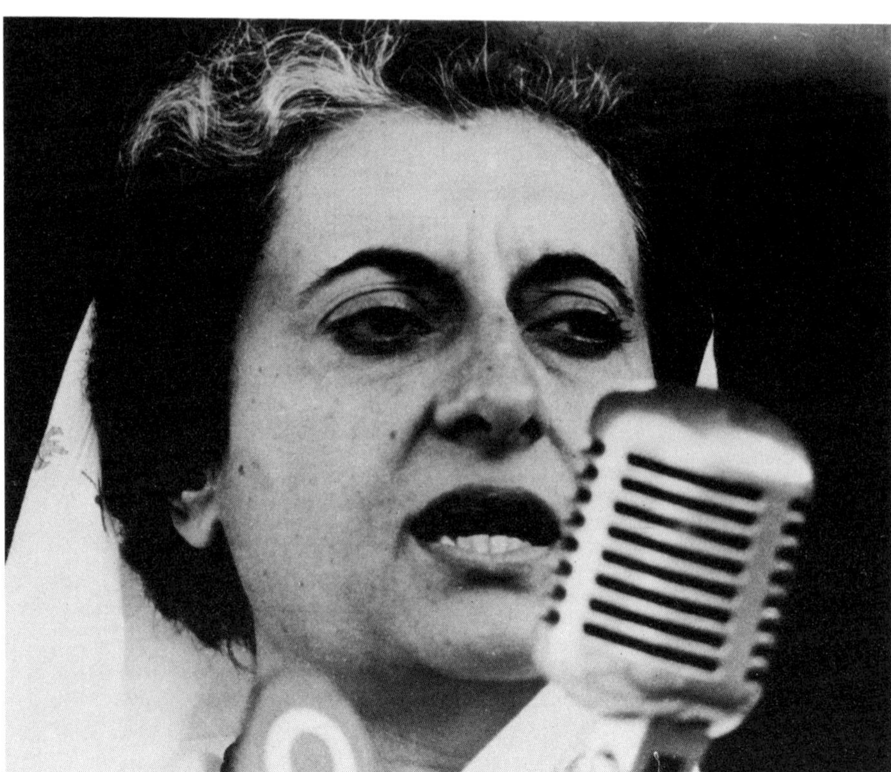

Some women, like Mrs Gandhi in India, have achieved powerful positions. But usually part of their success has been due to their family connections. Mrs Gandhi is the daughter of the first Indian Prime Minister, Nehru.

Women in New Guinea display their contribution to marriage payments.

On Chole Island, women have taken the second alternative. A characteristic of Islamic institutions everywhere is to separate women and men's spheres of activity and to prevent access by women to public forms of authority. Given this situation, women in Kanga village have developed their own leaders in women's activities, keep their own sources of income and control many of their own public activities, such as girl's puberty rites. Separation in this case denies women participation in certain important activities, particularly public office, but it does give them an arena of their own where they can develop some autonomy. Furthermore, because public and domestic spheres are not strongly differentiated, men do participate in household tasks, and women's household activities are not undervalued.

Above
For ceremonies women pound rice together usually with singing and dancing, all of which is organized by an elder woman.

Right
Gypsy women in California always sit in a group on public occasions and discuss matters of importance taking place in their own and other territories.

Gypsy women in California also benefit from a lack of strict separation between public and domestic spheres of activity, and through their role in the family they exert considerable influence on public decisions. As on Chole Island, they too gain independence and self-confidence by spending much of their time in groups of women. Their independence is diminished when they are isolated from other Gypsy women and are under the authority of a father or husband; however they become extremely powerful when they are elderly and widowed, and can control their sons and daughters-in-law.

I have dealt with two different but related questions concerning women and men. At the 'ideological' level, we must look at the way women and men are defined, perceived and symbolised. For example, in Bali women and men are seen as two complementary halves of a whole. This idea is symbolised by Balinese God images who come in male and female pairs but have the same name and are identical. In contrast, in Malta women are seen as intellectually inferior, morally weaker and tied to their biological function of motherhood. Some of these ideas are symbolised by the role of the Virgin Mary who achieved her identity as both virgin and mother.

Both of these different conceptions of the essential nature of women and men are reflected in what they actually do in their own society. However, the correspondence between ideal and real is not perfect. In Bali, roles for women and men are strikingly similar. Nevertheless, although women *can* participate in ward politics and hold religious office, statistically they are less likely to do so. On the other hand, in Malta, though most married women do not work and are primarily housekeepers and mothers, women are, more and more, pressing for the right to move into the public sphere of work.

Further general reading part one

POCOCK, D. F. *Understanding social anthropology* Teach Yourself Books, paperback 1976. This book argues that the vocation of social anthropology is to make the strange normal and exotic familiar. Professor Pocock aims to stimulate an anthropological consciousness in the reader as a social being, to make each one of us aware of our 'personal anthropology' – assumed notions about such social values as kinship, authority, status and money – in order that we might perceive these notions anthropologically and newly assess them and ourselves. It is written specifically for the beginner to the subject.

LEWIS, I. M. *Social anthropology in perspective* Penguin Books, 1976. A survey of the field of anthropology for the layman and first-year student. Designed to give a broad overview without being too technical.

LEACH, E. *Culture and communication: the logic by which symbols are connected: an introduction to the use of structuralist analysis in social anthropology* C.U.P, 1976. A lively introduction to Leach's use of structuralist analysis.

LEVI-STRAUSS, C. *Tristes tropiques* Cape, 1973; Penguin Books, 1976. An accurate translation of an influential early work by a great French anthropologist, discussing both his field work in Brazil and the nature of anthropology as an exploration of the human mind.

SMITH BOWEN, E. (BOHANNAN, L.) *Return to laughter* American Museum of Natural History and Doubleday. 1964. An entertaining account of how an anthropologist does field work. The author draws on her own experience as an anthropologist among the Tiv of Nigeria to provide a witty and perceptive story.

MARSHALL THOMAS, E. *The harmless people* Secker and Warburg, 1959 op; New York: Knopf, 1959, Random House 1965. A description of bushmen and their surroundings by a layman who accompanied her mother on an anthropological expedition to the Kalahari. Elizabeth Thomas writes sympathetically and vividly so that the reader gets to know these attractive bushmen personalities as friends.

READ, K. E. *The High Valley* Charles Scribner, 1965 New York. Anthropological field work in the highlands of New Guinea described with sensitivity and an honest awareness of the anthropologists own difficulties in understanding a very different way of life. A personal account by an anthropologist who worked in New Guinea in the early years of its discovery by the West.

Part Two

Five Ethnographies

Chapter Five The Maltese Islands

Jeremy Boissevain

Most people have heard of Malta as the home of the legendary Knights of St. John, but few can find it on the map. Even fewer have been there. The first thing that strikes the visitor to these islands in the centre of the Middle Sea is that they appear to be all rock. Houses, fortifications and huge churches form part of the tawny limestone landscape, from which they are built. Villages and towns cluster closely around the magnificent harbours, that thrust like deep pockets on either side of Valetta, the capital. The men appear prosperous, even handsome; the women are often strikingly beautiful. Away from city and tourist areas, women and men do not mix in public. By the standards of Western Europe in the last quarter of the twentieth century, the Maltese are deeply religious. Alongside pop culture, television, mass tourism and thriving industry, there is a religious pageantry usually associated with medieval peasant communities. In spite of industrialisation, rising prosperity and progressive involvement in Europe and North Africa, the scale of the annual parish *festas* and Good Friday rituals is increasing. Here lies a paradox.

The Maltese islands lie midway between Gibraltar and Lebanon. The south-east corner of Sicily lies just 60 miles to the north, Tripoli 220 miles to the south, and Tunis a little over 200 miles to the west. Malta has thus always formed a natural port of call between Europe and North Africa. Both the Christian and Muslim worlds have contributed cultural traits which the industrious Maltese have adapted for their own use. The language, for example, is basically semitic and related to North African Arabic. It contains a heavy overlay of French, Italian and English words. The flat-roofed houses with interior courtyards are more reminiscent of North Africa and the Middle East than of Southern Europe. In spite of this, the main features of the cultural and social organisation of the Maltese are more European than North African.

The Maltese archipelago consists of three inhabited islands, Malta, Gozo and Comino. Malta, the largest and southernmost island, is 17 miles long and nine miles wide. Gozo is only nine by five miles; the little island of Comino lies in a three miles' wide channel, which separates the two main islands. Altogether the archipelago has a land area of only 122 square miles (316 square kilometers). Since the islands have a total population of about

HUNGARY
ROMANIA
YUGOSLAVIA
BULGARIA
ITALY
ADRIATIC SEA
Corsica
ALBANIA
Sardinia
TYRRHENIAN SEA
GREECE
IONIAN SEA
Sicily
Malta
TUNISIA
MEDITERRANEAN SEA
GOZO
Victoria
COMINO
LIBYA
MALTA
Naxxar
Valetta
Vittoriosa
Rabat
MEDITERRANEAN SEA

315,000, Malta has a population density of just under 2600 per square mile. They are more than three times as densely populated as the Netherlands, commonly thought of as one of the world's most populated countries. In spite of the intense crowding, there is considerable open land away from the industrial conurbation around the harbours, and there are more than fifty villages and towns. These range in size from just under 1,000 to over 15,000. The island's isolation, its small scale and dense population have important social repercussions, for they contribute to a striking cultural homogeneity and a high level of social control. Everyone seems to know everyone else and, what is more, know or assume they know what is going on.

Malta's strategic location and its large sheltered deep water harbours have influenced its history in no small measure. Until it became independent from Britain in 1964, it belonged to a succession of major Mediterranean powers. Phoenicians, Carthagenians, Greeks and Romans successively occupied the islands. In A.D. 870 the Arabs occupied the archipelago for two hundred years, until they were replaced by the Normans under Count Roger. Malta thereafter shared the fate of Sicily and passed successively to the Swabians, the Angevins, the Aragonese and the Castilians. In 1530 Malta and Gozo with their protesting inhabitants were handed by Emperor Charles V to

There is a strong devotion to St. Paul, who was shipwrecked in Malta in AD60.

Malta's relative prosperity is very much a result of its centuries-old fortress economy.

the Knights of Malta, the Sovereign Military Order of St. John of Jerusalem. This powerful and wealthy body of celibate nobles, pledged to caring for the poor and sick and waging war on Islam, remained in Malta until Napoleon drove them out in 1798. Britain replaced France in 1800 after the Maltese revolted against Napoleon's garrison for trying to auction off church treasures.

The Maltese themselves regard the visit of St. Paul, in A.D. 60, as their most important historical happening. They are intensely proud of the apostolic origin of their religion. Virtually any Maltese can relate, as though it happened only a few years ago, how *Missierna San Pawl*, 'Our Father Saint Paul', was shipwrecked at the mouth of the bay on Malta's northeast shore that now bears his name; how he was miraculously saved; how following his miraculous removal of the poison from the viper that came out of the fire, built to dry his clothes, there have been no poisonous snakes in Malta; how he then passed through the village of Naxxar, whose inhabitants were the first to be converted; how he subsequently converted the Roman governor, who became Malta's first bishop; and how Malta since then has been an unwavering bastion of Christianity.

The legacy of this colourful history is still very much evident: relative prosperity, a high degree of centralisation, the power of the church and the dynamic way in which its inhabitants adapt to and select from new economic, political and cultural influences. Malta's relative prosperity is very much a result of its centuries old fortress economy. First the Knights of St. John and then Britain provided funds to construct and then man the island's massive fortifications and multitude of public buildings. Maltese were employed as masons, soldiers and sailors, book-keepers and servants and later as skilled

Oil rigs are now repaired alongside docks that once serviced the galleys of the Knights of St. John.

engineers and radar technicians to service the fortress. Times of international armed crises, such as the first and second world wars, were boom periods. Thus independence in 1964 came to a country with a developed infrastructure and a modestly prosperous population who had acquired technical, social and cultural skills, including a knowledge of English, by servicing its military masters. These were assests its governments put to good use to develop light manufacturing and tourism. Consequently, although the country's per capita income and gross domestic product are the lowest of Europe, they still compare favourably to most developing countries. Tourism, for example, has become a major industry. Since independence, the annual number of tourist arrivals has increased from 47,000 to 334,000 in 1976.

Democracy and the requirements of running a fortress are contradictory. The Knights and Britain gave Malta a highly centralised administration. Consequently, while there is a parliament composed of sixty-five district representatives, there are still no municipal councils, headmen or mayors to represent the interests of their respective villages and towns to higher authorities. Everything is run from the capital. Until the advent of modified self-government in the 1920's, mainly the parish priests represented the interests of the people. This arrangement reinforced the position of the church, whom Britain protected in order to provide its island fortress with a semi-religious form of indirect rule. Following World War II, however, universal suffrage and a series of Maltese internal governments culminated in independence in 1964. Not surprisingly, apart from the question of independence, the political role of the church provided perhaps the chief political issue until the late 1960's. Local politics are taken seriously, and the parliament is one of the liveliest in Europe. The country has been led by the mildly anticlerical socialist Malta Labour Party since 1971, when it replaced the conservative Nationalist Party in a closely contested election. The MLP was returned to power again in 1976. The Labour government has pursued with increasing success, a policy designed to limit the influence of the church to purely religious affairs, to achieve a greater degree of political and economic independence from major power-bloc affiliations and to provide for a more equitable distribution of the fruits of progress through social reform designed to reduce social inequality.

Social space

The way nature and culture of the past and present combine to form a dynamic continuity, is nowhere more evident than in the use of space. Maltese villages and towns, often perched on inland hills, are tightly clustered around enormous, cathedral-like churches. This settlement pattern is common to much of the European Mediterranean. It dates from a period when shelter was sought from marauding pirates and Moslem corsairs and from the malaria that flourished in the coastal marshes. The centre of every Maltese village is its immense parish church. The church is very much a symbol of the village, for it is the hub around which village life has revolved for centuries.

Every village is a parish; some towns are divided into two or more parishes. The *village* itself has no corporate unity, it has no official leader, it owns no property, it conducts no activities, it has not even a clearly defined territory. But as a *parish* it has a leader in the parish priest, a clearly demarcated territory, membership rules, and a busy programme of ritual activities which keep its members together. Last but not least, it owns valuable property, the most important of which is the parish church. This building is more than just a central place of worship. Its gilded ceilings and silver altar fronts, its damask tapestries and embroidered vestments, its precious votive offerings and ornate statues represent the parish's collective history and wealth amassed over

Maltese villages and towns are tightly clustered around enormous, cathedral-like churches.

centuries from the savings and bequests of generations. The patron saint to which the church is dedicated is both symbol and protector of the village. It is not surprising therefore that most of the important associations, shops and residences can be found in the parish square in front of the church or in the streets leading into it. The ancient hilltop parish of Naxxar, with a population of 5,000, in which my wife and I lived in 1961, then again in 1974 and 1976, illustrates clearly the concentric structure of a Maltese village. The village's six most important streets lead into the spacious square in front of the church. On the square, or no more than two minutes' walk from it, are located the house of the parish priest, the police station, the houses and premises of the notary and the chemist, the houses of four of the village's dozen or so priests, and the palace of the Marquis Scicluna. The town's four butchers, three of its five wineshops, two grocery shops, the tailor, the silversmith, the cobbler and several household bazaars are also to be found here. Moreover, all the important associations are located in this circle as well. These include the Peace Band club, the Victory social club, premises of several lay parish associations, the football club and, last but not least, the club houses of the Malta Labour Party and the Nationalist Party.

The small chapel of St. John, located at the north corner of the village, forms a mini-centre of one of the poorest neighbourhoods. There are

The Peace Band Club, Naxxar's oldest social club, provides music for important ceremonies and feasts.

two other chapels where daily services are held. The church's ubiquitous presence is also manifest in the statues of saints set in street corner niches, the madonna plaques at entrances, the statues, pictures and votive lights in houses, clubs, and even in buses, trucks and cars.

While the wealthier villagers have clustered in and near the parish church, the poorer people have, by and large, tended to live farther away from the square. The concentric pattern of the village thus reflects the distribution of economic and political power. Those with the highest moral and economic status have tended to live nearest the church and those with the lowest status farthest away in little alleys that backed on to open fields. The built-up section of the village conferred high status and prestige, for it has been associated with the culture of the town. The periphery of the village, which shades off into the fields, was associated with the country and agricultural work, which in Malta, in common with many Mediterranean countries, has very low status.

This traditional concentric pattern, which we found in Maltese villages in 1961, has subtly changed. In Naxxar the parish square has been opened up by two wide access roads to permit the ever increasing volume of cars and buses to move in and out of the village more freely. Many village families desired better housing and built large villas on the new avenues. They

Labour Avenue, opened to ease traffic in Naxxar, also marks the increasing involvement of the village with the rest of the island.

have thus by-passed the exclusive square and created two smart residential areas on the periphery. This changing settlement pattern reflects an increasing involvement outside the village. As more people work and marry outside the parish, as public and private transportation becomes more readily available, as the grip of television on leisure time grows, people are less dependent upon neighbours for work and leisure and look increasingly outward beyond the parish limits. The shift from a village-centred to a village-outward orientation is reflected in the way people have reoriented their social space. The community of interest and activity is no longer exclusively the village. The location of the houses that have been built in the last fifteen years mirror this; they no longer face the parish church.

If many of the new houses no longer face the square, most conform to the traditional perceptions of private space. The Maltese threshold looms very large. It separates the public from the private domain. Only very close family members have full access to the house. The formal hallway and the front rooms are used to isolate strangers and casual visitors from the kitchen or back-room where the family lives. In most front halls, near the door, there is a mirror and a pair of horns, perhaps in the form of a ceramic 'stag-at-bay' or a set of antlers. Mirrors and horns, it is believed, help neutralise the harmful effects of the 'evil eye' of envious visitors. Similarly, olive leaves blessed on Palm Sunday may be hung in a corner, and occasionally burnt to purify the house and ward off evil.

The house is normally inward-looking, with a private courtyard. The windows of the front rooms look out to the street, but are normally shuttered. On ceremonial occasions, such as the annual *festa* of the parish patron saint, weddings, baptisms, and the Easter blessing of the house, the front rooms are opened to the public. They are dressed in ceremonial regalia, much in the way the church is decorated for feast days. Special curtains are hung, carpets spread, dustcovers removed, chandeliers uncovered and the lights turned on full so that passers-by can look in and admire.

Visitors entertained in the front room ceremoniously receive a small glass of whisky or vermouth, presented on a tray. This offering of drink, and accepting it, is an important part of the ceremony attached to entertaining front-room visitors and so holding them at a distance in the house. We learned this, as we did so many other things, by stumbling over it. After the birth of our daughter Maria in Naxxar, many female neighbours came to call on Inga, my wife, to congratulate her, to look at the baby, and to bring a small gift. By then we knew that etiquette required us to provide them with a drink. I had consequently bought several bottles of whisky and vermouth, and assembled all the glasses that I could find in our sparsely furnished alley-house. This did not satisfy Guza, the fourteen-year-old neighbour girl who occasionally helped in the house. When she discovered, to her horror, that we did not have a proper tray and small glasses, she ran next door and borrowed them from her mother, thus protecting us from the pointed comments of the visitors. Guza again required us to use her mother's glasses and tray when the parish priest came to bless our house after Easter. He arrived at the end of a long afternoon during which he had blessed many houses and inhaled if not drunk large quantities of whisky. He put Guza's glass to good use and cheerfully sprayed holy water on us all, saying 'Here is a house that really needs blessing' (since we were not Catholic).

Men and women

The correspondence between public and private, illustrated in the separation between street and house, is found again in the separation of the spheres of men and women. The men's world is the public, that of the women the private domain of home and family.

In spite of recent pro-forma changes regarding the equality of sexes, the present generation of Maltese adults still believe that men are superior and women inferior. Men lead, provide and command. Women should obey, follow and care for home and family. Women are regarded as morally weak and easily misled. This propensity jeopardises a woman's ability to perform her roles as wife and mother, which, in turn, endangers the very existence of the family, the basic institution of Maltese society. In 1944 a prominent progressive academic argued against allowing women to vote, on the grounds that they lacked social education and hence the sense of responsibility necessary to vote. Consequently, to give the vote to women, he maintained, was tantamount to giving it to children and idiots, who also lacked a sense of responsibility. Fortunately many people thought otherwise, and women were given the right to vote.

Until very recently this attitude towards women was enjoined by the church, and reiterated from the pulpit, in the confessional, and by chaplains in schools, associations and work place. The rigid position of the church was modified somewhat following the second Vatican Ecumenical Council in the 1960's. The concept of marriage was redefined from a *contract*,

The men's world is the public, that of the women the private domain of home and family. Men gather at a public bar in Naxxar during the late afternoon to chat.

the prime purpose of which was to produce offspring so that the church might replenish itself and expand, to a *community* of love, only one of the objects of which was to beget and educate children.

The Maltese Civil Code reveals the same bias in favour of men as do the pronouncements of the church, though the government recently took some steps to lessen the inequality. Maltese law also reflects the principle of female incapacity. Until the early 1970's a woman could not hold public office, act as a juror, administer her own property or assume responsibility for her own children if widowed or separated. All women were barred from making donations of over £M50 without the consent of husband, father or court. Women shared this incapacity with the insane and minors. The present generation has been raised on these concepts. Although in the early 1970's the Malta Labour government removed some of the discriminatory clauses which applied to unmarried women, married women still may not fully administer their property. The husband is the legal head of the family and as such administers the joint estate. He can thus dissipate it with legal impunity. In fact, if husband and wife separate legally and guilt for the separation lies with the wife, her husband is permitted to keep the use of her dowry, as a sort of punishment for her misbehaviour. The most blatant form of discrimination, however, is in the field of employment. Women who work for government and many private firms are obliged contractually to terminate their employment on marriage. If a married woman is difficult to replace, she may then be re-employed on a temporary basis with a lower salary and without pension rights. Moreover, a new law, enacted in November 1974, stipulated that when a post which used to be filled by a man is vacated, it cannot be filled by a woman. This measure was taken to ease the unemployment situation. Although there was some grumbling, most Maltese women accepted it as morally correct. 'After all,' as one woman said to me, 'men are the providers'.

Considering the attitude of church and law to women, it is not surprising that there is considerable division of labour and segregation between the activities of men and women. In the church, *Missierna San Pawl's* dictum still holds: 'Let women keep silence in the churches for it is not permitted them to speak, but to be subject . . . if they would learn anything, let them ask their husbands at home.' None of the church's administrative offices are held by women, nor do they organise any of the activities important to the parish, except catechism for girls. In most churches women sit separate from the men, as I painfully learned.

During fieldwork in 1960, I arrived early for the first mass I attended in the village of Kirkop. I was determined to get a good seat to see what was going on. Since there was only a handful of people in the church when I arrived, I sat down on the right-hand side of the nave, in the third row from the front. Hardly had I settled down when a large group of giggling girls surrounded me. I turned selfconsciously around and saw three solemn-faced nuns seated on the aisle. The church remained painfully empty, for it was the 6.30 mass on a Monday morning. It suddenly dawned upon me that I was sitting in the place traditionally occupied by the nuns and their numerous little charges. After an embarrassing half hour of being peered and giggled at incessantly, I bolted. Later that day I met the parish priest, who discretely suggested that in future I sit in one of the lateral apses. He implied that this was not the way things should be, but it was the quaint custom in rural villages for men and women to sit apart.

Fifteen years later men and women in the rural churches still sit apart. Although in some of the larger rural parishes such as Naxxar, some young couples now occasionally sit together in the central section of the church.

Though women have low formal status, they of course play an extremely important role in Maltese society. They run the houses and take all the day to day decisions concerning finances and bringing up the children. They also occupy key positions in the kinship network, for children are much closer to their mothers than to their fathers. Consequently they see much more of the mother's relatives. In the political field women have also played important roles. For example, during the late 1950's and most of the 1960's there was intense conflict between the church and the Malta Labour Party. Women, who paradoxically are generally tied more closely than men to the church, were successfully mobilized by the church both as voters and activists to combat the socialist Labour Party. This manoeuvre was successful, for the Labour Party did not succeed in winning an election until it had made peace with the church. On the parish level, women are often most active in pursuing factional disputes and are involved more often than men in physical attacks on each other as well as, occasionally, on men during the course of neighbourhood skirmishes.

Although women voters outnumber men, they have played only a marginal role in parliamentary politics. For the past 25 years no more than three women have been elected to parliament. The Labour Party has been much more active in organising women's votes than its conservative rival. This is not only because the Labour Party has generally represented disadvantaged social categories. It has also desperately needed female votes to be able to challenge its rival's superior resources, which included church backing.

The measures introduced recently by the Labour Government to improve the status of women, modest though they are, are a sign of the times. Married women in increasing numbers are finding employment in manufacturing and tourism. Though it can scarcely be said that women's liberation has come to Malta, there are two important pressure groups: the older more conservative National Council of Women, and the younger, radical *Muviment ghall-Emancipazzjoni tal-Mara* (Movement for the Emancipation of Women). Both have been active and the N.C.W. in particular has had considerable success during the past ten years in presenting legislation and stimulating public debate on the position of women. It thus seems quite likely that as women come out of their homes and enter the labour force, they will assume a more active role in the political arena as they have elsewhere.

Social differences

In Malta, as in most societies, there are numerous ways in which people differentiate each other socially. Two important ways are what we may call a

Women visit in the street after the men have gone to work.

'*we–they*' principle, and a '*high–low*' or hierarchical principle. The 'we–they' distinction has to do with feelings of solidarity, of consciousness of kind, of membership in a *category or group*. The 'high–low' distinction is very often a *person to person* evaluation. These distinctions, of course, are not mutually exclusive and they very often overlap. A hierarchical criterion can become the basis of a 'we–they' distinction, as when a class-based consciousness and solidarity develops.

Perhaps the most striking 'we–they' distinctions important to Maltese are patriotism, parochialism and party solidarity. Maltese have been in touch with foreigners for many centuries and have developed social skills to handle these relations. They learned their masters' languages but continued to speak Maltese to each other. Language is very much an active symbol of belonging. Those who identified strongly with the English, tried hard to adopt the symbols of the group. They spoke Maltese with an English accent and interlarded their speech with English expressions. Even though Malta has been independent for ten years, there are still many who try to speak English at home. Shop keepers, ever sensitive to the wishes of their clients, are often obliged to speak English to customers they know to be Maltese simply to humour them. Country people, villagers and poorer Maltese did not have these identity problems. They were Maltese and had no pretentions of trying to adapt their language and behaviour to the mannerisms of their occupiers. They consequently spoke and still speak a much purer Maltese. Till the advent of tourism they also tended to identify all foreigners, irrespective of nationality, with English. Thus when we moved into Kirkop, my nickname was first *L-Ingliz*, although most knew I was American. Gradually they got to know me better, and as the social distance between us decreased, they called me by my Christian name. I became *Jerry, L-Amerikawn.*

Independence and the ever swelling stream of tourists have given the Maltese a new self-consciousness, and a more developed sense of patriotism. Maltese is now spoken more frequently as people become more conscious of their own cultural heritage. The way foreign tourists genuinely admire Maltese monuments, arts, crafts, music and even rural parish feasts, cause many citizens to view these in a new light. This newly 'discovered' cultural heritage has provided an important dimension to the search for a national identity. Thus, the ever increasing number of foreign visitors, in combination with the very visible colony of 'settlers', mostly retired English who have settled in Malta to enjoy the tax concessions, modest cost of living and pleasant climate, form a 'they'-category. This in turn is making the Maltese themselves more conscious of their own identity.

Tourists visiting the old capital at Mdina where several aristocratic families have converted their palaces into tea rooms and souvenir shops.

Parish patriotism or parochialism is extremely strong in Malta. People have a very keen sense of identity with their parish which is expressed in intense rivalry between parishes. The object of competition most often has to do with the honour of the parish. There is rivalry about the celebration of rituals, especially about the annual feast of a village's patron saint, and about the bestowal of rights which affect the rank and thus the honour of the parish *vis-à-vis* other parishes. All groups and individuals that are tied to the church are ranked. Each parish, each religious order, even each parish society has its fixed position in the overall order. Position in the hierarchy is determined by seniority of foundation, in the case of parishes and associations – or date of ordination or appointment to present office, in the case of the clergy – in combination with certain marks of honour conferred by the church authorities. Such honours carry with them a claim to higher precedence than seniority by itself would give. For example, any parish in which there is a collegiate chapter, or whose church has the title of basilica, or one of whose statues has been crowned, ranks higher than one that does not have these honours. To a considerable extent these honours are rewards for meritorious conduct, as measured by contributions to the decorations of the church, or the number of vocations, or special devotions performed in a parish. During certain religious processions and ceremonies this ranking becomes an important determinant of the order in which participants take part. Consequently, such events are often the occasion of active competition and hostility which can take on bizarre proportions.

In 1927, for example, the long standing rivalry between the collegiate chapters of Senglea and Birkirkara finally ended in the abolition of a centuries-old procession in which all parishes of Malta took part. Birkirkara and Senglea each claimed precedence in the procession. To resolve the dispute the bishops had decreed they were to take part in the procession side by side. Each year there were incidents caused by canons or confraternity members poking each other. But in 1927 there apparently was a free for all. Rival participants jabbed and thumped each other with crosses, ornate silver lanterns and heavy silver and damask banners. The archbishop, fed up with this annual confrontation, cancelled the procession forever. But not all disputes are limited to matters of precedence. In 1949 the people of Birkirkara smashed the archbishop's coat of arms and heaped rubble in the main door of their church, thereby symbolically denying him entrance. They were protesting because he had abolished, among other things, the right of their collegiate chapter to choose as canons only those priests born and baptised in Birkirkara. The Holy See was able to resolve the dispute, and a few years later it bestowed the title of basilica on the town's church, to the very great satisfaction of all loyal parishoners.

While parochialism in Malta is pronounced, in Gozo it is sometimes mind-boggling. During the 1960's, rivalry between the parishes of Nadur and Xaghra for the title of basilica escalated to incredible proportions. They spent thousands of pounds to decorate their respective churches. In Nadur a new marble pulpit cost the 1,800 parishoners and many migrants in

North America and Australia almost £M5000 and they spent more than £M20,000 to cover the walls with marble. The most acute parochial rivalry in Gozo, however, is between the parishes of St. George and Sta. Maria in Rabat, the island's capital. Because of this rivalry their annual *festas* are probably the Islands' most spectacular celebrations. But in spite of the enthusiasm with which the parishoners look forward to their *festa*, the parish of St. George cancelled the annual three-day tribute to its patron for almost ten years as an act of protest. The background to this act of apparent ritual self-destruction was Byzantine in its intricacy, but not unusual. In 1968, the new bishop of Gozo, responding to the recommendations of the Second Vatican Council, announced that the traditional Good Friday procession in Rabat would be transferred to the last two Sundays in Lent because it interfered with the church services on Good Friday afternoon. This new regulation favoured the partisans of Sta. Maria, who for many years had resented the control that their rivals had been able to exercise over the Good Friday procession, because most of the statues for the procession were housed in the church of St. George. By forbidding the procession to be held on Good Friday, the bishop abolished the monopoly position St. George supporters had over the procession via their control over the statues. Sta. Maria supporters were quick to take advantage of the opportunity the bishop's new regulations offered them: they petitioned for and received permission to organise a procession from their own church, the cathedral, on one of the last two Sundays in Lent. There would henceforth be two processions before Easter.

The leaders of St. George reacted by cancelling their traditional Good Friday procession, which had been transferred to Palm Sunday, and announced that they were also cancelling the external celebration of the annual *festa* of St. George in July. Moreover, to ensure as little interest as possible in the new procession of Sta. Maria on Passion Sunday, and to annoy the bishop, they hired a beat group to give a public programme while the procession was taking place. In place of the annual *festa* they held an elaborate song festival and invited pop-stars from more than a dozen countries.

Parochial confrontation continued. In order to channel the energy and funds of the parish's ardent partisans, normally applied to the preparation of the annual *festa*, St. George leaders decided to build a huge theatre. This in due course became Gozo's first public cinema, which, of course, was in its turn boycotted by the more ardent partisans of Sta. Maria. Not to be outdone, the latter built an even larger cinema and theatre. Their cinema also included a gigantic sunken dance floor. This parochial monument was opened to the public in 1976. That year St. George finally made peace with the bishop and celebrated its first *festa* in nine years.

Another form of 'we–they' identification is through party conflict. Although Maltese villages present a tightly united front to the outside world, all are divided internally. Cleavages cut across the community at various levels. Some of these divisions are only temporary, and disappear when the issues which created them are resolved. Others, which may have arisen over temporary issues, have become permanent by growing into formal associations. But regardless of their origin or duration, these divisions are painfully real to the villagers. Persons, made vulnerable through their network of personal relations, are forced to commit themselves to a particular division. In doing so they become opposed to neighbours and relatives who have taken the other side in relation to that division. This is particularly true of villages, such as those in Malta, in which the inhabitants are closely related through kinship. The Maltese call these divisions *partiti* (sing.: *partit*). The foremost divisions of this kind are caused by politics and band club rivalry related to the cult of saints.

Politics cut across Maltese society at all levels. They are related to the competition at the national level between the Malta Labour Party and the more conservative Nationalist Party. This division, of course, also represents a hierarchical 'we–they' ordering, for the political parties are class-based. Because the church sided with the Nationalist Party against the socialist MLP in the late 1950's and the 1960's, the confrontation between the parties has sometimes resembled a religious war. In the recent past it divided Malta into two bitterly opposed camps. Although the religious element is no longer so important in political alignment, the Maltese continue to take politics seriously. No less than 95 per cent voted in the 1976 election. People are labelled as either Nationalist or Labour supporters. Their respective parties try to keep them mobilised in preparation for the next election. Although the elections take place every five years, Malta always seems on the verge of an election.

The other type of permanent cleavage into 'we' and 'they' groups that exists in a number of villages is caused by the competition between supporters of rival band clubs. This rivalry is usually related to the cult of saints. In addition to the patron saint, every parish celebrates many other saints, some of which are honoured by special feasts. These secondary feasts are not normally celebrated on the same lavish scale as the annual *festa* of the patron. There are a number of villages, however, which celebrate two annual *festas*: one for the official patron of the parish, and the other for a secondary saint who has assumed almost equal importance. Where this occurs, the village is divided into two *partiti*, each of which has his own band club. Each *partit* celebrates one of the saints and competes with its rival in a public display of devotion. They vie with each other over almost every aspect of the *festa*: the decoration of the streets, the adornment of the statues, the number of bands invited to play, the number of candles and flowers displayed in front of the Saint's statue and, especially, the quantity and quality of fireworks. Since all innovations concerning the *festa* must be approved by the parish priest, he is frequently subject to heavy pressure. This sometimes results in hostile intrigues that periodically flare up into anti-clerical action and violence between rivals. In Kirkop, for example, there was a dispute between the *festa partiti* over which band had the right to march down a certain street. When the parish priest finally came down in favour of one *partit*, the furious rivals exploded a gigantic fire-cracker in the drainpipe under his house, early in the morning. The priest was so shaken that he persuaded the archbishop to transfer him to another parish. The *festa* partisans who had panicked the priest gleefully recounted to

Village *festa partiti* vie with each other over almost every aspect of the *festa* including the quantity and quality of fireworks. St. Leonard partisans in Kirkop display some of the fireworks for their patrons centenary.

me how he had been so frightened that he had insisted on a police escort to move round the village during the weeks pending his transfer.

The most intense clashes between rivals take place just before and during the celebration of their respective *festas*. Then police are often required to keep the frequent confrontations between rival partisans from escalating into a free for all. During the course of a year, numerous fund-raising fairs run by the band clubs are also occasions on which the village divides along *festa partit* lines. While supporters of the *partit* running the fair flock to it, their rivals either stage their own fair, or usually, they hire several buses and leave the village for a picnic or pilgrimage to some shrine of their saint.

Within a country as small as Malta, there thus are numerous ways in which solidarity in terms of a 'we' group versus a 'they' group is expressed. It seems most intense where it cuts across bonds of loyalty that link people to each other in group context at the community, club, or family level. It often sets brother against brother and neighbour against neighbour. For this reason, people deplore the effect that political and *festa* factionalism has on personal relations.

There are also other, more overtly hierarchical, forms of social differentiation which fundamentally affect people's lives. In Malta, as elsewhere, people also differentiate each other by status and moral reputation. Two important ways in which they differentiate social status is in relation to education and occupation. Education frees people from dependence on patrons willing to interpret the printed word for them. It also leads to better employment opportunities. Since entrance to the civil service, the professions and many commercial concerns is by competitive examination, people attach great importance to formal education. There is also a considerable difference in the social status ascribed to various jobs. Non-manual occupations, for example, have the highest status, while manual occupations the lowest. Professionals, such as priests, doctors, lawyers, chemists and – though slightly lower – teachers, are at the top; while farmers are at the bottom. Wealth is another determinant of status. It is generally related to occupation. Wealth also permits people to be less dependent upon others. Wealth can be used not only for better education, but also to acquire symbols which are associated with high status. New houses, cars, modern furniture, and even holidays abroad have become tangible indices of success and status. People grade each other partially according to the number of these symbols they have acquired.

Education, occupation and wealth are thus important criteria by which people attribute status to each other socially. Age was also an important determinant of status. Age meant wisdom, experience and position as the head of a large family, which also operated as an agricultural production unit. But, in a society where sons and daughters are working as skilled labourers, clerks, teachers and maids, while their fathers still farm or dig ditches, and where school children read letters, newspapers and voting instructions to their still illiterate parents, the words of the elders are often not heeded. The social and cultural gap between old and young is wider now than it was in the past. Leadership in the villages today is in relatively young hands. The old parish registers give support to the claim of the present generation of elders that this had not always been the case.

In addition to factors already mentioned, the moral reputation of a person is also an important determinant of the respect he receives from others and the status he is accorded. Because of the strength of the church, the Ten Commandments are important moral precepts. The moral worth of a person is judged according to the way in which he performs his duties as husband, father or mother, brother or sister. People should be good neighbours, and not fight with each other or gossip. In all these areas, women seem to be more vulnerable than men.

Some years ago I tried to understand how people viewed each other in moral terms. The way people judge each other differed slightly from person to person, so that it was difficult to generalise. But it may be interesting to examine how a Maltese friend viewed the people of his village, which is small enough so that he knew everyone. It appeared that he discerned six rough prestige classes in the village. The people in the highest prestige category (9%) seemed to possess all the factors which provided prestige. They were noted for their correct moral behaviour. They were often older persons who had demonstrated that they could take good care of their children. As teachers and civil servants, they also had high status occupations. These factors were also present, although to a lesser degree, among the persons my friend placed in the second category (19%). There were rumours associated with some of them, their education was not quite as good and their occupations were consequently less prestigious. One was not as religious as he ought to be. The daughters of another were a bit too friendly. Yet another was too much of a political fanatic, etc. People in this category were often young married couples who could still move up or down. Most persons were placed in the third, or middle group (55%). These were simple people, without much education or ambition. Their occupations were not particularly presitigous, for two-thirds were unskilled labourers. There was little chance they could move higher, but in moral terms they were good people. According to my friend, they were reasonably content with their position.

The lowest three categories consisted of people whose honour – either because of their own weakness or a fault – was blemished. People in the fourth class (7%) were generally more intelligent than those in class three and were trying to improve their prestige and reputation. They were found morally wanting, because of fights between spouses or siblings, because they worked too hard, or because they had a baby too soon after marriage. Those in the fifth class (5%) were not trying to improve their reputation. They were not as intelligent as those in the fourth class. Their families had a bad name, they were separated from their spouses, the women were too sexy, or the families had used violence, or had gone to prison. The sixth and lowest class (also 5%) consisted of persons who were actually outside the moral community of the village, and were hence unable to improve their position. Their reputation had been destroyed by immoral or violent behaviour. These included several cases of illegitimate birth and one case of murder which resulted in a long prison sentence. People in this category mostly lived in little farmhouses at some distance from the village centre. Figuratively and physically they were outside the village. It thus appeared that the relative importance my friend attached to moral reputation increased as other criteria which accorded prestige, such as occupation, education, decreased.

Finally, I think that it is worth noting that the principle of hierarchy is deeply imbedded in Maltese society. There exists in Malta what might be called a hierarchy of infallibility. It is believed that the view of persons who occupy superior positions should not be questioned. If a person is superior in rank or office, he is therefore right. This attitude permeates Maltese society. It is obviously derived partly from the recent colonial past; but it also stems from the very strong position of the church. Both the colonial government and the church are hierarchially organised institutions. Neither tolerate questioning. Commands, sermons and ex-cathedra pronouncements allow little room for discussion. New ideas usually enter institutions with young people who question the established order controlled by the older generation. The older generation usually has a vested interest in maintaining things as they are. These questions are thus healthy. They must be listened to and answered. In a hierarchy this does not usually take place. Those who have superior positions take decisions which their subordinates are expected to obey. Questioning is regarded as insubordination. Insubordination is punished. Here again a premium is placed upon conformity: a person who asks no questions is not punished. Nowhere is this hierarchical attitude more pronounced than in Maltese families. Father's word, generally speaking, is law. He does not discuss or invite opinions. He commands. Time and time again we have been struck by the way Maltese children, and especially sons, remain silent when their father is present. Visitors from countries where a more democratic spirit of consultation prevails in family and workplace, are often amazed at the passiveness with which Maltese children and wives accept the shouted, and often abusive commands and opinions of father and husband. The hierarchical world view is congruent with much of Maltese society and obviously incubated in many families.

Ritual

Ritual expresses in dramatic form the various organisational principles important in Maltese society discussed in the foregoing sections. Even time is ritualised. As the church bells mark out the important hours of the day, so the principal divisions of the year are set out by the annual national and parochial religious feasts and processions. Besides being important religious occasions, they are looked forward to as recreation. Though such secular spectacles as political rallies, the government-run carnival procession, cinema and, increasingly, football draw large crowds, the principal amusements of the Maltese still

Our Lady of Sorrows' procession in Naxxar is followed by most of the village.

generally have some connection with their religious ceremonies. Moreover, while celebrations such as St. Joseph the Worker, Corpus Christi and Christ the King, which are organised at the diocesan or national level, are important, the principal religious spectacles are parish rituals.

During the course of a year in Naxxar, for example, there are fourteen major celebrations and religious processions. The greatest concentration of ceremonies is around Easter. The cycle starts with the feast of Our Lady of Sorrows on the Friday before Palm Sunday. Virtually all the inhabitants escort the statue through the principal streets of the village. This is followed by the Palm Sunday procession from one of the village's smaller chapels to the parish church. On Maundy Thursday there is a long service during which the parish priest washes the feet of twelve village laymen. Immediately after this service the church is draped in black damask, and a huge wooden rattle replaces the church bells as a sign of mourning. On Maundy Thursday and on Good Friday in the morning, family groups visit the church and, passing before the statues depicting scenes from the Passion, which are later carried in the procession, they stop to pray at the elaborate altar of repose that is constructed in one of the chapels. Members of each of the village associations and clubs, including the Labour club, visit the altar of repose in groups. Many families make pilgrimages to the churches in the other parishes which hold Good Friday processions. At each they offer prayers before the altar of repose and pause to examine the statues and funeral hangings of their rivals before going on to the next village. Thus on Thursday evening after the services, and on Friday morning, visitors stream into Naxxar to see the church. Then, at two in the afternoon, there is a three-hour sermon on the Passion. This is followed by the Good Friday procession.

The Good Friday procession in Naxxar is one of twelve that take place in Malta. It is a spectacular parish production with the village streets as a stage and a cast of hundreds. In 1976 the procession lasted from five in the afternoon till 9.30 at night. Roughly 425 persons took part. They were watched by the rest of the village and many visitors who had come by bus and car. There were also some sixty foreign tourists, brought to the village by two agencies and seated on chairs rented for them from the band club. A subdued commentary broadcast by one of the religious associations via speakers in the square explained in both Maltese and English the details and meanings of Christ's Passion. There were nine large statues depicting scenes of Christ's Passion. The largest of these was the monumental gilded glass-covered mausoleum in which the crucified Christ was laid out. This heavy statue was carried by ten men, accompanied by four attendants and guarded by four Roman soldiers. It was re-gilded in 1974 at a cost of £M900 donated by a returned emigrant who had spent 43 years in New York. In addition there were seventy-nine costumed figures representing personages from the Old and New Testament in some way associated with Christ's Passion. Then there were two bands. Twenty masked penitents dragged extremely heavy chains tied to their ankles, and six penitents followed the procession on their knees. It was a most solemn and impressive spectacle, which took the organisers and participants months of intensive work to prepare and finance. The people of Naxxar are extremely proud of their Good Friday procession. They maintain that it has much more solemnity than those of their rivals.

Very early on Easter morning bells rang out to announce the Resurrection. The sacristan and his assistant removed the black damask from the church walls. Later in the morning a small procession with the statue of the risen Christ passed quickly through the village. This procession drew little attention.

If in Naxxar the Good Friday procession is the most spectacular ritual, and the annual three-day *festa* of Our Lady of Victories, the parish patron, the most joyous, the procession of Our Lady of Sorrows is probably the parish's most solemn and sacred religious experience. Seen analytically, this procession, like most others, is a ritual which links the religious with the secular. The procession originates in the church, the holy place; it then passes into the secular domain through the square along a set route of streets in the village, before returning once more to the church. The procession joins the inside with the outside, the religious with the secular, the sacred with the profane. The way in which a religious procession is organised reflects the linking function which it performs. It is composed of a secular head and a religious tail. That is, the order of precedence is inverted, with the least important leading and the most important bringing up the rear. The laymen, who have the lowest prestige and rank, lead the procession. The celebrant, often the bishop or the parish priest or their delegates, bring up the rear, the place of honour. Only men and youths take part in the procession. Women and children follow it.

In a procession the social ordering of sex and age are given a spatial dimension. Even class is reflected, for those laymen who carry the statues, lanterns and banners, and in general participate in the procession, are manual labourers. White collar workers watch and organise. For example, of the 425 people who took part in the 1976 Good Friday procession, only the ten clergymen and a few of the bandsmen did not work with their hands.

With these general principles in mind, we can examine the important procession of Our Lady of Sorrows which took place in Naxxar on Friday, 9 April 1976. The procession was headed by the enormous purple damask banner of the confraternity of Our Lady of Sorrows. Immediately following it was the leader of the confraternity, who carried a cross and was escorted by fellow confraternity members carrying beautifully wrought silver lanterns. Behind these came three more members of the confraternity. Each was dressed in an ankle-length white vestment covered by the purple cape of the confraternity of Our Lady of Sorrows. Following these was a man carrying a tableau setting out the significance of Our Lady of Sorrows. He was escorted by two men each carrying a silver lantern. Then came an altar boy with a censer. He was followed by another boy carrying a cross, in his turn escorted by another altar boy. They were followed by twelve seminarists and altar boys who preceded the celebrant, who in turn was escorted by five village priests. They were then followed by four men carrying silver lanterns, who brought up

It takes months of hard work to prepare parish celebrations. Here street decorations are being erected for Naxxar's annual festa.

the rear of the sacred portion of the procession. Then came the statue of Our Lady of Sorrows carried by eight men. The villagers followed the statue, but they were also grouped. First came the village boys, followed by the village priests. Then came the village girls. The boys and girls were supervised by members of the lay associations who taught them catechism. The mass of villagers followed the girls. Men, women, boys and girls were all mixed up. Sometimes they walked in family groups, sometimes with friends, sometimes alone. Virtually the entire village of 5,000 appeared to be participating in the procession, which, because of the bad weather, did not go the full course normally followed by processions. There was also a loud-speaker van leading the recitation of the Rosary.

This procession brought into relief a number of important structural principles that have been emphasised already. First the central position of the church in the village was made apparent, for it was the hub around which the procession moved. The hierarchical organisation of the church was again emphasised by the position of both clergy and laymen. The associations and different grades of clergy were also carefully positioned, as were men and women, boys and girls. The passage of the procession from the church through the streets of the village and back into the church also pointed to the concentric form of the parish. In addition to these principles, the procession also highlighted a number of pairs of structural oppositions which I have summarised as follows.

Religious	*Secular*
last	first
old	young
inside	outside
centre	periphery
right	left
men	women
high prestige	low prestige
powerful	weak

I should emphasise that, though I have distinguished these dyadic pairs in the procession, the people of Naxxar do not do so themselves. Participation in rituals is a normal event. Processions are as much a part of life in a village as gossiping and shopping and going to work. The religious and the secular are not seen as two opposing poles. The way in which these elements are built in the procession and the various rituals are examples of the way in which religious and secular threads make up the social fabric of Maltese society. The same is true in most of the small-scale, face-to-face societies that anthropologists study.

There, are, of course, many other examples of the way sacred and profane intermingle in Malta. For example, priests live at home and not in presbyteries. Many pass much of the day outside their religious roles by teaching, farming or administering their private property. Images of saints abound and can be seen on street corners, in houses, offices, even in the Labour Club. Village and countryside are dotted with small chapels and at Easter time the parish priest blesses the house of each parishoner in good standing, thus bringing the church to every home. Secular associations, religious clubs and political clubs, are also blessed. Many Maltese cross themselves and say a short prayer when they leave their houses in the morning, or when they step into a car or a bus. Religion permeates the structure of Maltese society. Most Maltese move unconsciously from the religious to the secular and back again. They do not draw a clear line between those two fields.

I formulated much of the above analysis in virtually the same words almost fifteen years ago. Since then Malta has been caught up increasingly in such secular activities as industrialisation and tourism. The secular impact of mass-media, television, modern films, and journals, and the relaxation of censorship has been quite significant. Due to these influences, and also because of the concerted effort made by the Malta Labour Party to limit the church's power to purely religious matters, the hold the church had over people in the recent past has weakened. People no longer go to church quite as often as they used to, nor do they hold the clergy and the precepts of the church in quite such high esteem.

If attachment to the church is diminishing, why then are many public religious ceremonies growing? For growing they are. In 1976, for example, the Good Friday procession in Naxxar was a great deal more complex and larger than in 1961. There were seventy-nine new costumes. These were personal property and each had cost its proud owner an average of £M60. The bands were larger, and a second band had been hired. The statue of Judas was new. Christ's monument had recently been regilded. There were ten more penitents with heavy chains. In all 130 more people took part in the 1976 Good Friday procession than in 1961, although there were fewer black-clad and veiled female penitents walking behind the procession. The same

In Malta sacred and profane intermingle.

The people of Naxxar are proud when foreign tourists come to watch their processions.

increase in scale is noticeable in the annual village *festas*: more participants, more spectators, more hired bands, more elaborate decorations and more intricate and colourful fireworks. Why should there be this increase in scale?

The growth of these public rituals can be explained in a number of ways. To begin with, during the past fifteen years transportation has improved immeasurably. There are both more buses, and more people have cars. Improved transportation makes it easier for the public to come and watch. This is an incentive to those holding the celebration. Second, the pressure to innovate, to improve the feast, to be one up on rivals, remains constant. Third, a rising standard of living has enabled fewer people to spend more. If a number of people have ceased to participate in the pageantry – and several villages now pay labourers to decorate the streets and even to carry some statues – they have increased their contribution which, together with those of others, enables them to be replaced. Fourth, innovations to improve ceremonies such as the Good Friday procession are cumulative. Fifth, through television, people have increasingly become conscious of how spectacles can be staged and how they appear to others. Sixth, with independence there has become an increased support of Malta's cultural heritage. The government, particularly the Tourist Board, has taken pains to point out that rituals such as Good Friday processions form part of that heritage. Seven, tourism has provided an extra, important, dimension to the public of such spectacles. As one friend in Naxxar told me, 'We are proud they have come from so far to see our procession. They could have gone to other villages. They chose to come to Naxxar.'

These rituals also provide a way in which outsiders – who are increasingly moving into the village as spouses or simply because they find housing there – can take part in communal activity and so feel, if not become, a part of their adopted community. Thus by taking part in such rituals, outsiders can integrate themselves. Participation need not involve carrying a statue or dressing up. It can also take the form of a financial contribution or of enthusiastic watching. Ritual provides a bridge from 'they' to 'we'.

It is also possible that the greater enthusiasm for spectacular rituals such as the Good Friday processions and the *festas* that emphasise the 'we-community' of the village, is related to the fact that people who live together in such villages have increasingly less to do with each other. Formerly the people of Naxxar worked together and spent most of their leisure time together. They were much more dependent upon each other. Now they are more isolated, withdrawn into individual family units. Perhaps because of this isolation, they find themselves periodically drawn to events that celebrate their solidarity as a village, their sense of community, their parish, their 'we' as opposed to other 'they' groups. These communal rituals thus provide a sense of identification and solidarity with a group larger than the family, at a time when such communal solidarity is no longer reinforced by work and leisure.

Further reading

AQUILINA, J. *Papers in Maltese linguistics* Valletta: Royal University of Malta, 1961.

BLOK, A. *South Italian agro-towns* in *Comparative Studies in Society and History* vol. 11, part 2. April 1969. pp. 121–135.

BOISSEVAIN, J. *Saints and fireworks: religion and politics in rural Malta* (LSE Monograph on Social Anthropology, 30) Athlone Press, 1965.

BOISSEVAIN, J. *Why Maltese ask so few questions* in *Ferment* University of Malta vol. 7, 1969. pp. 18–22.

BOISSEVAIN, J. *Hal-Farrug: a village in Malta* Holt, Rinehart and Winston, 1969.

BOISSEVAIN, J. *Fieldwork in Malta* in *Being an anthropologist: fieldwork in eleven cultures* edited by G. D. Spindler. Holt, Rinehart and Winston, 1970. pp. 58–84.

BOISSEVAIN, J. *Some notes on the politics of women in Maltese society* in *Nord Nytt* vol. 3, 1972. pp. 196–213.

BOISSEVAIN, J. *A causeway with a gate: the progress of development in Malta* in *Perceptions of development* edited by S. Wallman. CUP, 1977.

KNOX, R. J. ed. *The documents of Vatican II* New Delhi: St Paul's Publications, 1966. pp. 47–52. (Gaudium et Spes).

Lehen -il-Malti vol. 14, 1944, Editorial.

PITKIN, D. S. *Mediterranean Europe* in *Anthropological Quarterly* vol. 36, part 3, 1963. pp. 120–129.

SCIBERRAS, L. *Women and Maltese politics* in *Malta Yearbook 1975* Sliema: de la Salle Bros., 1975. pp. 372–383.

United Nations Statistical Yearbook 1976 New York: UN Statistical Office.

XUEREB, C. *Women and the law* in *Malta Yearbook 1975* Sliema: de la Salle Bros., 1975. pp. 357–363.

Left
The parish owns valuable property of which the most important is the church. Its gilded ceilings and ornate statues represent the wealth of the parish amassed over centuries from bequests of generations.

Below
The Grand Harbour at Valetta, Malta. The first thing that strikes the visitor is that these islands appear to be all rock, and the fortifications form part of the tawny limestone landscape.

Above
The devotion of Maltese to their religion is reflected in the many shrines found even in buses.
Right
The Good Friday procession in Naxxar is a spectacular parish production with the village streets as a stage and a cast of hundreds.

The Palm Sunday procession goes from one of the parish's smaller chapels to the parish church.

Above
Cooking for the family is usually done in a small separate kitchen made from a frame of poles covered with plaited coconut leaves. When guests have to be served a large pot of rice is cooked in the open courtyard. The women wear *kangas* – two pieces of brightly coloured material wrapped around the body, one covering the breasts to the ankles and one the upper part of the body including the head.

Right
Using only hand tools, it takes a few months to make a dug-out canoe. This kind of skill is possessed by only a few men in the village. When it is fitted with outriggers, the canoe will be used for fishing.

The Swahili of Chole* Island, Tanzania

Chapter Six

by Patricia Caplan

Introduction

Chole Island[1] lies some twenty miles off the southern coast of Tanzania, and covers about 200 square miles, roughly half the size of Zanzibar Island which is 100 miles to the north, but twice as large as our other island community, Malta. Chole, along with the other islands lying off the east coast of Africa, has shared in the long and interesting history of the area. The east coast forms a part of the Indian Ocean littoral, and the peoples of this region have been traders and sea-farers for centuries. It is an area exceptional in Africa because it is mentioned in written accounts which go back as far as two thousand years. The earliest is a Greek text, the *Periplus of the Erythraean Sea*, which is dated around A.D. 110. Most subsequent accounts, up to the arrival of the Portuguese on the coast in the fifteenth century, were written by Arab geographers.

By the end of the first millennium A.D. there had been established a number of Islamic city-states, based on trade, the most important of which were initially on Zanzibar and Pemba Islands. (The earliest inscription on the coast is found at Kizimkazi on Zanzibar, and bears the date A.D. 1107.) By the thirteenth century, however, the chief settlement on the coast was Kilwa Kisiwani, a small island lying about 80 miles to the south of Chole. Kilwa owed its prosperity mainly to the fact that it controlled the gold-trade from Sofala (now in Mozambique).

One of the earliest documents relating to the coast is the Kilwa chronicle, of which two versions survive, one in Arabic, and the other in Portuguese. In this book, Kilwa is said to have been founded by the sons of a sultan from Shiraz in the Persian Gulf, who migrated in the tenth century A.D. However, the archaeologist Neville Chittick, who has excavated the ruins at Kilwa, suggests rather that the 'Shirazis' came to Kilwa from the Somali coast and that they did so not in the tenth, but the twelfth century. The Kilwa chronicle goes on to record that some of the sons of the first Kilwa sultan settled on Chole Island, at its southwesternmost tip, which is today called Kisimani Chole; there they tried to establish an independent polity. On the whole, however, Chole remained subject to Kilwa during this time, with only one of two brief periods of independence.

*Chole Island is also known as Mafia Island

The Great Mosque of Kilwa which was probably first built in the twelfth century.

The period between the twelfth and the fifteenth centuries was the hey-day of the coastal civilisations of Muslim city-states; their rulers and merchants built mosques, tombs, and palaces, and minted coinage; they also imported pottery and other goods from most of the known world, including China. These towns were inhabited by a mixture of Africans and traders coming from elsewhere in the Indian Ocean, particularly the Persian Gulf region. While Arabic was their literary language, it is probable that they were using a vernacular not far removed from modern Swahili. The immigrants must have married local African women, giving rise to the physically mixed Swahili speakers of the coast.

The Portuguese arrived on the east coast of Africa in 1498, and remained there for exactly two hundred years. They took control of the Sofala gold-trade, thus causing the decline of Kilwa. However, they have left little impression on the coast, beyond a few large fortresses such as those in Kilwa and Mombasa, and a handful of Portuguese words in Swahili, such as *meza* – table, or *almeria* – cupboard.

The Portuguese were eventually ousted by the Omani Arabs, who dominated the coast and also much of the interior from the beginning of the eighteenth century until the coming of the British and Germans, who colonised Kenya and Tanganyika respectively. During the Omani period, the most important settlement on the coast was Zanzibar town, the seat of the Sultan of Zanzibar. It was during this period that the links between the coast and the interior were forged, largely on the basis of the trade in ivory and slaves. There was a saying at this time that 'When they play the pipes in

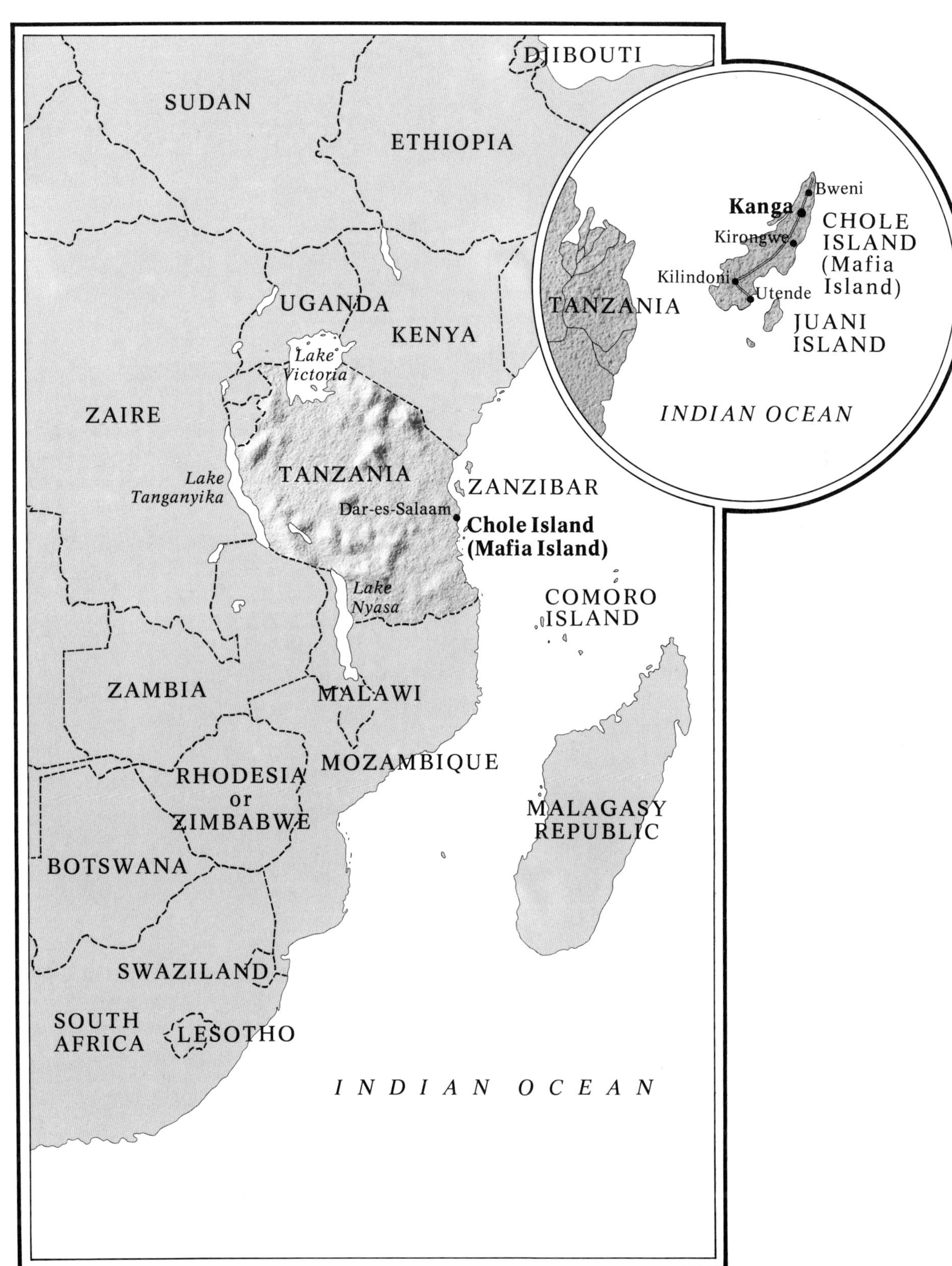
DJIBOUTI
SUDAN
ETHIOPIA
UGANDA
KENYA
Lake Victoria
ZAIRE
TANZANIA
Lake Tanganyika
ZANZIBAR
Dar-es-Salaam
Chole Island (Mafia Island)
Lake Nyasa
COMORO ISLAND
ZAMBIA
MALAWI
MOZAMBIQUE
RHODESIA or ZIMBABWE
MALAGASY REPUBLIC
BOTSWANA
SWAZILAND
SOUTH AFRICA
LESOTHO
INDIAN OCEAN
Bweni
Kanga
CHOLE ISLAND (Mafia Island)
Kirongwe
Kilindoni
Utende
TANZANIA
JUANI ISLAND
INDIAN OCEAN

Part of the interior of the Great Mosque at Kilwa.

Hoisting the sail of a boat (mashua) which is about to sail to the mainland.

Zanzibar, they dance as far away as the lakes' – that is of course the great lakes of East Africa. This expansion of trade carried Swahili, by now a well-developed language with a rich written literature, into the interior of the continent. It is now spoken as a second or third language by millions of people from Mozambique to Somalia, and even as far into the interior as Zaire – indeed, it is the most widely understood language in Africa, as well as being the national language of both Tanzania and Kenya.

During the period of Omani Arab rule, which continued until European colonisation in the mid-nineteenth century, Chole Island continued to be an appendage, but this time of Zanzibar. Many Arabs settled in the southern part of the island, and set up large coconut plantations, run mainly by slave labour brought from the mainland. The original inhabitants of the island, who call themselves Mbwera or Shirazi, were pushed into the northern half, where the soil is less suitable for coconuts but more favourable for subsistence crops. It is in the north of the island that people live in nucleated villages, and it was one of these villages – Kanga – that we filmed.

The north of Chole is even nowadays somewhat more remote and under-developed than the south of the island. In the southern half is located the capital of the island, Kilindoni, with its hospital, air-field, and government headquarters. A network of roads covers the south, but only one fair-weather road runs to the north of the island. However, northern villagers have always kept contact with the mainland by sailing their dhows there in order to sell coconuts, and buy cloth and other goods not produced on the island. Nowadays, contact with the mainland, and with Dar es Salaam (capital of

Tanzania) has been increased by the growing number of radios in each village, and by government personnel sent to live and work in the villages as teachers, para-medics and development officials. So even in the north of Chole, people do now think of themselves as 'Tanzanians', although in certain contexts they still regard themselves as 'coastal people' (and thus rather different from Tanzanians who live up-country) or even as 'northerners' (in contradistinction to the people of the south of Chole).

Kanga village

Kanga village has a population of just over a thousand people. The centre of the village consists of three shops, a mosque, a community building, and a clinic. The school, which is also attended by children from another village, lies some way to the north, and school-children from Kanga face at least a two mile walk each morning and evening.

The villagers' houses, which are built among their coconut trees and grouped in small family clusters, are usually constructed of a framework of mangrove poles filled in with mud. Those who can afford it plaster and white-wash the walls, whereas poorer people may simply construct walls of plaited palm fronds. All houses are roofed with palm-leaf thatching. A house is generally divided into the covered veranda, which faces the road or path, a main room (or several rooms in a large house) and a court-yard at the back, which houses the kitchen and bathroom areas. Generally speaking, men sit on the veranda to receive their visitors, while women entertain theirs in the courtyard.

The coconut trees growing throughout the village separate clusters of houses from one another. Houses which are built next to each other generally belong to close relatives. It is usual for people to build houses amongst their coconut trees. The veranda of a house often adjoins a path and is a meeting place for male visitors.

In northern Chole each nuclear family (i.e. parents and their unmarried children) has its own house, unlike other societies where there are joint or extended households (i.e. nuclear family plus other relatives). Boys move out of their parents' houses when they are adolescents and build small huts for themselves. When a young couple marries, they build a house of their own – this may be next to that of the husband's or the wife's parents, although the former arrangement is somewhat more usual, but it is always an independent structure, and cooking arrangements will be separate. People who are divorced or widowed may choose to come and live near to one of their relatives, and in some cases, for example when extremely old, may even be fed from the kitchen of the focal household, but they will almost invariably have houses of their own. People feel very strongly that privacy is important and that in houses which are relatively flimsy this is impossible to obtain if several families share a single dwelling. For instance, one close friend of mine is now divorced, and has gone to live with her widowed mother. They do share the cooking arrangements, but each woman has her own hut. My friend explained that in this way, she can entertain her friends without disturbing her mother.

Kanga village is divided up into wards, each of which is associated with one of six descent groups. A descent group is composed of all the people who can trace their descent back to a founding ancestor or ancestress, and so are entitled to use the resources of the group. The main resource of the descent groups in Kanga is land for cultivating but residential land in the village is also held by descent groups. The descent groups on Chole are unusual because they are *cognatic* – this means that membership of them is obtained through both father and mother. So if a person's parents are members of different descent groups, then he or she will have multiple membership, and be able to obtain rights to land and other resources through more than one group. Our own society is also cognatic, of course, in that we inherit property from both parents, and we trace ties to relatives through both the mother and father, but these links do not make people members of organised groups like those in Kanga.

One of the descent groups is considered to be of somewhat higher status than the rest because a famous Sheikh (Muslim scholar and leader) from Zanzibar married into it a couple of generations ago. Many of the members of this group are renowned for their piety and Koranic learning. Another group is considered to be of lower status than the others because many of its members are very involved in spirit possession cults, which are condemned by the very pious. Members of these two groups tend to marry fellow members, and are thus less likely to have multiple membership than people who belong to other groups. Even so, more than half of the people in the village are members of more than one group, and they may have quite a lot of choice about where they are going to live; a married couple has an even wider choice for they can choose between the husband's and the wife's descent groups. However, in order to obtain land on which to build a house a person should not only be a member of the descent group which 'owns' the area of the village, but also have some coconut trees there. Since people inherit coconut trees through their fathers and mothers, just like they do their descent group membership, this means that they usually inherit trees in those wards where they also have descent group membership.

Most villagers move their residence every few years or so, particularly in the early years of married life. Some, who have rights in other northern villages on Chole, may even move from one village to another, although this is less common. Even if people do not take up all their potential residential rights, over a period of time most of them will use all their cultivation rights, for land in Mafia is cultivated on a shifting system, by which

Felling coconuts – a difficult task which is carried out by specialists in the village who are paid by the tree owner for their work.

This house has three rooms. On the left of the door is the main room where the couple sleep. On the other side are two smaller rooms for the children and for storage. The veranda floor is covered in mats and in the evening a group of men may sit there talking. Prayer mats hang on the wall behind.

a particular piece of land can only be cultivated for a single season and then has to lie fallow for a number of years in order to allow the soil to recover.

In short, then, this is a very flexible system of organising social relations. If one descent group has no available land in a particular year, then a couple goes to another of their groups in order to obtain land. If a couple decides to move their house – perhaps to be nearer to the centre of the village, or else to be further out and so nearer the fields – then it is not difficult for them to do so. However, this system may begin to change in the near future. The Tanzanian Government is very anxious to encourage each household in the village to cultivate a one-acre kitchen garden around its house. Furthermore, in Kanga, as in other parts of Tanzania, there has been a considerable effort by the government to concentrate villages in a single area, rather than allowing them to remain spread out. This of course makes it easier to provide the villagers with essential services. Recently, then, people in Kanga who were living away from the centre of the village have been moved in, and allocated land, although not necessarily on the basis of their descent group membership or of their ownership of coconut trees. It is not yet clear what effect this movement will have on the traditional system. What people can do, if they wish to preserve their original system of land rights, is to buy or exchange their coconut trees, so that they will have rights on the land where they are not living. However, in many instances, this may not be necessary if a kinship link can be traced with the owner of the trees, who may then give formal permission for a house to be built.

The government also states that anyone may cultivate any piece of unused land, which means that, in theory, any villager may take any piece of bush land and cultivate it. But, there have been relatively few cases of villagers simply taking up land in such a way. Most people continue to get land through their descent groups or those of their spouses. Perhaps one reason why the traditional land tenure rules are adhered to is that other villagers might make life difficult for people who contravened them, such as for example refusing to help build the protective fence around a recalcitrant person's field.

The economy of the village

The economy of the village is a varied one – agriculture, fishing, growing coconuts as a cash crop, and animal husbandry. Cultivation of the bush begins in early November when after deciding where each family shall cultivate, the men cut the bush and then set fire to it. Planting, which is women's work, begins in early December, and the men meanwhile begin to build fences around their fields in order to keep out wild pigs, or stray cattle, which could spoil the crops. Fences are usually built around a number of fields together, and the men do the work co-operatively. The crops planted are mainly rice, but also corn, millet, beans and pumpkins.

In February, people generally move out to their fields to live in small temporary huts. They are thus able to guard the ripening crop from birds and monkeys. Some villagers stay as long as five months in their fields until everything has been harvested and in this way they also avoid the long walk from their village houses to the bush fields every day.

Picking over rice after the main harvesting in the low lying meadow land. Small, temporary huts, which can be seen in the background, are built in the fields to house the family before and during the harvest period. Sleeping out in the fields is considered essential to protect crops from monkeys, birds and wild pig. The palm trees mark the edge of the village.

Rice is threshed and winnowed as it is required for cooking. In preparing a meal for a wedding the young women pound the rice and the older women sit under the eaves at the back of the house winnowing by gently tossing the rice in shallow baskets. The chaff provides food for the chickens kept by most households.

In addition to the bush fields outside the village, there is also a limited amount of meadow land within the village which can be cultivated on a permanent basis, provided that cattle dung is used as a fertiliser. Since there is no bush to be cut down, women can, and often do, cultivate this land on their own if they are widowed or divorced, or else women may manage to cultivate a small meadow field in addition to the main bush field. The rice yield from meadow land is high, but it does not support any other type of crop.

Although rice is the main staple, and the most valuable food, cassava is becoming increasingly important with encouragement from the government. Cassava is a hardy crop which gives yields for most of the year and needs relatively little attention. Aside from the root crop, which can either be cooked like potatoes, or else dried and pounded into flour, the leaves make excellent spinach. All households in the village have a cassava field, mostly in the areas set aside by the government.

Although most people work hard in their fields, the simple technology, relatively poor soil, lack of fertiliser and large numbers of pests of all kinds means that the yields are not high enough to enable them to feed themselves all the year round. (However, with the increase in cassava production the situation is certainly better now than when I visited the village for the first time ten years ago.) Accordingly, people buy food from the shops when their own harvest runs out – rice if they can afford it, or else flour which is made into a stiff porridge. Money is thus needed to buy supplementary food, and for other purposes too – clothing, kerosene for the small wick lamps which are the sole source of light after dark, and also for fish, the main accompaniment to the evening meal.

For most villagers, their coconut trees are the chief source of cash. People obtain their trees, as I have already said, by inheritance from their parents, but they may also acquire them by buying or planting seedlings. A

Large quantities of rice are cooked for wedding feasts. Rice is the staple food and the most valued. Weddings and other ceremonies are held after the harvest to take advantage of the availability of rice. Each of the six descent groups has its own cooking pot.

coconut tree takes about seven years to start bearing, and then it continues to give nuts for about 80 years. The nuts are felled when ripe and then the outer husk is removed, the nut is split open and the flesh is dried, either in the sunshine, or else if it is the wet season, in a specially constructed kiln. The dried flesh is known as copra, and this can either be sold to the large estates in the south of the island or sold directly to the mainland markets. Copra is used for making soap and many other products, and oil for cooking can also be extracted from it.

There is almost no part of the coconut tree which is not useful. When the coconuts are green, the milk makes a refreshing drink; later when the nuts are ripe, they are covered in a husk of coir which can be used to make rope and other coir products, such as doormats. The villagers themselves tend to discard the husk, except for one or two rope-makers, but the government is anxious to encourage the development of a coir industry, and has already made a start in this direction.

When the nuts are ripe, the flesh can not only be dried for sale as copra, as already described, it can also be ground up to extract the coconut oil which is used for cooking rice or cassava and gives it a most delicious flavour. One villager, whose father had come from the Arabian peninsula to settle on Chole told me 'Of course, I'd like to go back some time to visit where my ancestors lived. But I don't think I could stand to eat dry rice cooked without coconut like they do there, so I suppose I'll never go!'

The fronds of the coconut palm likewise have many uses. A frond can be plaited into a sort of mat which can be used to form a hut wall, or else the leaves can be cut off and attached to a stick to make thatching material for roofs. Another form of plaiting provides a handy little basket. Fronds can also be stuck upright into the ground to make the fencing around a courtyard. And the rib of the palm leaf can be dried and strips cut to make toys like model cars, boats and houses. It is thus small wonder that coconut trees are a person's most valued possession and that people like to live near to their trees.

Villagers can also obtain cash in a number of other ways – some are fishermen, and can sell their catch to others in the village, or else dry and smoke it, and then take it to the capital, Dar es Salaam, to sell in the markets. Fishing is carried out on a small scale in Kanga: individuals use lines and a canoe, or else a small group of men may take out nets in a larger boat, or set traps on the beach to catch the fish on the outgoing tide.

Another source of income in the village is animal husbandry. Cows, goats and donkeys are all kept, the two former to provide meat on festive occasions, and the latter are used to transport goods to the south of the island. Cows are also kept for their milk, but the yields are very small indeed.

Another way of earning a cash income from the village is by trading – buying up dried fish or coconuts to sell in Dar es Salaam, and using the money to buy manufactured goods such as cloth, kerosene, cooking pots and crockery which are not obtainable in the village.

All of these activities – fishing, animal husbandry and trading – are carried out mainly by men, although some women do own cattle. However, the main source of cash income for women, apart from the sale of the nuts from their coconut trees, is the sale of mats. All women in the village make mats – small girls learn at a very early age, and even old women, who are incapable of agricultural or other work, plait away as they keep an eye on their grandchildren. Women plait at every conceivable opportunity, rather in the way that some women knit in our society – on Chole one even sees women walking along the road and plaiting.

The mats are made from the leaves of the wild date palm which are cut and dried in the sun, then split into a kind of raffia, and plaited into long strips. These are then dyed various colours, and cut into uniform lengths which are sewn together to make a mat which measures about eight feet by four feet. Some women who are more skilled dye the raffia first, and then achieve very intricate designs by plaiting the two colours together in a single strip. The mats are bought up by village traders, who take them to Dar es Salaam or Zanzibar; they are also willing to buy the raffia, and this too provides a source of income for women. Money earned from the sale of mats or raffia belongs entirely to the women who have produced them and can be used in whatever way they choose. Generally women buy clothes for themselves or their children or else they may buy extra utensils for the household. Unsupported women, that is widows or divorcees, will, of course, have to use their money for daily expenses.

Mat-making is thus extremely important for women's economic independence – married women have a source of cash income to spend as they please while women who are divorced or widowed are not forced to look to their male kin for support. Even young girls can earn a few shillings and buy an extra set of clothes which their parents might not otherwise afford, while old women, even those past agricultural work, are not totally dependent for their every need on their children.

There are, however, few new sources of cash income in the village – although there are increasing opportunities for earning money outside. In the last decade there has been a growth in the migration of young men, and even a few young women, to seek jobs in other parts of Tanzania. They work in factories or hotels, or as teachers and para-medical staff. Since this is a recent phenomenon, it is difficult to know whether people will return to the village but certainly until now, it has been very rare for anyone to leave permanently. Previously, young men would spend a few years working at unskilled jobs in Zanzibar or Dar, and then return to the village to marry and settle down. Certainly, the young migrant workers, home on leave, whom we met in the village intended to return after a few years, and as long as the village continues to have enough land to be able to offer a living to its population, this is likely to continue to be the case.

The point that I want to stress in this description of the village economy is that no one is either very rich or very poor. Certain people are

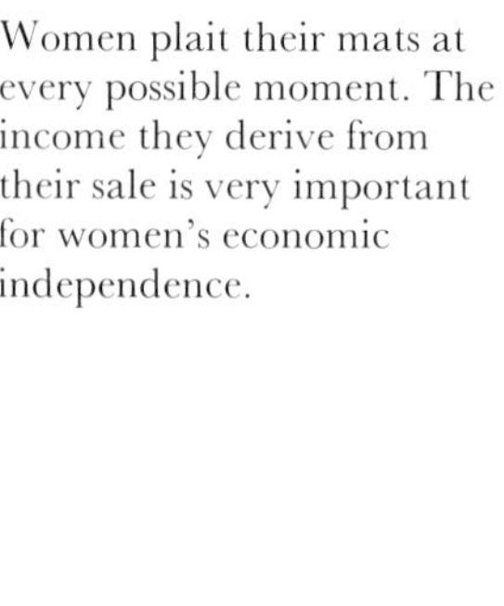

Women plait their mats at every possible moment. The income they derive from their sale is very important for women's economic independence.

relatively well off, in that they own large numbers of coconut trees, and/or cattle, but even they depend to a large extent on their own labours to feed themselves. Some are relatively poor, but these are often young people who have not yet inherited or planted coconut trees, or else a handful of elderly people who are reputed to have 'squandered' their property.

Since there is plenty of bush land, each person can have what he or she is capable of cultivating; there are no landless people in the village, although there are people who own no coconut trees. But even these can acquire trees by planting them, or else they can try to earn money, either through migration or trade, and buy some trees. Furthermore, there are no labourers who will cultivate other people's fields for cash – all have to work their own fields, although occasionally people who are having problems (such as sickness) may pay someone to do a specific task if they are unable to find a relative to do it for nothing. There is, in short, no class of landless labourers or idle land owners.

By the standards of Tanzania, which is a poor country, the people of Chole are relatively well off – they have enough land, which is reasonably fertile, to grow food for most of the year, and enough cash earned from their coconut trees to buy clothes and other goods imported from the mainland, and to pay their taxes. Because they also fish, they have a balanced diet, which includes grains, pulses, vegetables, fish and occasionally chicken or meat. Although the villagers work hard, there is sufficient leisure to permit a varied and rewarding social life, as I shall show in the ensuing pages.

The life cycle

Childhood

Children on Chole are born into a society which values them very positively, and accords them a degree of respect which many westerners would find surprising. Children are rarely coerced into doing things against their will, and they are not often punished. Unlike western children, they grow up surrounded by a large number of adults with whom they have close ties – their parents, grandparents, aunts and uncles, many of whom will live in the village, or perhaps in an adjacent village. Many children after babyhood are taken to be brought up by relatives other than their parents – a grand-parent, an older brother or sister, or an aunt or uncle. This is in no sense an adoption – the children know perfectly well who their 'real' parents are, and call the foster-parents by whatever kinship term is appropriate, not 'mother and father'. They visit their natural parents frequently and inherit property from them, not from their foster-parents. However, strong ties are created between foster-parents and children, so that the latter may choose to remain near to them when they grow up.

What is the reason for this custom of fostering? One factor is, as I have said, that children are very much valued. People *like* having children around, and older people, once their own children are grown up, beg for grandchildren to care for. Secondly, fostering is a good way for a large family which may have difficulty in feeding all the members adequately, to solve its problems by helping a childless couple and allowing them to foster a child. Thirdly, it also helps to alleviate the difficulties created by divorce and re-

Young women and girls sometimes wear dresses instead of *kangas*.

marriage, since the children of a divorced couple are usually taken by the mother of the wife, usually only until the latter establishes herself in a new marriage, but sometimes on a permanent basis. Of course, it also means that one almost never finds old people living alone. During the time that I did field-work on Chole, a quarter of the children in Kanga were being fostered in this way.

Even if children are not fostered on a permanent basis, many of them visit relatives frequently – perhaps in another village where they may stay for several days or weeks when they are older, or just for short stays of a few hours with relatives in the same village.

When children are small, they are cared for mainly by their mothers, although other female relatives may do a certain amount of child-minding; this is particularly likely if the mother is very busy, or has to attend a ritual. The traditional 'father's hour' is the late afternoon, when the men return from the fields or the beach and relax while waiting for supper. While the women cook and pound the rice, the men will usually play with their children. Until they are weaned at two years, children are rarely away from their mothers for long periods, but after that, they may be taken out by an older sister or brother who goes out to play in the neighbourhood. It is not uncommon to see a small girl of five or six with a baby clinging to the hip.

Children do not begin school until they are at least eight or nine. One reason is that the school is too far away for small children to walk to, but a second is that the Tanzanian government, recognising that most children will only have seven years of schooling, encourages late entry; this means that most children are almost adult when they complete their basic education. All children now attend primary school, which is a considerable improvement on the situation a decade ago, when hardly any girls, and only about half of the eligible boys attended.

Some children do go to the traditional Koranic schools when they are six or seven. Here they learn to read the Muslim's holy book, the Koran, although they do not understand the Arabic in which it is written; however, they do learn to write in Arabic script. There has been a high percentage of literacy on the coast for many years because people knew how to write their spoken language, Swahili, in Arabic script. The present generation which attends government schools, learns to write in Roman script as well. Sometimes children leave the Koran school when they start attending the government school, but others continue to attend the former part-time, on holidays and at weekends.

Children also begin to work at a relatively early age – girls particularly are required to look after small children, and to help with pounding and cooking. Boys tend to help rather less, although they are often sent on errands; at adolescence they begin to help with such activities as agriculture and fishing. This does not mean that children are exploited – in this society, everyone has to work, and even the most routine tasks, like the preparation of foods, require many hours of physical labour. Children learn at an early age that one must work in order to eat, and their efforts to help and imitate adults are regarded by encouragement and sometimes by payment. One friend of mine was relating to me how the cash from the sale of the family's sim-sim harvest had been divided up – he and his wife had taken equal shares, and then their children had also received varying amounts according to their age and the amount of work they had put in to growing it.

Both boys and girls seek relative economic independence as soon as possible. Girls plait their mats and also begin cultivating a small meadow field next to that of their mother or other relative. Boys also begin to cultivate their own fields long before marriage. The ensuing crops may be given to the family, which continues to feed them, but in theory, it is theirs to dispose of as they please. Nowadays, since most teenagers are at school where they are required to wear a basic uniform, they usually make efforts to raise the money for this themselves, knowing in any case that their parents can ill-afford to buy it for them.

During childhood, boys and girls go through a special ritual, or rite of passage. Boys are circumcised, and girls have their ears pierced. Both of these rites can be performed any time up to the age of about nine. Normally, a number of related boys, perhaps the sons of brothers or sisters, are circumcised at the same time.

Circumcision

A circumcision ritual can be divided into three parts – the preparation for an operation itself, the period of seclusion while the wound heals, and the coming-out feast and rejoicing.

Preparations begin several days before the event, and a large part of the time is spent collecting together enough rice to feed all the guests who will attend. A large number of relatives come the day before to help pound the rice, and at night, there is usually a Koranic reading, after which the boys' ancestors are 'remembered' and their blessing sought. Finally, the chief circumcisor and his assistants perform a special dance for the mothers of the boys and their female relatives, who reward them with small amounts of money.

Early the following morning, the boys are circumcised, and then placed in a special hut built for the purpose a little removed from the house where the ritual is being held. (It is said that formerly this hut had to be built in the forest, far away from the village.) Older youths act as their attendants and help to look after their wounds, for their mothers are not allowed to see them. Sometimes, if the boys are old enough, and the attendants

Koran school teacher and his pupils. Girls and boys are sent to the traditional Koran school when they are seven or eight. They learn to read (though not understand) the Koran and to write in Arabic script. They continue to attend the Koran school part time even after starting at the Government run school at about ten years.

know something about the traditions surrounding circumcision, the former are taught songs containing lessons about sexual behaviour with women, and respect for elders. The boys stay in the circumcision hut for a period of between one and two weeks; they are examined frequently not only by the circumcisor, but nowadays also by the paramedical officer, who can use modern antibiotics if there is any danger of an infection.

When the chief circumcisor decides that they are well enough, the preparations begin for the coming-out feast. Once again, the rice is collected and pounded on the day before the feast is due, and that evening, there is often an all-night dance in which all the guests participate. The next day, the boys are dressed in new clothes, and brought out of their seclusion hut to be placed in a room of the house, where their mothers are allowed to see them for the first time, followed by the rest of the guests. It is on this occasion that the sisters of the boys have their ears pierced, although this is not attended by any elaborate ritual.

The girls' puberty ritual

For girls, ear-piercing is in fact much less important an event than one which comes later when they reach the age of puberty. This is a ritualised form of sexual and marital counselling which goes on for a whole afternoon, night and part of the following morning. During this time, other adult women led by a woman expert, teach the young girl what will be expected of her as wife and adult woman, through songs, dance, mime, and lectures. Some girls do not go through the entire process, but are only ritually 'washed' by their female relatives when they first menstruate, and then told how to cope with menstruation, and are also given some sexual instruction. Of course, girls do not grow up in ignorance of sexual and other relations between men and women; such things are fairly openly discussed in this society. However, recognising the problem that parents often have in communicating such matters to their children, each girl is given her own 'marriage counsellor', who is usually a close older female relative, such as an aunt, or grandmother or sister. It is this woman who is responsible for ensuring that the girl knows all that is necessary, who later takes her to her wedding, admits her husband to consummate the marriage, and finally conducts her charge to her husband's home.

Marriage

Traditionally, girls were secluded from the time of their puberty ritual until their marriage, which would follow as soon as it could be arranged. This generally took place within a year, but in a few instances could be delayed for several years, during which time the girl was not supposed to leave her house, and even within it, had to be chaperoned at all times. However, since girls are at school nowadays, this is less likely to happen.

The ritual which marks adulthood for both men and women is their first marriage. For girls, this happens between sixteen and eighteen, for boys a year or so later. In theory, first marriages are arranged by the parents of the boy and girl concerned, or more likely by their grandparents, but in fact, the young couple are generally from the same or neighbouring villages, and so will know each other; they may also have attended either government or

Koranic school together. Also, as often happens in Islamic communities, there is a preference for cousin marriage. Although marriages are arranged by parents and grandparents, nowadays the opinion of the young couple is also taken into account.

For Muslims, marriage is a contract, not a sacrament, and the essential elements are simply the agreement of the couple before witnesses to marry each other, with a specified amount of bride-price given by the groom to the bride. However, as happens in most other societies, the wedding is embellished far beyond the minimum legal prescription.

Generally a marriage takes place at the girl's house, although if her parents or foster-parents have only a small house, it may be held at the house of one of her grandparents. In any case, grandparents, both maternal and paternal, play a major role in arranging the match, and also in organising the wedding itself. Contributions of rice and money, given by a wide range of relatives to help defray the expenses, are generally handed over to the girl's grandparents rather than her parents.

None of the delicate negotiations preceding a marriage takes place directly between the parties concerned. The suitor and his family employ a go-between who carries all the letters and receives the replies. When the relatives have decided who will be a suitable husband for the girl, the go-between is sent to tell him to write a letter formally proposing marriage. When this proposal arrives, the parents do not have the right to open it until all the relatives are assembled again, and the oldest man present is generally asked to open and read it. A small sum of money is always enclosed, and this is divided up among all the relatives present, both male and female. The acceptance of the money signifies acceptance of the proposal, and the suitor now becomes known as the girl's fiancé.

If the boy does not know the girl well, he sends some of his close female relatives with a few presents for her; on their return, they are able to give him a full report about how she looks and behaves. Usually, he chooses relatives with whom he has what anthropologists call a 'joking relationship' – this means just what it says, and it also means that sexual matters can be discussed with such people. On Chole, one's joking relations are grandparents, grandchildren, and cross-cousins (that is mother's brother's or father's sister's children).

Shortly after this, the young man is invited to be 'shown the house' which means that he has to meet his future wife's family. This is regarded by most youths as a considerable ordeal. The fiancé must dress respectably, that is in the long white gown and embroidered cap which is worn on formal occasions by older men. He takes three or four male relatives with him, and they are given tea or coffee by his future in-laws. After this he is introduced to all the men. Then, as one young man told me, 'If you are really unlucky, you are taken to the courtyard to meet the women!' To each woman, even the youngest girl, he has to give the respectful greeting, 'I touch your feet', which he normally only uses for elders. He is particularly told to note his fiancée's mother, because after marriage he must maintain a respectful relationship with her – he must keep his distance, never be alone with her or make sexual allusions in her presence. He does not, however, meet his future bride, even though he is aware that she is probably able to see him through a window or a crack in the wall of the house; he is even more painfully aware that her relatives are using the opportunity to 'look him over' very thoroughly!

By this time, the amount of the marriage payments has been decided, and the money which is to be paid immediately has been handed over to the go-between. There are three payments – the first two go to the bride's father (known as his 'turban'), and to her mother (known as her 'belt') and are a recognition of their role in bringing up their daughter. The third payment is made to the bride, but in actual fact, only half may be paid before the wedding, and the rest remain a debt, even for years; this might seem to be unfair, but women can often turn this fact to their advantage later, as I explain below.

Weddings are extremely expensive affairs for both the bride's and groom's families. The father of the bride has to provide a cow for the feast, while her mother must collect together a large number of mats; generally these are sewn by mother and daughter, but some will also be contributed by other female relatives. The mother also makes the bedding for the large four-poster bed which is bought and given to the girl by her father. The girl's marriage counsellor has the duty of providing all the household utensils – buckets, pans, crockery and so on. The groom and his family have to provide the trousseau which consists of a large number of the pairs of cloths worn by women (*kangas*), as well as the black veil worn when travelling (*buibui*), underclothes, cosmetics, jewellery and so on. In addition, he himself is expected to wear new clothes for his wedding.

The night before the wedding, everyone stays awake to dance and sing. The following morning, the brief marriage ceremony takes place on the verandah of the house. Before this can happen however, the girl's male cross-cousins come forward and try to prevent the groom from sitting down. They point out that they as cross-cousins have the right to marry the girl, and only when the groom gives them a few pence do they allow the marriage to proceed. The girl's grandfathers, with whom she also has a joking relationship, then complain 'Who will shave our beards for us now that our grand-daughter is getting married?' And they too receive a token monetary compensation from the groom.

Only men attend the ceremony, which is conducted by an Islamic teacher. The bride is inside the house, and a messenger is sent to ask for her consent (although this can be dispensed with if she is still a minor i.e. marrying for the first time); the actual agreement to marriage is made between her father and the groom, but must be witnessed by the bride's and groom's relatives; care is especially taken that there should be representatives of both the mothers and fathers. Once the ceremony is finished, the groom is conducted inside the house to the room where the bride is waiting. However, he finds the door is barred by her female relatives, who refuse to admit him until he has given them some money. For most it is again a few pence, but to the marital counsellor he must give a substantial sum known as the 'gift of her (i.e.

Above For the wedding feast, the *Kadhi* (Islamic official who conducts weddings and funerals) slaughters a cow in the prescribed Islamic way using a knife. *Facing page* The old man looking on is the bride's grandfather and sponsor of the wedding. The meat is then shared according to the degree of relationship to the couple being married.

the bride's) hand'. He is then allowed to enter the room, and he places his hand on his wife's head and reads a section of the Koran.

Meanwhile, as soon as the wedding ceremony is over, the cow is slaughtered and the feast prepared by the women and eaten by all the guests. As on all such feasting occasions, men and women stay separated, the men eating at the front of the house and the women at the back in the courtyard. Before the women eat, there is a lot of dancing and singing, and much ribald joking between them.

Generally, the bride moves to her husband's home the next day, although sometimes she remains living in a house built near to that of her parents, and the groom joins her there; this is only likely to happen, however, if the groom already has a wife. The bride remains secluded in her new home until the husband's relatives have come to greet her formally – they each give her a few pence, and she replies to their greeting. After this, her marriage counsellor comes and takes her to a public ritual, which is only attended by adults, such as a funeral or wedding, and after that, she is treated as an adult woman.

Divorce

Quite a high proportion of marriages, especially first marriages, end in divorce, sometimes within a year or two, particularly if there are no children. A man can divorce his wife simply by repeating the Islamic formula, but for a woman, it is somewhat more difficult. She can take him to court if he fails in his

obligation to maintain her, and, given the poverty of most villagers, this is not usually difficult to prove. However, court cases are expensive. If the husband refuses to divorce his wife, she can use the weapon of the unpaid debt from the time of their marriage, and demand that she receive it immediately. In order to avoid paying it, which he is legally bound to do, he may agree to give her a divorce providing that she 'buys' it for the cost of the unpaid bride's money; this means in fact that he pays her nothing, but she gets her divorce.

Usually, on divorce, the wife returns to her parents or if they are also divorced, to her mother, while the husband remains in the house. The wife usually takes any children with her, and, as I have already explained, these are likely to be fostered by their grandparents when their mother remarries. Second and subsequent marriages are arranged by the couple themselves, and the wedding is a less elaborate affair.

Childbirth and parenthood

Women usually return to their mother's house for the birth of first and second children. Subsequently, they may stay at home, and their mothers come to help them with the delivery. Nowadays, the para-medical officer can assist with difficult cases and women can be brought to the hospital in Kilindoni if necessary.

A woman remains secluded for forty days after a birth, during which time she is supposed to rest, and is given good food. Formerly, on the fortieth day, a Koranic teacher would come to give her a ritual washing (rather like 'churching' in England), but this is rarely done today. Instead, the woman takes a specially thorough bath and changes her clothes and is then free to resume her normal life.

Sometimes on the fortieth day the child has its head shaved for the first time, and this event may be accompanied by the reading of a religious poem, called a *Maulid*, which is attended by a small number of relatives. However, this *Maulid* reading and hair-cutting is more likely to be deferred until the child has survived the first few months of life, which are considered the most dangerous, and passed a milestone like being able to sit up on its own. There is still a high rate of infant mortality on the island, although it has improved considerably over the last ten years. Most women have lost children at some time during their lives, either through still births, or death in the first few weeks after birth. Because of the importance of the mother's milk to the child, women try not to become pregnant again until they wean the baby at two years, but since there is no effective method of contraception, some women do not succeed in spacing their families as widely as they would wish.

There are, of course, some women who never succeed in having children at all, or whose children all die young. While such women do regret this fact, childlessness is not the terrible fate on Chole that it is in other societies. There are perhaps two reasons for this: one is that, as I shall discuss later, women are not defined simply as bearers of children, nor is marriage seen only as a means of reproduction. A woman who is or has been married (and marriage is virtually universal) is defined as an adult, and her status does not change materially with the birth of children nor, conversely, does she have a lower status if she fails to bear children.

Before girls could join in a Maulid a screen was erected to separate them from the boys and men.

Women bear most of the responsibility for looking after children but they have help particularly from older female relatives. Grandmothers will even foster children. And it is customary for fathers to look after babies in the early evening while mothers cook the supper.

Women bringing water to a feast where rice is being cooked. Although it is more usual for women to fetch water, men also do it on occasions.

A young man embroiders a *kofia* – a cap worn on formal occasions. Only men do this work.

Secondly, as I have already said, almost all childless couples will be 'given' at least one child to bring up by a more fortunate brother or sister, so that there is rarely a home in which there are no children. Furthermore, on Chole, as in many other societies where kinship is very important, we find the categories are extended to include as close kin those whom we might classify as more distant. For example, mother's younger sister is called a 'little mother' and her older sister a 'big mother'. The same applies to the grandparents generation, so that the brothers and sisters of grandparents are also referred to, and, in many ways, treated as grandparents.

Middle age

For both men and women, an increase in age almost inevitably means an increase in status. By middle age, they usually own a number of coconut trees, they have children who are marrying and bearing children of their own, and they may also have acquired status in certain specialised spheres – they may be office-holders in one of the Sufi mystical orders, members of the village council, shamans who are leaders of a spirit possession guild, or simply elders who are recognised by others as having ability and experience, and thus asked to organise rituals or mediate disputes. Let us look briefly at some of these activities.

Islamic Institutions

The people of Chole are, as I have already indicated, Muslims. They belong to the Sunni, or orthodox division of Islam. In each village there is a central mosque, used on Fridays, the Islamic holy day. There are also four other mosques for daily use in different areas of the village. At first appearance, they look like ordinary houses, but closer observation reveals the extra little niche on the wall which faces north (i.e. in the direction of Mecca), and the tank of water outside the door, which enables people to purify themselves ritually before they enter the mosque. The Friday mosque has a *muedhin* who calls people to prayer, and also an *Imam*, and two deputy *Imams*, who are the prayer-leaders and give the sermon during the Friday service. All such people are accorded high status in the village, for they are generally very pious and learned in the Koran.

Aside from the mosque, the other important Islamic institution is the Koran school; there are three such schools in the village, and their teachers are also people with high status, who are accorded a great deal of respect by the community.

As on much of the rest of the East Coast, many people are followers of Sheikhs who lead Sufi mystical orders known as *tarika*. In addition to following ordinary Islamic practices, Sufis are supposed to perform devotional exercises daily, particularly using breathing techniques, but on Chole they rarely do so. However, each year every village branch of a Sufi order holds a celebration of its founder's anniversary, known as a *ziara*. Each branch of an order has allegiance to a particular Sheikh, and sometimes there is a fair degree of rivalry between the Sheikhs and their societies.

The organisation of all branches is basically the same. There are four types of officials:, the most important of whom are the deputies of the

Sheikh. Secondly there are those who carry the banners used in the procession to the site of the *ziara*, and who also oversee the cooking which takes place at the *ziara* site. Thirdly, there are the people who lead the chanting and singing; and finally those who issue the invitations and also procure the animal which is cooked for the feast. There are at least two officials of each type, one man and one woman, in each village branch of a Sufi order.

The *ziara* rituals involve a great deal of organisation, as they are attended by hundreds of people – indeed, some famous Sheikhs, such as the one living in Kilwa, have a *ziara* to which thousands of people are drawn. In Kanga, a *ziara* usually attracts around five hundred participants. There are two different orders in the village, one whose members are the followers of a Sheikh who lives in Kanga, while the other is composed of followers of a Sheikh living in another village in central Chole, who only visits the village on the occasion of his *ziara*. So each year, the village witnesses two such large celebrations, and of course, many Kangans go to the *ziaras* in other villages. Like other large rituals, *ziara* provide the opportunity to meet dispersed friends and relatives. They take place at night, and the combination of torch and firelight, colourful banners, and large crowds of men and women singing, chanting or performing the special breathing exercises, is both exciting and dramatic.

Spirit possession

Another dramatic ritual is the spirit possession dance. Much illness on the coast is thought to be caused by the intervention of spirits – either sent by a malevolent human, or else one who has been annoyed in some way by the victim. When people are sick, they may consult a diviner who will suggest the reason for the sickness, and also the best means of effecting a cure. Islam itself has several remedies – for example, the writing out of holy verse either to be worn as charms on the arm or around the neck, or else to be burned and the ashes drunk with water. Alternatively people learned in Islam, like Koranic teachers or Sheikhs, may exorcise bad spirits. However, the majority of curative measures lie not with the Islamic experts, but with the spirit shamans. A shaman is a man or woman who is thought to be able to control spirits and so can, at will, become possessed in order to divine or heal.

Shamanism and possession are condemned by orthodox Islam, which, while recognising the existence of various categories of spirits, states that trafficking with them denies the oneness and omnipotence of God. However, many people, albeit Muslims, do participate in the curing rituals of the spirit possession guilds each of which is centred on a particular shaman. It is believed that a cure will be effected by 'coming to terms' with the spirit causing the sickness, and this generally involves giving a cow, a goat, or a tray of delicacies to the spirit, during the course of a dance ritual, under the direction of a shaman. There are a number of shamans in Kanga, the majority of them men.

In addition to their ability to control a spirit, shamans also have considerable knowledge of herbs and their curing powers; other villagers too can be specialists in herbal medicines, and there are a few who treat certain diseases by cupping (i.e. cutting the skin and placing a vessel over it containing

After dancing all night to make the shaman and spirit possession guild members possessed, a white heifer is slaughtered and its blood drunk by some of the participants in the ritual. 'The spirit wants to drink blood from a cow'.

hot ashes; the ensuing vacuum causes the blood to be drawn out. Cupping was once a favourite remedy in the west). Curers do charge for their services, unlike the village government-funded dispensary, which is free, but villagers prefer to use both traditional and modern methods of treatment, the main reason being that they feel that traditional methods treat the 'real cause' of illness (i.e. witchcraft or spirits), whereas western-type medicines merely relieve symptoms. Curers in the village are rarely rich people, with the exception of successful shamans, who often demand and get an animal as the fee for a successful cure.

What is very striking about curative methods on Chole is the link stressed between the body and the mind. Spirit possession rituals would seem to be essentially concerned with the phenomenon of the apparent invasion of a person's mind by a spirit, that is, with mental disturbance. However, many patients display mental and physical symptoms, and even those who do not are treated by some curers, particularly shamans, as if they did. In addition, most cures involve not only a single patient, but a whole family, all of whose members have to contribute to the necessary ritual and/or payment to the curer. Also, if the patient does go as far as to become possessed in a ritual, the family must agree to whatever demands are made upon it by the spirit concerned. Furthermore, in the process of investigating an illness, the curer will question the patient closely about his or her problems, giving an opportunity for 'letting off steam' that might not otherwise be available.

In short, then, there are a number of areas of village life which provide occasions for important and dramatic rituals. They also endow certain people with positions of authority and are the areas in which social differentiation is most clearly marked – Islamic office-holders are most likely to be members of one descent group in the village, shamans of another; both are more likely to be middle-aged than young, and male than female, although none of these are inviolate rules.

Until quite recently, people who were Sheikhs or who held office in the mosque, or were Koranic officials, or Sufi order officials, were generally drawn from one descent group in the village. These were also the people who tended to hold political office in the village, to be Chairman of the Council, or the representative to the District Council. People who participated in the spirit possession rituals, and particularly members of guilds, were extremely unlikely to be elected to political office. However, this situation has changed quite a lot in the last decade. The Sheikh and his relatives are still accorded a great deal of respect, but the village council and its officials now show a wide spread of members drawn from all the groups in the village, including the spirit possession guild members. It seems likely that the egalitarian ideology of TANU, the political party in Tanzania, is beginning to have some effect.

Old age, death and burial

On Chole, independence is preserved for as long as possible. People continue to cultivate, even though the size of their fields may decrease with the years, and they continue to cook for themselves until very old or infirm, when they may go to live near to a son or daughter who will look after them. Very old people are

A woman asks the diviners why her child is sick. The ritual was performed for the woman standing. She is still possessed.

The chief shaman (back to camera) is asked about a child's illness. He will tell the parent the cause and what action should be taken.

accorded a special sort of licence, in that they can demand gifts, such as small amounts of money, food or tobacco from a wide range of younger people, who would be ashamed not to acquiesce in such a request.

When people are sick in Chole, they have many visitors, and if seriously ill, some of these remain at the house until the outcome of the illness, either recovery or death, is known. These people, who are usually close relatives of the patient, also assist in nursing, and participate in curative measures.

When death is known to be imminent, people gather to read the Koran, and at the moment of death, the women in the house begin to wail. Young male relatives are quickly chosen to take the news of the death to all relatives living in other villages, and one is also sent to buy the shroud. Other male relatives begin to dig the grave. Burial, unlike the other rites of passage already discussed, constitutes a public event, that is, virtually all the adults living in the village are expected to attend, and so are many people from nearby villages. Almost all will come with some sort of contribution for the funerary feast and other expenses, either food or cash.

The corpse is first washed by close relatives, and then by a Koranic teacher who knows the correct ritual method, and is placed in the shroud. It is then ready for burial, but this cannot proceed until the joking relations of the dead person have received their token dues which are taken from the deceased's estate. Provided that all the most important close relatives have arrived, burial takes place as soon as possible, and the Koranic teacher officiating pours water on the grave.

There are usually three days of intensive mourning, during which close relatives sleep at the house of the deceased. On the third day, there is a final Koranic reading, and, if possible, the main funerary feast takes place. However, if the relatives have problems in raising the money necessary to buy an animal for slaughtering, and also for obtaining sufficient rice, then this may be postponed until the fortieth day after the death, when the inheritance is normally decided, or even later at the time when the headstone and footstone are placed on the grave.

If the deceased was a man who left a widow, then her period of mourning is extended beyond forty days to three months and ten days, during which time she is supposed to remain secluded. The ostensible purpose of this custom is to ascertain whether or not the widow is pregnant, for even a posthumous child is entitled to share in the inheritance. After the period of seclusion, the widow is ritually bathed and given new clothes, after which she is free to marry again if she so wishes.

Death involves a change of status for both the deceased and the relatives left behind. The deceased now becomes an ancestor, for whom an annual Koranic reading is held, and after whom children must be named, for the belief is that if this is not done he or she may cause sickness. For the bereaved, on the other hand, other adjustments must be made, and his or her roles in society filled by others. Obviously the death of an old man or woman with many roles involves more adjustments than that of a young child, and indeed, the ceremony surrounding the funeral of a child is much simpler and shorter.

On Chole, then, certain crucial phases in the individual's life cycle are marked by elaborate rites – circumcision for boys, puberty rituals for girls, marriage, childbirth and death. There are certain features common to all of these rituals – one is the seclusion of the persons central to the ritual, and later their 'coming out' to rejoin society with a new status. Frequently they are washed to purify them before they emerge from their period of seclusion. The rituals take a similar form – an all-night vigil before the event, which is marked by singing and dancing, and Koranic readings, a feast of rice and meat after the event has taken place. At all such rituals the joking relations interrupt the proceedings and demand their dues; by doing this they act as a point of reference in the complex kinship system, and serve to remind everyone present how they are related to one another.

Men and women

It is very difficult to arrive at a satisfactory method for measuring the status of women in any given society, nor is it always useful to try and do so. However, in this concluding section, I want to make a few points about men and women on Chole, and relate them to some points about other aspects of this society.

One question which we might ask when considering the position of women in any society is the extent to which they are dependent on men – fathers or husbands, for example. On Chole, women's status is to a large extent their own – it is not derived from that of their husbands. For instance, women on Chole retain their own names throughout their lives, and this symbolises the fact that women on Chole are independent individuals. What does this mean in real terms?

First and foremost, women are not necessarily economically dependent upon men. Many women can and do manage on their own when divorced or widowed. They have the right to obtain land, and they have a source of cash income through their mat-making. Even within marriage, a woman retains her own property – there is no community of property, which is found in other societies, and which often works to the advantage of the men. Women also have specific rights over joint property in marriage; if a couple gets divorced, she is entitled to a half share of whatever food and harvest they have produced, and also half of whatever coconut trees have been planted during their marriage by her husband. Furthermore, she is not obliged to turn over her earnings from mat-making or the sale of coconuts to her husband, or indeed, even to use the proceeds for the maintenance of the household, although of course, many women in lasting marriages do so.

As in all other societies, there is a division of labour in northern Chole based on sex, however, it is not a particularly rigid one. Men, for example, may cook when their wives are sick, or when no women are present (e.g. groups of fishermen). Most men will help with the arduous task of fetching water. Men also play an active part in child care; they take sick children to hospital, register children at school, and frequently play with them and talk to them when they are small. In agriculture, there are a number of tasks which are sex-specific; planting is done by women, while cutting down the bush and building fences is always done by men. People who are without a partner have to recruit a relative to perform these tasks for them. But other jobs, like weeding and harvesting, are carried out by both sexes.

Furthermore a number of tasks which occur in our own society are regarded as the preserve of women are on Chole, performed by men. For example, the intricately embroidered caps worn by men are made by men, and so are most of the clothes worn by villagers. Men use exactly the same arguments as people in our society do for rationalising the reverse situation, 'Women's hands aren't capable of such delicate work'. Another task which on Chole is usually done by men is shopping, although the reasons for this are somewhat different, and are related not only to the fact that men are supposed to provide for their families, but also to the fact that in theory, women should not go to a public place like a shop.

Another point which may be made about the division of labour on Chole, as compared with our own society, is that there is not a sharp division between domestic and non-domestic labours. Many tasks which in our society are carried out by specialised agencies are performed in and around the home, for example, the preparation of food. Food comes from the labour of the household members, both men and women and often children too. Perhaps as a result of this, women's work is not devalued. One never hears phrases like 'only housework' or 'only a housewife', or 'I'm not working' from women on Chole. All work, whether done in the field or around the house is equally valued in a non-wage economy.

Let us now turn to the political arena and consider the role of women there. Students of politics sometimes distinguish two kinds of 'political' power – authority which is generally recognised, legitimate power and informal influence, or power that is not overtly legitimised. Women in Chole have less formal political power than men. No women in Kanga sit on the village council, for instance, nor do they hold office in the mosque, although they are office-holders in the important Sufi mystical orders, and they can also be shamans and mediums in the spirit possession guilds.

Women do, however, have a considerable amount of informal political power – older women, just like older men, provided that they are considered intelligent and experienced, can become elders to whom others turn for advice, or who are asked to mediate disputes or organise rituals. Another important political role which women collectively have is their singing of impromptu *kalewa* songs at rituals during the all-night vigil. These songs are full of double-entendre, and frequently refer to, and can influence, current events and disputes in the village by bringing private gossip into the open for all to hear.

A third aspect of women's position in society is concerned with marriage, divorce and motherhood. Although first marriages are generally arranged, women can and do obtain divorces if they cannot get on with their husbands, and are then free to choose their own partners. If they are unhappy in their marriages, they have the option of returning to their natal family, particularly to their mothers, and are assured of their support. This is also given in the form of help with child-rearing. The wife's mother often takes her grandchildren to live with her if her daughter re-marries, which lessens potential problems of rivalry between half-siblings.

On Chole, children belong to the descent groups of both parents, and both have equal rights in the child. At a wedding, as I have shown, the relatives on both sides of the family must be present as witnesses. Carried to its logical conclusion then, this even means that a child born out of wedlock is not without rights; as one woman friend of mine remarked only half-jokingly, 'a child can't really be illegitimate on its mother's side, only on its father's'. It is thus not surprising to find that in this society, both girls and boys are equally desired. Both are economically productive, both will retain their connections with their natal family, and produce children in turn for the descent groups of both mother and father. This situation, of course, contrasts sharply with other societies, where the birth of daughters is less welcomed than that of sons, because daughters marry away from their families and bear children for their husband's descent groups.

It is thus hardly surprising to find that in this society, sex is treated fairly matter-of-factly. Since women are not regarded as the property of men, or primarily as the producers of men's children, they are not hemmed in by the sort of restrictions which we find in other societies where this is the case.

I am not trying to present a picture of life as ideal for women on Chole; in many ways their lives are more difficult than those of men. Women certainly work harder, in that they share more or less equally in agriculture, but have a greater burden of household and childcare tasks. They also have fewer economic resources than men, because they inherit coconut trees at a 1:2 ratio to men, and have fewer opportunities for acquiring them by buying or planting. Nevertheless, women are in this society independent individuals, and not appendages of men.

I would suggest that there are two important reasons for this fact, not only, as I have already said, that women are economically productive, but also that women have equal membership of the descent groups which control the major economic resource in this society – land.

Conclusion

Every culture and every society constructs boundaries, in space, in time, and in relationships. In some societies, the boundaries are rigidly demarcated, and the sanctions for those who try to cross them are severe. But on Chole, we have an example of a society with relatively flexible boundaries, as I have tried to show in my discussion of the roles of men and women. It is a society in which a great deal of choice is 'built in' to the system. Most people are members of a number of descent groups, and can 'move around' both literally and figuratively, in order to maximise their opportunities. They have a choice about where to cultivate, where to live, and whether to identify with the very pious people in the village, or participate in the spirit possession guilds. For most people, the choices are not once and for all, but can be varied according to time and circumstance.

Further reading

CAPLAN, A. P. *Cognatic descent groups on Mafia Island, Tanzania* in *Man* vol. 4, no. 3. September 1969. pp. 419–431.

CAPLAN, A. P. *Choice and constraint in a Swahili community: property, hierarchy and cognatic descent on the East African coast* OUP for the International African Institute, 1975.

CAPLAN, A. P. *Boys' circumcision and girls' puberty rites among the Swahili of Mafia Island, Tanzania* in *Africa* vol. 46, no. 1, 1976. pp. 21–33.

CHITTICK, N. *Kisimani Mafia: excavations at an Islamic settlement on the East African coast* (Occasional paper no. 1) Tanganyika Ministry of Education, Antiquities Division, 1961.

CHITTICK, N. *The Shirazi colonization of East Africa* in *Journal of African History* vol. 6, no. 3, 1965. pp. 275–294.

FREEMAN-GRENVILLE, G. S. P. *The mediaeval history of the coast of Tanganyika* OUP, 1962.

HARRIES, L. P. *Swahili poetry* OUP, 1962.

NYERERE, J. K. *Freedom and unity* OUP(EAf), 1967.

NYERERE, J. K. *Freedom and socialism* OUP(EAf), 1968.

OGOT, B. A. and KIERAN, J. A. eds. *Zamani: a survey of East African history* East African Publishing House and Longman, 1968.

PRINS, A. H. J. *The Swahili-speaking peoples of Zanzibar and the East African coast: Arabs, Shirazi and Swahili* International African Institute, n.e. 1968.

TRIMINGHAM, J. SPENCER *The Sufi orders in Islam* Clarendon Press, 1971; Galaxy Books, OUP(NY), 1973.

WHITELEY, W. H. *Swahili: the rise of a national language* Methuen, 1969.

Chapter Seven The Gypsies of California

by Anne Sutherland

Most people have heard of the Gypsies. You have probably seen their caravans on the roadsides in Britain or come across their fortune telling signs in Scarborough or Brighton. They may have come to the door selling paper flowers or asking to buy scrap metal. Some of you may live near Gypsies and see them frequently, and others have only heard tales of the strange power of the Gypsy woman's curse or been warned by your parents that Gypsies steal children. Because they are somewhat familiar, most people have some preconception of Gypsies that bears little relation to what they are really like. One problem is that there are several contradictory stereotypes of Gypsies. On the one hand, Gypsy men are thought to be dirty, lying, thieving good-for-nothings. On the other hand, Gypsy women are often represented as sensual and sexually provocative, or as old crones with mystical powers who see into the future and can curse with a glance. The stereotypes that people form about Gypsies also depend on the kind of contact they have with them. Social workers and school teachers often see the main 'problems' as lack of fixed abode, crowding into sub-standard housing, untidiness, illiteracy, and refusal to send children to school. The police are concerned with Gypsies as confidence tricksters or pickpockets and find them elusive and hard to catch. And yet there is also a romantic view of Gypsies that is found in literature, art and music. The Gypsies are depicted as carefree, wild, fun-loving or as mysterious, uncanny, dark people unfettered by convention. They may also be seen as sensual, artistic, individualistic roamers. When Shirley Bassey sings about 'the Gypsy in my soul', we all know what she is talking about.

It is easy enough to show that all these stereotypes are wrong, but I want to go much further than that. I want to avoid preconceptions of the Gypsies and show how the Gypsies see themselves, how they understand their own society and their position in the wider society. The questions I shall answer are: 'Who are the Gypsies?' and 'What are they really like?'.

Who are the Gypsies?

There are Gypsies living in virtually every country in the world, but they are now more concentrated in Russia, Western and Eastern Europe, and North America, and in smaller numbers in India, the Middle East, South America,

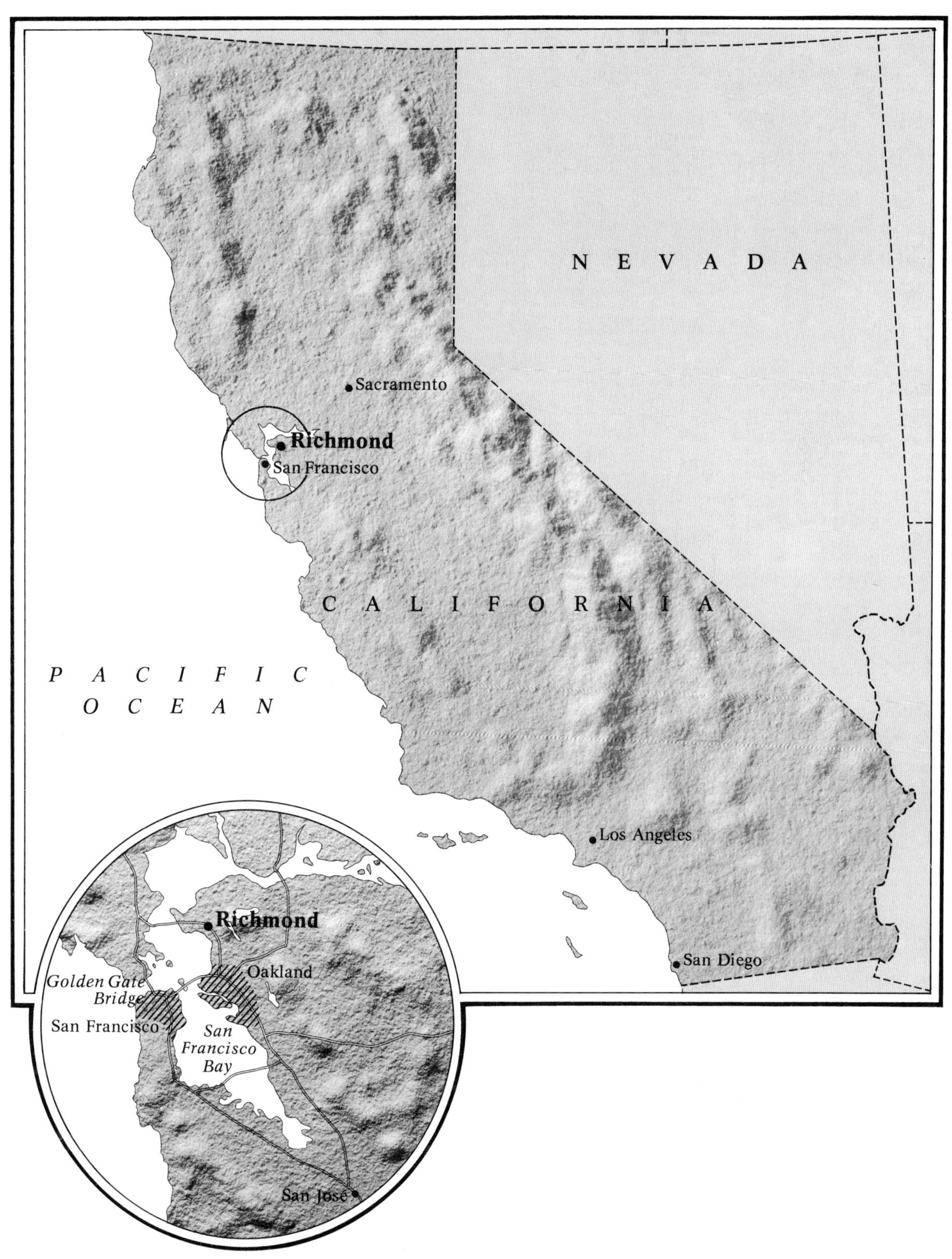
NEVADA
Sacramento
Richmond
San Francisco
CALIFORNIA
PACIFIC
OCEAN
Los Angeles
San Diego
Richmond
Golden Gate
Bridge
Oakland
San Francisco
San
Francisco
Bay
San José

Australia, and Hawaii. No one really knows how many Gypsies there are because Gypsies have little interest in staying in one spot and even less interest in being counted. Estimates range from one to three million.

Because they live in so many different countries, and therefore adapt to vastly different societies and languages, there are a proliferation of groups that might be classified under the general term, Gypsy. There has been a lot of debate among those who study Gypsies, and among the Gypsies themselves, as to which groups are really Gypsy and which are not. Some Gypsies and Gypsy scholars feel very strongly that unless the group speaks some dialect of *Romanes*, the Sanskrit-derived language that most Gypsies speak as a mother tongue, they are not really Gypsy, and others argue that the group must be nomadic as well. Then there is the problem of defining individuals as *truly* Gypsy. Some argue that you must be born a Gypsy, others that you must also live and work as a Gypsy. The problems arise from the great diversity of Gypsy groups as well as the differing degrees to which individual Gypsies conform to their own group's way of life. The only true consistency that comes out when talking with Gypsies, is that each individual Gypsy will describe very emphatically who are the real Gypsies and who are not, and his description will depend on which group he happens to belong to, who he is talking to, and his own individual life circumstances. Although it is a topic of great interest to

Gypsy women on a caravan site in America. A woman trains her daughter-in-law to tell fortunes. Skill at fortune-telling is a great asset for a woman.

both Gypsies and non-gypsies who have contact with them, during my eight years of experience with both, I have yet to encounter two identical definitions of the *true* Gypsy.

In spite of what I have just said, the situation is not as hopelessly confused as it sounds. Most Gypsy groups are easily indentifiable as 'Gypsy' according to some criteria. Most readers will feel that the *Gitanos* of Spain who dance Flamenco and live in caves, and the Hungarian Gypsies who play moving rhapsodies on the violin, fit perfectly with their image of a Gypsy. Ironically neither of these groups speak the inflected *Romanes* language nor are they nomads, though there is still a certain emphasis on mobility. Besides, there are many other less publicised European groups: the Rudari, the Sinte (or Manush), Aurari, Ursari (bear tamers), Boyash (Romanian Gypsies), and the British travellers. In North Africa, there are the Xoraxai and the Afrikaya; in India, the Dom and the Luri. These groups are all socially and linguistically distinct from each other and rarely intermarry. They are also all identified with a specific locality. British travellers, who are not one uniform group, for example, do not speak inflected *Romanes*, though they use some *Romanes* words, but are on the whole nomadic and live a 'Gypsy' life style.

Apart from these groups, there are a large number of people who live in many different countries (and therefore may be referred to incorrectly, as 'Russian' Gypsies, 'American' Gypsies, or 'French' Gypsies) who call themselves Rom. Whereas it may be difficult to classify some groups as 'Gypsy', the Rom must definitely be considered Gypsies. An individual Rom may of course leave the group, or a specific group of Rom may no longer be nomadic, but the Rom all speak a dialect of Romanes that is generally intelligible to other Rom. Unlike other Gypsy groups (which includes British travellers), all Rom belong to one of four 'nations' (or tribes): the Machwaya, the Lowara, the Kalderasha, and the Churara. Apart from the Machwaya, who seem to be concentrated in the Americas, these nations are found all over the Western world. Each nation (or *natsia*) has its own particular dialect, customs and appearance, but the differences between the four nations are insignificant when compared with the differences between the Rom and the other Gypsy groups listed above. Consequently marriage between the four nations is common. So the Rom are clearly identifiable by four criteria: (a) they call themselves Rom (which means 'man'), (b) they speak *Romanes*, (c) they belong to a particular sub-category of Rom, a nation or tribe, and (d) they frequently intermarry. There is another characteristic of the Rom that may be significant. Whereas all Rom recognise each other as true Gypsies, regardless of their mutual differences, they tend to regard non-Rom Gypsies as inferior or inauthentic. The Rom are the 'élite' of the Gypsy world.

If there are so many diverse Gypsy groups, is it possible that all Gypsies are of the same origin? Where do the Gypsies come from? These questions are thorny because the evidence is so sparse. The Gypsies are a non-literate people. Apart from the work of a few recent scholars, *Romanes* has been for centuries an unwritten language. So our main evidence on Gypsies comes from non-gypsy records. These written records show that bands of people entered Europe in the fifteenth century, claiming to have come from Egypt (hence the name 'Egyptians' that has been modified to 'Gypsy') fleeing Muslim persecution. Like all Christian refugees, they received alms and the occasional chicken from the villages they passed through. But there is a bit more evidence than this. By studying the language carefully, a philologist named Potts confirmed in the eighteenth century that *Romanes* derived from Sanskrit and broke off from it about the same time as Hindustani, some one thousand years ago. It seems reasonable, therefore, to suppose that the Gypsies came originally from India, probably from Northern India and most likely from more than one group there. Why they left, we do not know, but again from further study of the language, it is clear that they spent a long time in Persia (where there are still many Gypsies today) before migrating further into Russia, Europe and Northern Africa. And of course they are still moving. At the turn of the century, large numbers immigrated to North and South America and westwards to Hawaii and Australia. Nowadays they fly to various parts of the world seeking new territory.

Before I leave this general background on Gypsies to discuss the particular group of Rom that this essay is concerned with, let me conclude with some general truths about Gypsies. The first and by now most obvious to the reader, is that they defy generalisation. The minute I make a general statement such as 'Gypsies avoid nine-to-five jobs', I can think of an example of a Gypsy in a nine-to-five job. There are so many different groups of Gypsies living in so many different situations in so many different countries, it is not surprising that general statements about them are so difficult. Nevertheless it is not impossible, so what I shall do is begin with the generalisations with the least exceptions and work towards those with the most.

First of all, Gypsies always live within another society. So, in one sense, they are always 'strangers' to the wider society, though obviously not within their own society. The consequences of this particular situation are very significant. All Gypsy groups that have been studied have one word for themselves and one word to describe outsiders. For British Gypsies it is 'travellers' and 'Gorgios'; for Spanish Gitanos it is *Kale* and *payos* (meaning peasants); and for the Rom in America and Europe it is 'Rom' (meaning 'man') and *gaje* or *gadje*. Invariably the word for themselves has superior connotations such as man, or human, or nomad, and the word for non-gypsies has inferior connotations, such as peasant or fool.

Gypsies are strangers in a hostile world and thus have developed methods of self-protection. Since they are, as a group, always threatened from the outside, they have ways of binding themselves together that are, not so much different, as more emphatic, than in most societies. In other words, it is not that their techniques are unique in kind, but that they are unusual in degree. Everything written on Gypsy groups indicates that they all have a very highly developed sense of themselves in opposition to others, which comes out in these emphatic techniques for keeping outsiders out. Perhaps the best way to illustrate some of these techniques for dealing with outsiders, is to recount my own personal experiences in getting to know the Rom in America.

The first Gypsy I met was a young fortune-teller who opened the door to me, thinking I was a prospective customer. She smiled, in an ingratiating manner, until I asked for her father by his non-gypsy name. Though I did not know it at the time, this use of his non-gypsy alias immediately indicated to her that I was a suspicious stranger, and she leapt at me, screaming and cursing, 'what you want?'. Later I went up to a man who I knew to be a relative of other Gypsy acquaintances and asked 'are you a Gypsy?'. He replied, 'Gypsy, what's that?' and looked appropriately puzzled. And when I attempted to get into conversation with his wife, she began mumbling to herself and staring wildly into space so that I would think she was either crazy or an imbecile. Polite imperviousness, pretence of mental retardation or insanity, or even appearing blind or deaf, straightforward lies or simply disappearing altogether – all these are time-honoured techniques for avoiding the inquisitive non-gypsy. The methods are extremely flexible and effective. They may create a public scene in one instance with screaming and fighting or decide to fade from sight in another. They may flatter, cajole or feign extreme humility at one moment and switch effortlessly to aggressive, threatening behaviour. They may appear overtly sensual or full of rigid moral indignation. The idea is to confuse the non-gypsy, keep him guessing, reveal as little correct information as possible, and carry on, unhampered, with their own lives.

What is important about such confusing and contradictory behaviour is that it keeps all but the most persistent outsider from penetrating Gypsy society, and it keeps the individual Gypsy from forming many lasting relationships with the outsider. It is the strong sense of *themselves* in opposition to the *outside* world that is expressed emphatically in every-day behaviour. But of course this inside-outside opposition goes much deeper into the society than simple problems of dealing with casual non-gypsy contact. There is the much more difficult problem of how to earn a living from the outside society without being drawn into it.

Gypsy work

In western industrialised countries, there are very few examples of a self-perpetuating nomadic society that is largely independent of wage-labour. There are, of course, migrant workers who move from one area to another, but they take settled, wage-labour jobs at the end of their move. In non-industrialised societies, there are pastoral nomads and hunting and gathering nomads, but these also differ from Gypsies because their migrations are partly influenced either by grazing requirements or the availability of wild fruit and game. In contrast, the livelihood of the Gypsies is directly dependent on a sedentary or 'host' community within which they live and travel. The dependence of the Gypsy population on the host community can be demonstrated, in Britain, by looking at the places British travellers choose to live. Like the sedentary population, Gypsies have shifted from a major concentration in rural areas to concentration in urban areas. For the romantics, this shift is bemoaned as a sad loss of traditional life styles, but a more realistic interpretation is that it demonstrates the continuing flexibility of the Gypsy. In our highly mechanised and specialised society, the Gypsy's flexibility in work situations is very much to his own advantage. In Britain, the odd jobs that Gypsies used to do for farmers, such as fencing and pest control, they now do in an urban setting, either in scrap clearance or laying tarmac. In America, the Rom have dropped occupations no longer useful to the host population, such as coppersmithing and horse trading, and now engage in car bodywork or the second-hand car business. While nomadic societies all over the world are being drastically changed by the encroachment of industrialisation, the Gypsies take modern technology in their stride (*Okley, 1975a; 113–116*).

Consequently, Gypsy occupations all over the world are constantly changing, with new ones being added to the old. These changes, however, follow a specific pattern, so rather than list all the possible occupations, let us look at their common characteristics.

1 First of all, Gypsies prefer *self-employment*. Self-employment allows mobility and avoids a situation of working directly for a non-gypsy. Furthermore, the Gypsy can then work in large family groups or in partnership with other Gypsies. Gypsies generally only take wage-labour employment for short periods when in dire circumstances.

2 Gypsies prefer work that depends on *mobility*. This is not only suited to their life-style in other ways, but it allows them to perform tasks that other individuals or businesses in a sedentary society would find difficult or uneconomical to perform. Seasonal occupations such as crop-picking, and situations where the demand is irregular in time and place, such as laying tarmac driveways, selling Christmas decorations, carnival entertainment, knife grinding or telling fortunes, are the sorts of services Gypsies prefer to provide. Because of this mobility, and low overhead costs, Gypsies can often provide services less expensively, though not necessarily of better quality, than a regular business. Car bodywork, collecting and selling scrap metal, and the hawking of household goods would be examples of this.

3 There is a *style* of work that is common to most Gypsies. This style depends on being a good talker, on fast thinking, and on an ability to size up a prospective customer. In fortune telling or hawking, the style is really essential to the business, but Gypsies use it in all kinds of situations, from convincing a person he needs his car fixed to buying antiques.

Now that we have some idea of the background to Gypsy society in general, let us turn to a specific group – the Rom in California, U.S.A.

The Rom

The Rom in California belong for the most part to one of two 'nations', the Machwaya or the Kalderasha. The Machwaya are generally prosperous, drive new Cadillacs, and make their livelihood either from buying and selling used cars or from lucrative fortune telling businesses. The Kalderasha are generally less prosperous than the Machwaya, drive used Cadillacs and make their living in a variety of ways: soliciting car bodywork, seasonal farm labour, occasional fortune-telling, tarring roofs or driveways, repairing copper boilers or pneumatic drills, and frequently, welfare (social security). Though they have

Left
Staley's half-brother 'Rattlesnake Pete' with his handlebar moustache. Older men are invested with great authority over their families.

Below left
Mary Marks at her granddaughter's wedding, with characteristic rose in her hair. Old gypsy women also have a great deal of authority in their family groups.

Below right
A Gypsy fortune-teller.

Right
Staley Costello and his wife Persa posing with the state flag of California. They both control Gypsy matters in the Richmond territory.

Below
Three young girls watching a wedding.

intermarried for generations, the members of the two nations regard each other with suspicion. The Kalderasha say that the Machwaya try to take over Kalderasha territory to set up businesses there and then treat the Kalderasha as inferior. The Machwaya point to lack of economic success among the Kalderasha and then lean over conspiratorially and add that they are not as 'clean' either. The Machwaya are the 'elite' of the Rom world.

The state of California is divided up primarily into Machwaya and Kalderasha territories. Each territory consists of a city or a section of a city, and within their particular territory, each community of Rom tries to control all the possible sources of Gypsy livelihood, whether it be fortune-telling

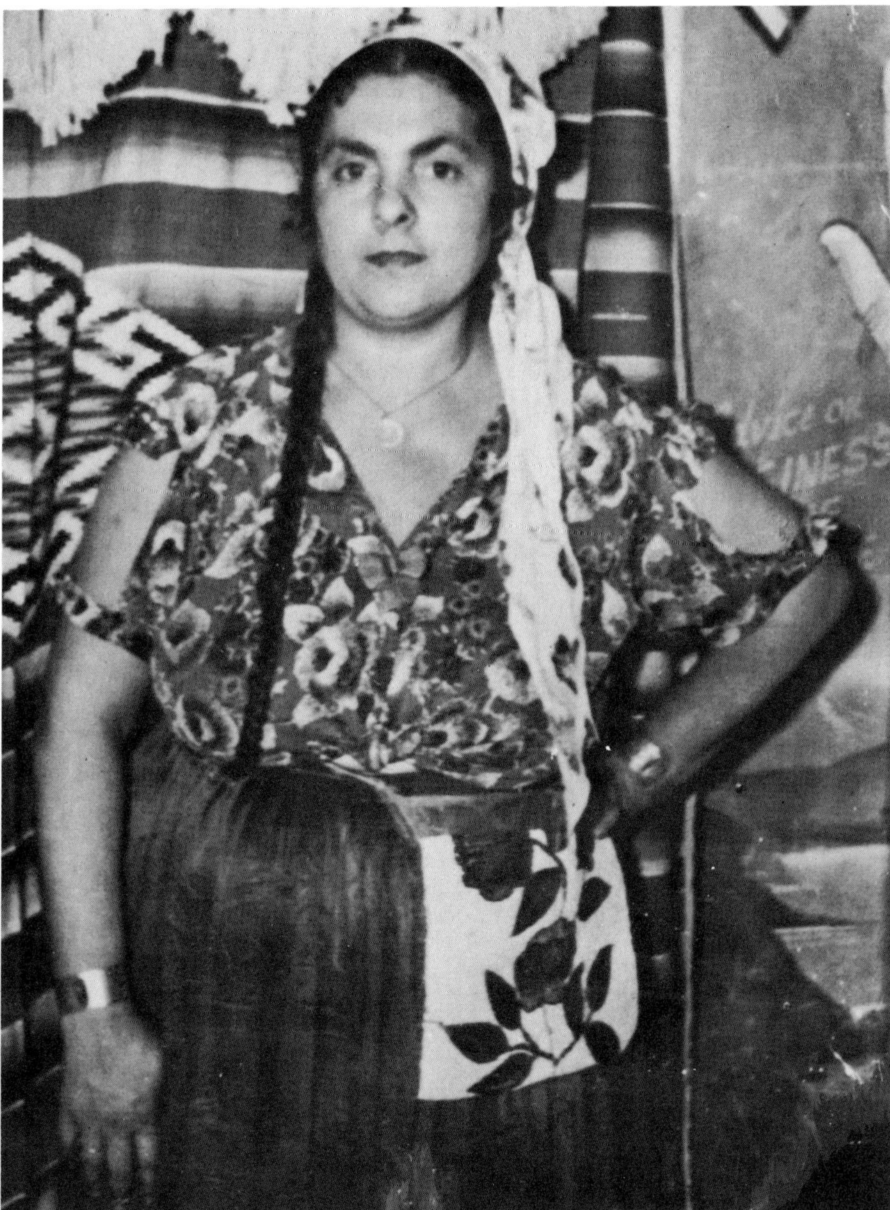

A Kalderasha gypsy fortune-teller posing as an American Indian.

A Machwaya and a Kalderasha man talking about recent events in their territory.

customers or welfare. Within each territory, one group of Rom, who are generally related to each other either by kinship or marriage, divides itself up into various households. The households may consist of a single nuclear family for periods of time, but there is such continuous interchange between households that relatives in extended families frequently share food, work, living quarters, child care, and leisure time. The houses tend to be clustered together so that visiting is easy, and they tend to be located on main streets so that business opportunities will not be missed.

When a family of Rom first occupy a house, they mould it to their own ideas of cleanliness and aesthetics. First they scrub the entire house with cleansers and disinfectants and then burn incense in each room to purify it. Then they knock out inside walls, except for the bathroom and kitchen, hang brightly flowered curtains in the resulting alcoves and windows, lay down plush red paisley carpets, and fill the house with mirrors, satin sofas, elaborate coffee tables, plastic covered silk lamps, baubles, and glass grapes.

It would be easy to assume that because they control a specific territory and live in houses, the Rom in the U.S. have become sedentary. But this is not the case. They use the territory mainly as a base, but they travel to and from it (on average they spend half their time there) and even within the territory they may change house frequently. Except for old people or territory leaders, houses are seen primarily as temporary stopping places. But more importantly, travelling is very much part of their entire life style and is imperative for a large number of social and religious reasons. Families will travel long distances to visit a sick relative or to attend one of the four funeral feasts that accompany each death. Since families are large (nowadays an average of five children per couple, formerly much larger), each Rom has several hundred relatives over four generations that he must visit. Furthermore, families will travel to contract marriages, attend a wedding or baptism, take part in a *slava* (a religious feast that occurs six times a year) or a *pakiv* (a feast in honour of a visiting leader). Women who have married out come to their parents' territory to give birth to their child. There are also a number of political reasons for travelling. Whenever a conflict occurs in the territory, the families usually move until the situation has resolved itself, and if it does not then a *kris* (trial) must be called, and another gathering of families in a neutral territory takes place. Any scandal, breach of morality, or of purity rules (*marime*), results in a great upheaval until it can be resolved.

Travelling does not usually take place in a random fashion. Some families travel within a limited area to follow seasonal occupations (such as picking crops during harvest time). Others travel primarily between two places where they have winter and summer headquarters (e.g. fortune-telling). Others may stay in one territory for the winter (e.g. on welfare) but spend the summer continuously on the road, tarmacing drives and roofs. The amount of travelling that each family undertakes depends on the sort of occupations the members pursue and their general age and state of health. Young, healthy families travel more than their elders, work more, and contribute part of their income to their parents or grandparents.

Authority

Each territory usually has a leader called a *rom baro* (literally, a big man) who is responsible for controlling economic resources in the territory, negotiating and solving problems with non-gypsy authorities and maintaining relations with the leaders of other territories. This leader, therefore, must function well, both in Rom society and in non-gypsy (*gaje*) society. No leader lasts for long if he fails to be effective with *gaje* officials in smoothing the way for his families, or cannot command the respect of Rom families in his internal dealings with them.

First of all, what sorts of problems arise with *gaje* authorities? There may be economic problems, such as how to negotiate work contracts with farmers for picking crops, how to obtain a fortune telling licence or a driving licence, or how to cope with the elaborate bureaucracy of welfare departments. There are also problems of a more political nature, such as how to avoid arrest, or if in trouble with the police, how to cope with the legal system; how to deal with school authorities, the office of employment, or welfare fraud investigators; how to get around hospital regulations and ensure the kind of care they want for their relatives. In all these cases, the *rom baro* either deals with the problem directly himself through his personal contacts with *gaje*, or if this is not possible, advises the family on how to deal with the problem themselves. In either case, he not only helps the Rom families, but by helping them, he makes himself indispensable to these families and therefore also reinforces his own position of authority.

Staley, the *rom baro* of Richmond, for example, has considerable influence with many families because he has worked out effective methods for coping with the California welfare department. Welfare regulations may theoretically be public information, but they are so complicated and obtuse that they are often difficult for social workers to understand. Staley, partly through careful questioning of social workers and partly through trial and error, now knows exactly how much he can spend on a car or have in the bank or earn from working, without being denied welfare. He can calculate which benefits each family is entitled to, and he can advise them on the manner they should adopt with different social workers. For example, some social workers prefer obsequiousness, while others are attracted to the exotic behaviour of the Rom. There have been occasions when new families in Richmond believed, quite falsely, that the only reason they got welfare was because of Staley's influence.

Recently, Staley has been expanding his empire to include setting up fortune-telling places in the county. Fortune-telling, which has been

Staley with two other contenders for leadership in Richmond. Since physical size is important for a *rom baro* (leader) Staley does not have any serious competition.

Staley Costello is the leader of the Richmond territory. He first came to Richmond about 12 years ago and since has established his position there and gathered all his large extended family around him.

illegal in Richmond until this year, can be a very lucrative business, and the change in the law has come to the attention of Machwaya from other territories in California. Staley's first reaction to these proposed changes was to try to prevent the legalisation of fortune telling because of his fear of Machwaya encroachment on his territory. When he realised this was not possible, he turned to threats. One Machwaya family who quickly rented a store front near Staley when they heard the news of legalisation, found that Staley had gone to the landlord to offer him twice the rent if he would kick out the Machwaya and rent it to Staley. He also called a meeting of his families and urged them to be diligent in harassing new Machwaya families. Staley's unswerving support from his relatives in Richmond will be a great help to him in his attempts to keep control of his territory.

The second aspect of leadership that is crucial for the *rom baro* is support from other Rom in the territory. How does a leader emerge and what is the basis of his influence within the community? Leadership depends, first of all, on age. Authority and old age are very closely linked. The older a person is the more respect and authority he is due (the *Romanes* word, *pakiv*, means both authority and respect) because his knowledge of Rom custom and law (*romania*), as well as *gaje* custom and law is greater. This knowledge is essential for arranging marriages, funerals, religious feasts and upholding standards of public morality. A leader must be an elder, but he must also be an elder with a sizeable family following. His wife and sons will always support him, but he must also try to bring his daughters and their husbands and as many of his cousins', nephews' and nieces' families as possible under his sphere of influence. In any situation of conflict, he can rely on his relatives to support him against unrelated Rom. A third factor is the reputation of his relatives as well as his own personal reputation. A reputation for cleanliness, high moral standards, good luck, and prosperity will help establish his position with other Rom leaders in other territories, and this public recognition of his authority gives it an air of legitimacy.

Finally, a *rom baro* must look impressive. As his title implies, he should be big, obese if possible, tall, and with a large head. Clothes should add to his impressiveness. Staley, who weighs close to four hundred pounds (28½ stone), wears a large, white Stetson hat and sports a handle bar moustache. On formal occasions he wears a shiny white western suit, a string tie clasped in silver, and elaborately tooled leather cowboy boots. When he really needs to impress, he puts on his gold sheriff's badge, smokes a pipe, and uses his carved and painted walking stick to punctuate a point.

Until now, I have been talking as if all authority was vested in men. As in so many societies, Rom men seem to preside in the most overt, publicly recognised political roles, such as the leadership of a territory. Rom men, in conversation, describe the women as powerless in the public sphere and inferior to men. The Rom would appear to be, on the surface, a highly male-dominated culture. On the other hand, women are strikingly aggressive and independent in behaviour, they are often the main financial support of their families, and they are dangerous to men because of their ability to pollute them. To explain this apparent paradox, we need to know more about the important values of Rom society.

I have mentioned that an individual's position in Rom society is based on the notion of respect (*pakiv*) which is linked with age, good luck and prosperity, a reputation for high moral standards and cleanliness. This is true for both men and women. Such a reputation depends on two things: the behaviour and personal attributes of the individual and the combined reputation and behaviour of his or her kin. When assessing a person's reputation, the Rom evaluate all these factors, but they generally refer to only one criterion, cleanliness, as a metaphor for expressing this evaluation. Their idea of 'cleanliness' is somewhat different from ours and is based on a particular view of the body.

The body

The Rom perceive the body as two opposed halves, an upper and a lower half, divided at the waist. The separation of the body at the waist into two halves is the basis of their conception of purity and pollution. Purity (*wuzho*) is attained by avoiding polluting substances and areas emanating from the lower half of the body. Pollution (*marime*) is the failure to keep these two halves separate; it is the mixing of what should be kept separate. There is another dimension to the body that is very important: the distinction between the inside and the outside. Anything that enters the body, such as food, must be even more pure than things that stay on the outside of the body.

In every-day activities, the implications of this ideal separation are far-reaching. It is not easy to prevent contact between the two

Gypsy women wear long skirts that must not be allowed to touch anything connected with food or man. The lower part of women's bodies is particularly dangerous to men.

halves of your body, but the Rom are trained very carefully from puberty onwards to observe standards of personal cleanliness that adhere as closely as possible to this ideal. Each individual is particularly conscious of the movement of the hands, because hands are constantly crossing the upper and lower boundaries of his own body. If the hands have touched the genitals or feet, they must be carefully washed before being used to handle food or wash the face. The Rom keep one bar of soap and one towel to be used for their face and another soap and towel (usually of a different colour) for their bodies. When taking a bath they are careful not to splash the bathwater onto their faces. Or if a man accidentally drops his razor on the floor when shaving, he will need to wash it carefully or even buy a new one. Women wear long skirts that must not be allowed to touch tables, cutlery or anything connected with food. If a woman sits on a coffee table, it must be thrown away. The lower part of women's bodies is particularly dangerous to men. Women are careful not to step over men's clothing, especially a man's hat, or brush her skirts against him or pass in front of a man. But a woman who has menstruated, will also take steps to prevent pollution of young girls by not sharing the same clothes or sleeping in the same bed. Women must be particularly careful to control their menstrual blood so that it does not contaminate clean items.

Given this conceptual division, washing takes on a special significance for the Rom. The Rom are concerned with removing 'every-day' dirt, but they are much more concerned with avoiding a mixture of the two halves of the body and with the purity of their inner body. Consequently any items used for food – table cloths, dish towels, dishes and cooking utensils – are washed separately from all other items and in a separate bowl that is used for nothing else. If someone inadvertently washes his hands in the bowl reserved for dishes, the bowl cannot again be used for this purpose. Clothes are also separated for washing so that men and women's clothes, children's and adult's clothes and upper and lower clothes are washed in separate loads. Pillowcases must be divided from sheets; face towels from body towels and so on. The house also becomes an extension of these divisions. Anything used in the bathroom or on the floor is kept separate from items used in the kitchen for food. It is considered impolite and embarrassing to be too obvious about using the lavatory and, if there are many people in the house, many Rom prefer to 'take a walk' outside rather than be seen entering the bathroom. The floor is generally an unclean area; therefore items that fall to the floor are either discarded or must be washed carefully before re-use. If a spoon falls to the floor, for example, it will be thrown away unless it is very valuable, in which case it will be soaked overnight in bleach.

Food, because it enters the body, is subject to even more stringent regulations. For the Rom, sharing food with another person is a statement of respect, friendship and acceptance of his cleanliness standards. Refusing to eat with someone is a serious insult, a statement that the person is not pure and clean. The most serious punishment the Rom as a group impose on an individual who breaks their laws is to refuse to eat with him. This is a public statement that the person is no longer pure, but *marime* or polluted.

At public feasting it is particularly important to ensure that food, which enters the body, is pure. Eating together is a statement of respect and friendship.

Thus in situations of public feasting, in particular, it is so important to ensure purity and prevent any defamation of character by refusing to eat the food, that special preparations are undertaken. Fruit and vegetables are bought in unpacked crates and drinks in cases or kegs; meat is bought on the hoof and butchered by men rather than women. Buying in bulk is not only economical for large gatherings, it is the best way to guarantee a minimal amount of handling by *gaje*. Also in large gatherings all cups, plates, napkins and table cloths are disposable paper or plastic because anything that is unused cannot have been contaminated by improper washing.

In spite of their careful precautions, mixing of the separate parts of the body may occur. Carried to their literal conclusion, many of these rules would be intolerable. Besides, away from the eyes of public condemnation, many Rom are more lax in their concern with purity. Privately, in her own home, for example, a woman may not be concerned if she should sit on her husband's coat, though she would probably still avoid sitting on a table. On the other hand, laxness in purity standards is considered to be one of the causes of disease as well as generally being an unlucky omen. Rom who become ill or are plagued by bad luck are, in the channels of public gossip, assessed according to their standards of cleanliness and blamed at least partly for their own misfortune.

These concepts of purity and pollution have far-reaching structural significance for the Rom. Concepts of purity and pollution, based on the inside/outside and upper/lower divisions of the body, are metaphors for expressing a number of social divisions or boundaries in Rom society. There are three areas of social organisation that are evaluated by the Rom in terms of relative purity: 1) the inside/outside division between the Rom and the *gaje*, 2) the divisions between the various nations of Rom, and 3) the age statuses of each individual Rom in the life cycle.

The division between Rom and gaje

The boundary between the Rom and the *gaje* is crucial to their sense of identity. I mentioned earlier in the introduction to this essay that all Gypsies have a word for themselves as opposed to non-gypsies and that these words always have superior/inferior connotations. For the Rom at least, and for many other Gypsy groups, these connotations are expressed most often in terms of the relative purity of the Rom in relation to the relative impurity of the *gaje*. An aspect of this is that non-gypsies, of course, fail to maintain proper separation; they are 'dirty' because they mix what should not be mixed. A Rom who associates too closely with the *gaje* is also in danger of becoming polluted. This metaphor is used by non-gypsies as well, since they too consistently think of the Gypsies as 'dirty'. Far from wishing to counter this image, the Gypsies appear to promote it – by leaving scrap metal by the roadside, sweeping rubbish out of the back door of the house, maintaining a grubby appearance, or scratching exaggeratedly for fleas in public places – since this stereotype keeps the non-gypsy at his distance and, ironically, helps to keep the Gypsy 'clean'.

Close personal contact with *gaje* is obviously fraught with danger of pollution. Eating in the home of a non-gypsy, associating in public places continuously, and in particular, any sexual contact with a non-gypsy is likely to result in illness or rejection by the group because it is *marime*. The *gaje* are generally felt to be lacking in sexual morality, and sexual relationships with them are feared as a source of veneral disease. In public places, in particular, the Rom generally avoid prolonged contact (hence their strong aversion to a regular job, a stint in jail, or attending school) and try to touch as few surfaces as possible. In restaurants, for example, drinks are taken from paper cups; in public toilets, paper towels can be used to turn taps, and so on.

This general association of the *gaje* with pollution obviously has implications for economic relations with them. Let me summarise briefly what I said earlier about the pattern of economic relationships among the Rom. First of all, they have a strong ethos of co-operation with each other. Rom work together in partnerships or in family groups, they share income in families or households, relatives are expected to help one another when in need, and relatives generally co-operate in putting on ritual feasts by each making a contribution or by taking up a collection among the participants. Even unrelated Rom show a degree of co-operation and mutual aid that is unlike non-gypsy society. A family that is seriously in need will always be offered a home and money from a collection taken up in the territory by the *rom baro*. This is a kind of Gypsy insurance policy, since those who give generously reckon that the day will come when they too may need some assistance.

In contrast to the generosity and co-operation they show with each other, economic relationships with the *gaje* are pure business: maximise profits and minimise losses. Cleverness in extracting as much money from the *gaje* with the least capital investment is highly valued. So a confidence trick such as the *bujo* (whereby a fortune-teller gets a customer to bring all his or her savings wrapped in a 'bag' to remove a curse on the money and then switch the bag for one containing cut up newspapers) as well as services (such as breaking up scrap metal or mending bumpers) that require very little cash output are both consistent with their principle of economic maximisation.

This pattern of internal reciprocity and external maximisation makes more sense in light of the understanding we now have of the boundary that the Rom perceive between themselves and the *gaje* in terms of a contrast between moral purity and immoral impurity. The opposition between Rom/*gaje*, inside/outside relations operates both on moral and economic levels, through the metaphor of purity/impurity. The Rom concern for avoiding what is *marime* means that they must avoid close, prolonged contact with *gaje*, and focus their relations with the outside world exclusively on making a living. The code for this behaviour could be summarised as: purity is to impurity as inside (Rom) is to outside (*gaje*) and as reciprocity is to maximisation.

The Rom nations

I have already mentioned that the Rom are divided into four 'tribes' called *natsia* (a nation) or *raza* (a race). These nations are not really *groups* in the sense that they are each spread over various parts of the world and therefore do not ever function as a group nor do members of a nation ever come together as a group. The nation is primarily a status *category* or a 'name' for identification of one's position. The status of the four nations is fairly fixed; the Machwaya and Lowara are small in numbers and enjoy superior status; the Kalderasha are the largest nation composed of a very varied 'middle' status; the Churara are generally conceded to be the lowest status.

The situation is somewhat more complex, however. Each nation is composed of a number of cognatic or bilateral descent groups (see page 147) called a *vista*. The Kalderasha, who have a large number of *vista*, also have a method of determining the status of each *vitsa*. Relative wealth or power in the territory, reputation for generosity and fairness towards fellow Rom and a reputation for high moral standards and cleanliness are all factors in determining the position of each particular *vitsa*. The reputation of the *vitsa*, of course, is not fixed and depends on the changing fortunes of each *vitsa* member.

The point that I want to emphasise is that both the status of the nations and the reputation of each *vitsa* are understood and expressed through the purity metaphor. The Rom do not tick off each factor in the reputation of a *vitsa* or talk about the 'status' of each *natsia*, because none of this is necessary for them. What they discuss is how 'clean' or 'unclean' the members of a *vitsa* or *natsia* are, and this acts as a kind of shorthand. The Machwaya consider themselves to be 'cleaner' than the Kalderasha, and this alone establishes their superiority. A Kalderasha *vitsa* with wealth, power, good fortune, and more correctness will develop a reputation for being 'clean' in relation to other *vitsa*.

Age statuses in the life cycle

A third set of boundaries marked by pollution categories are the stages of an individual's life cycle. Rom have four categories of age:

1	*sha*	boy child	2	*sha baro*	post-puberty male
	shey	girl child		*shey bari*	post-puberty female
3	*rom*	man, married adult	4	*phuro*	old man
	romni	woman, married adult.		*phuri*	old woman

Each of these ages is associated with a condition of purity or impurity that is in turn linked with notions of sexual activity and shame. Basically the idea is that during puberty and adult married life, that is during the sexually active period of one's life, the individual is in a condition of impurity relative to the sexually inactive periods, childhood and old age. Most of the stringent regulations on washing, separation of clothes, and special behaviour for women are relevant only during this period of sexual potency, particularly after marriage. Children of course must be protected from contact with pollution so their clothes are washed separately, but apart from that they are virtually free agents; they are always intrinsically pure and innocent. Children can even eat 'polluted' food, e.g. food handled by *gaje*, with impunity. Old people are a bit more susceptible than children to the dangers of pollution and still, for example, are careful about the purity of food. On the other hand, old people are expected to be sexually inactive, and old women, in particular, are freed from many restrictions in behaviour because they have gone through the menopause. As in other aspects of social life, the Rom attribute secular qualities, such as political power, to a condition of purity. Old people are respected and their authority is accepted because they are, like children, pure once again. The Rom do not share the attitudes of our society towards old age, and if you jolly an old *phuri* along by saying how young she looks, she will be highly offended. Old age is the crowning glory of a person's life, and every Rom's ambition is to reach old age as quickly as possible. Death, before old age, is considered a terrible tragedy, but at old age death is carefully prepared for, accepted and openly discussed. So in a sense we can say that the Rom look at time in terms of three phases in an individual's life:–

Marriage

It would be relevant to discuss one of the rites of passage that mark a change in status in the life cycle of an individual. Marriage is a particularly interesting ritual because it 'says' a number of things about both the individual and the society. First of all, marriage is an exchange and an alliance between two groups (either two *vitsi* or two extended families within a *vitsa*). This is an exchange because one group gives a bride (called *bori*, also meaning daughter-in-law) and the other group reciprocates with a *daro*, a payment of money that ranges from 500 to 5000 dollars, depending on the purity status of the bride and her family. In this particular instance, purity has a price. Most marriages, therefore, are arranged by the parents of the bride and groom, through an agreement on a marriage payment. Thus, marriage is an alliance between the two families, an alliance that creates a new set of relationships, obligations and expectations from each other.

Secondly, marriage marks a change of status for the individual. In Rom society the word for adult and for a married person are the same (*rom, romni*) so that an individual attains full adult status only upon being married. But, unlike in our society where adult status is associated with independence and full responsibility, in Rom society adult status is, at the beginning, associated with restrictions and low status, due to the individual's new condition of impurity. This is particularly true for women. Whereas an elder daughter in a household is haughty, independent, and indulged, a daughter-in-law must be modest, subservient, and work extremely hard. A new daughter-in-law, while she lives in her parents-in-law's house during the first few years of marriage, is expected to do all the housework and cooking, serve her parents-in-law, care for any children there, and provide the major supply of income as well. Until the birth of her first child, she is the virtual slave of her mother-in-law.

All of this is dramatised in the marriage ritual itself. The marriage ceremony centres entirely on the woman, while the husband remains to one side as a kind of casual onlooker. Before the wedding, the marriage payment has been agreed upon and paid in a ceremony called the *tomiala*, when the two prospective fathers-in-law drink whisky from a specially prepared bottle called a *plotshka* that is decorated with a scarf, red ribbons, and gold. Each of these items has a special significance. Red is the colour of happiness; gold, of good luck; and the scarf or *diklo* symbolises the married state. At the day of the wedding the bride arrives, usually in red, and is led by her new sisters-in-law to greet the important guests at the wedding, in a public show of her entrance into the new group. During the general dancing and drinking, her future sisters-in-law take her aside to change her into her wedding dress, white if she is a virgin, and her hair is unbound and combed out. This marks the beginning of the transition phase for the bride. Hair which in public must normally be bound up, is now allowed to flow freely. The reluctant bride is then dragged crying, and sometimes protesting, into a dance called the *kola* (meaning tail), in which one of her new male in-laws leads her and the wedding guests in a winding, twisting line of dancing. At the head of the line the man from the groom's group holds the marriage pole that is decorated with marriage scarves, red ribbons and a rose. The rose symbolises her virginal blood, for it is said that when a woman loses her virginity, the blood on the sheets will form a rose.

The next point in the ceremony is a brief exchange called a *geita* (gate) between a man chosen by the bride's father as his representative and male representatives from the groom's family. The two 'gate-keepers' argue over the giving up the 'lamb' (the bride; a lamb represents innocence) and the bride's representative makes a show of reluctance and may even come to blows with the men of the groom's *vitsa*. Eventually, however, the 'lamb' is handed over in exchange for a symbolic payment of a few gold coins. At this point the bride's hair is veiled by her sisters-in-law with the marriage scarf.

Now the wedding guests can sit down to eat at a large feast table and during the meal, another representative of the bride, called the 'godfather' (*pivlo*), takes up a collection for the newly married couple. This collection, like the marriage payment, is also called a *daro*. The godfather walks from guest to guest with the bride behind him holding a hollowed out loaf of bread filled with salt and the groom behind her with a tray of drinks. The godfather takes a gift from each guest, makes a speech proclaiming how much has been given, stuffs the money into the bread, and puts a marriage scarf around the neck of the donator. The groom then hands the donator a glass of beer, and a toast is made to the new couple. All this is accompanied by cheering and clapping. Part of the function of the *daro* is to obtain a public statement of

The bridegroom with his red sash for good luck at the wedding feast.

acceptance of this marriage union on the part of the guests present. A man who wishes to register his disapproval of the exchange may refuse to give a donation. Sometimes a relative of the bride, to show how much he cares for her welfare, will make a mock refusal and then finally relent. Or anyone who has knowledge of improper sexual behaviour on the part of the bride may throw his red rose to the ground, thus indicating that he knows the bride is not a virgin.

But if all goes well, the bride is taken back to the house of her parents-in-law where her first duty is to serve them food in a symbolic gesture of her new role of subservience. Only that evening is the marriage consummated, and the next day the bride's new mother-in-law, in a short ceremony, blesses the bride and groom, who share a symbolic meal of bread, wine, and salt. The mother-in-law then ties up the bride's hair and binds it with the marriage scarf that will be the symbol of her married status. In spite of all these ritual preparations, the bride is not truly established with the new family until the birth of her first child, when she contributes an addition to the *vitsa* in the form of a new descendant.

Let us see then how the Rom marriage fits with the usual form of a transition rite. The woman goes from the initial 'normal' condition of non-adult, pure status to a final 'normal' condition of married impure status. During the marginal or transitional period of time, the girl is not a free agent. She is a 'lamb' passed through the 'gates' (symbolic boundary) of two groups, dragged through a winding twisting dance, argued over in a collection, and finally initiated into sexual knowledge. It is interesting that b oth the rites of separation and incorporation focus on her hair. The loosening of the hair moves her out of the bounds of normal society; the binding and placing of the marriage scarf moves her back into those bounds, but in a new position.

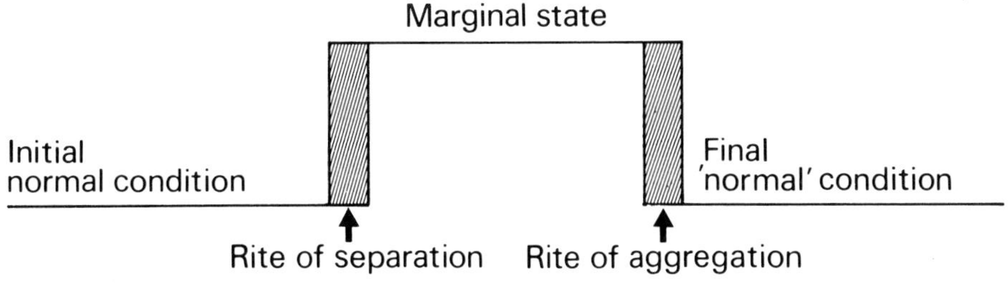

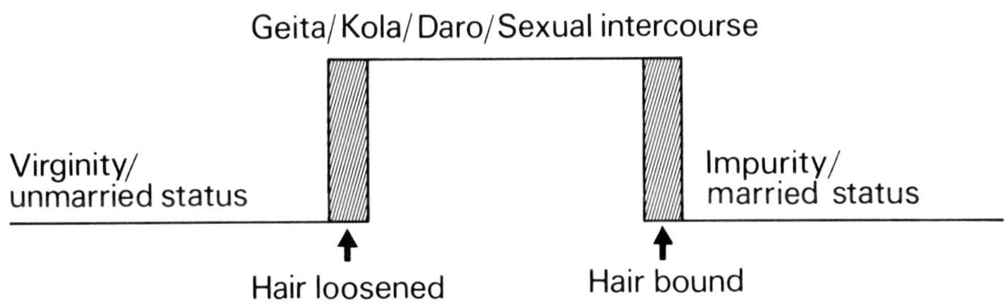

Women

It may seem strange to leave a discussion of women until the very end, but I have purposely done so because it will take me back to the beginning, not only the beginning of my argument but also back to first principles. In discussing the role that women have in Rom society, I want to pick up several threads in my argument. One is the apparent paradox between the exclusion of women in publicly recognised political roles and their important economic and 'purity' role in the family. Another is the presence of several contradictory stereotypes of women within Rom society and outside it.

In the beginning of this essay I described the non-gypsy stereotype of Gypsy women as sensual, sexually provocative, mystical, with supernatural powers. This stereotype may take the form of a fantasy of unobtainable sexuality, or it may represent Gypsy women as prostitutes. As we have learned, Gypsy women in their own own society are, in fact, hedged in by restrictions and are expected to conform to an ideal of chastity, sexual fidelity and morality, and adherence to domestic duties. So how do we explain this extraordinary contrast between the outsider's stereotype of the Gypsy woman and the ideal behaviour expected of her by the Gypsies themselves? Judith Okely, in a recent study of English Gypsies (Ardener, 1975), suggests that this contrast can be explained by relating it to the English Gypsy woman's 'calling' role. English Gypsy women earn money from non-gypsies by 'calling' at houses either to collect rags (that they recycle), hawk goods, or tell fortunes, and they are often most effective at this by exploiting their image as seductress (particularly in fortune-telling), destitute mother or old crone. While women are calling, they are in contact with non-gypsies and in danger of polluting Gypsy men, particularly through the threat of sexual relations with outsiders. Yet while her external role is polluting, it is she who is responsible for keeping men pure in her internal role as wife and cook. A standard anthropological model of this situation would show the women in an intermediary position between inside and outside, culture and nature. *(Okely, 1975:62)*.

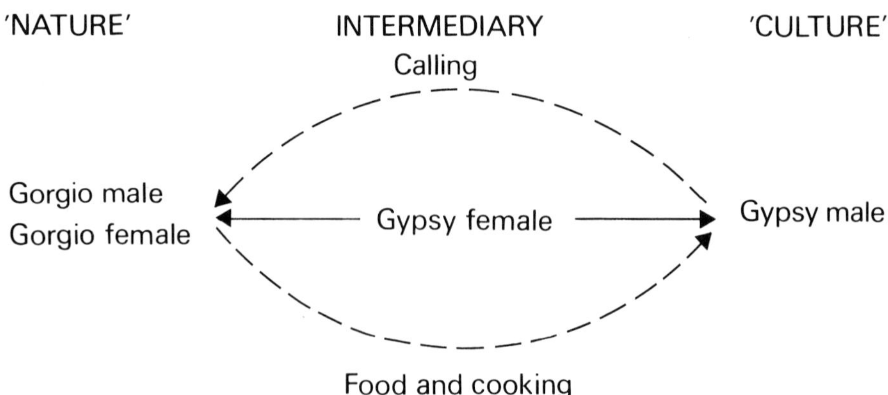

This model implies that Gypsy women are little more than an intermediary between two male-dominated societies, but it is Ms. Okely's contention that although in their own society English Gypsy women have a

Above
A young gypsy wife and her child at a wedding. Until the birth of her first child a woman is the virtual slave of her mother-in-law.

Left
During the wedding, the reluctant bride is dragged crying, and sometimes protesting, into a dance called the Kola (tail) in which one of her new male-in-laws leads her and the wedding guests in a winding, twisting line of dancing. At the head of the Kola dance a man from the groom's family holds the marriage pole that is decorated with marriage scarves, red ribbons and a rose.

Right
Shrecha who has knowledge of many medicines and curses, is respected by many for her ability to deal with the unknown forces.

Below
The godfather takes up a collection for the newly married couple. He puts the money in a hollowed out loaf of bread. The bridegroom gives a drink and a marriage scarf to the contributor.

restricted and subordinate role, in their external calling role, they undertake independent, self-employed work that requires decision-making independent of men, a multiplicity of skills, and training that sometimes includes very aggressive behaviour. Their work outside is not an extension of a domestic, supportive servicing role, as most women's jobs in our society are. So they resolve the subordinate role they have in their own society by playing on the stereotypes of themselves outside their society. They can 'fool' non-gypsy men by being the seductress while getting money from them, and they have a polluting power in relation to their own men because the threat of illicit sex with an outsider is always a danger to the purity of men.

This situation with English Gypsy women is comparable to the situation with the American Rom, but with an important difference. The American *romni*, like the English Gypsy woman, fully accepts the pollution beliefs that place on her the major responsibility for keeping men pure. But unlike the English Gypsy woman, the American *romni* has one advantage: she can pollute a man and have him rejected from the group (*marime*) for a long period of time by throwing her skirt over his head. The penalty for being 'rejected' or *marime* is very severe. The *marime* person can no longer eat with any other Rom or have close contact with them until he can call a trial (*kris*) and become reinstated. Reinstatement is a long, difficult and expensive process. A person can become *marime* or rejected by committing a serious breach of the moral or pollution code, that is, through his own actions, or he can become *marime* when his wife throws her skirts over his head. The latter is much more rare than the former, but it does happen, and it is the ultimate threat that women have over men.

So although men do not recognise women as part of the public decision-making process, in practice the woman recognises the power her polluting role gives her in her own society and the power she obtains from being an aggressive and effective money-earner. For example, in verbal statements, men assert that women have no rights in important decisions such as those taken by the *kris* (on questions of inclusion and exclusion from the group, divorce, etc.) Yet when pressed, it was admitted that a man was expected to take his wife to the *kris* and that her opinion was consulted by the man in the decision-making process. Other men's wives were still not recognised by men, but obviously, looked at as a whole, it is clear that the decision-making group was composed of an equal number of men and their wives, each of whom could influence her husband. Another strange paradox is that Gypsy men state that it is not possible for a woman to become the leader of a territory. Yet it is also not possible for a man to attain the position of *rom baro* unless he has a wife to back-up his leadership. Because of her ability to curse and pollute, a wife is an essential part of every man's political career. Furthermore, on the death of his wife, a man almost immediately loses his position of authority. On the other hand, widowed women can and do head a *vitsa* alone. Since women tend to outlive men, statistically female-headed *vitsi* are very common. In Staley's territory in Richmond the *vitsi* elders that he relied on to support his leadership were mainly women, and his wife's influence was crucial to his position.

Old women such as Persa and Rachael can head an entire extended family group.

One factor related to the political importance of women is the great respect for the aged, regardless of sex. Both old men and old women are considered more 'pure' and gain status by the supposed cessation of sexual activity. However, unlike men, women have increased powers at old age because they now have knowledge of the supernatural, of curses, and medicines, while being relieved of some of the most odious restrictions in behaviour due to their inherent pollution. Old women, therefore, are in a position to manipulate pollution rules to improve their situation in the political structure, while young women are still under the thumb of a father, husband or mother-in-law, as well as the stringent restrictions on behaviour.

Conclusion

This description of the Rom and other Gypsies is necessarily brief and incomplete and therefore hardly does justice to the complexity of their culture. It may even leave the reader with more questions about Gypsies than he had before reading it. I certainly hope so, for one of my purposes has been to jar some of the usual preconceptions that we all have about Gypsies. But I also hope that the reader is now in a position to see the Gypsy's viewpoint as well.

The problem is that the study of a group like the Gypsies, living in our midst, presents certain methodological difficulties because Gypsies are 'familiar' to us all. First of all, we have many preconceptions and prejudices about them that must be countered. Secondly, the Gypsies are extremely secretive and insular, and so they conceal and sometimes misrepresent their society to outsiders. This too must be countered. There is a third and even more difficult question of the role of Gypsies as an ethnic group in modern, industrialised society. How do they cope with such a complex and alien society? Will they continue to live as they do, or will they change so drastically they become assimilated?

It is as difficult to predict the future of the Gypsies as it is to generalise about them. But it is quite clear that Gypsies are under pressure to conform to their host society. Sedentary societies are generally hostile to nomadic groups. Attempts to settle Gypsies, however, have mostly been unsuccessful. Industrialised societies are intolerant of people unwilling to enter the wage-labour system and educational institutions and attempt to force them into it. Gypsies in England, for example, are officially defined as 'persons of no fixed abode' and therefore denied certain rights under the Race Relations Act because they are not considered to be an 'ethnic group'. They are considered by both officials and the general population to be parasites on society, and their children are 'deprived' because they do not participate in anything but the most rudimentary formal education. And yet Gypsies in England fill a niche in the industrial system that is greatly needed. As a highly mobile work force, they can profitably earn a living by recycling waste (rags, scrap metal, etc.) or provide intermittent but important services (sharpening knives, entertainment, Christmas decorations, etc.). Furthermore, their main alternative to such work so far has been to settle down and depend on state social security. At

When the gypsies settled down in houses they had to face the problem of how to remain separate from the rest of the community. This has been particularly difficult in the field of education and for a short time it was solved by the establishment of a separate school for gypsy children. The school was set up by the author in conjunction with the local social services department.

'Rattlesnake Pete' and his wife Rusha on the road in the 1930s.

the moment, Gypsy children learn important skills that English children entirely lack. A Gypsy child is taught to be flexible enough to earn a living in a multitude of ways. Like the big corporations, Gypsies diversify, and so when an old skill is no longer viable, they are already learning new ones. In a world of specialists, there is still a need for the jack-of-all-trades. A Gypsy child who chooses formal schooling loses this flexibility, and more often than not joins the mass of unskilled and unemployed. The Gypsies are not unaware that their flexibility and mobility are their main economic advantage over non-gypsies, and they are unlikely to give them up easily.

The historical evidence on Gypsies indicates that they have an ability to adapt and to survive that is unmatched by any other ethnic group in our society. Facing technological changes, new countries and languages, and periods of persecution has been a part of their life experience for their entire recorded history. In a sense, their whole social organisation, economic system and life style is geared towards coping with change. Their particular combination of moral rigidity and economic flexibility has resulted in a system that is highly adaptable to change.

Certainly we should not give the impression that there are never specific instances in which individual Gypsies, or even, though more rarely, whole groups of Gypsies lose their cultural identity. There is clearly a certain amount of movement of individuals from Gypsy society to *gaje* society and back, though no one knows exactly how frequently this occurs. But it is equally certain that the Gypsies on the whole will cope with new situations with their usual flexibility. The Gypsies are here to stay.

Further reading

OKELY, J. *Work and travel* in *Gypsies and government policy in England* by B. Adams and others. Heinemann, 1975. Chapter 5.

OKELY, J. *Gypsy women: models in conflict* in *Perceiving women* edited by S. Ardener. Dent, 1975.

REHFISCH, F. ed. *Gypsies, tinkers and other travellers* Academic Press, 1975.

SUTHERLAND, A. *Gypsies: the hidden Americans* Tavistock Publications, 1975.

SUTHERLAND, A. *The body as a social symbol among the Rom* in *Anthropology of the body* edited by J. Blacking. Seminar Press, 1977.

WOOD, M. F. *In the life of a Romany gypsy* Routledge and Kegan Paul, 1973.

YOORS, J. *The gypsies* Allen and Unwin, 1967.

Chapter Eight A Village in Bali

by Anthony Forge

Bali is one of the tourist centres of the world. It is widely advertised as having golden beaches, palm trees and all the conventional attributes of a tropical paradise plus magnificent dances, fascinating rituals and in general a rich and intact culture which the tourist is invited to share. But before it became such an intensely publicised and highly successful international resort, it was in many ways unique in Indonesia, and much of its present attraction comes from its unusual history. Lying only a few miles from the rich and populous island of Java, across the dangerous Bali Strait, it has often formed part of various Javanese kingdoms and often been independent. Many different influences were brought with the various rulers, and there are today many remains indicating that a variety of forms of Hinduism and Buddhism have at one time or another been the dominant religion of at least the aristocratic class. The history of the various rulers, both Javanese and Balinese, is full of intrigue and revolt. Much of it has a mythological character with the attribution of great magical powers to kings and holy men, but it is clear that the present form of Balinese society only starts with the conquest of the island by Gadja Mada, a famous general of the Madjapait empire in the fourteenth century. Gadja Mada overthrew the last independent Balinese king Dalem Bedaulu, who was reputed to have the head of a pig. Some of the aristocratic families in Bali trace their ancestry back to Gadja Mada or members of his expedition. The establishment of a Hindu–Javanese kingdom in Bali as part of the Madjapait empire lasted about one hundred and fifty years, before Madjapait itself fell to the adherents of the new religion – Islam – that swept away all the old kingdoms and established new Sultanates throughout the island of Java. The heir of the last king of Madjapait is said to have fled to Bali with many of his Brahmana priests, courtiers, artists and musicians, and established a new Balinese kingdom centred on Gelgel in the south-east of the island. Almost all the Balinese aristocrats – the *tri wangsa*, 'three races' of Brahmana, Ksatriya and Wesia, claim descent from either Gadja Mada's expedition or the flight from the fall of Madjapait. Some of the most powerful Brahmana used the power of their learning and religious and magical skills to fly direct from Madjapait, rather than risk the dangerous crossing. Descent from Madjapait is still very highly

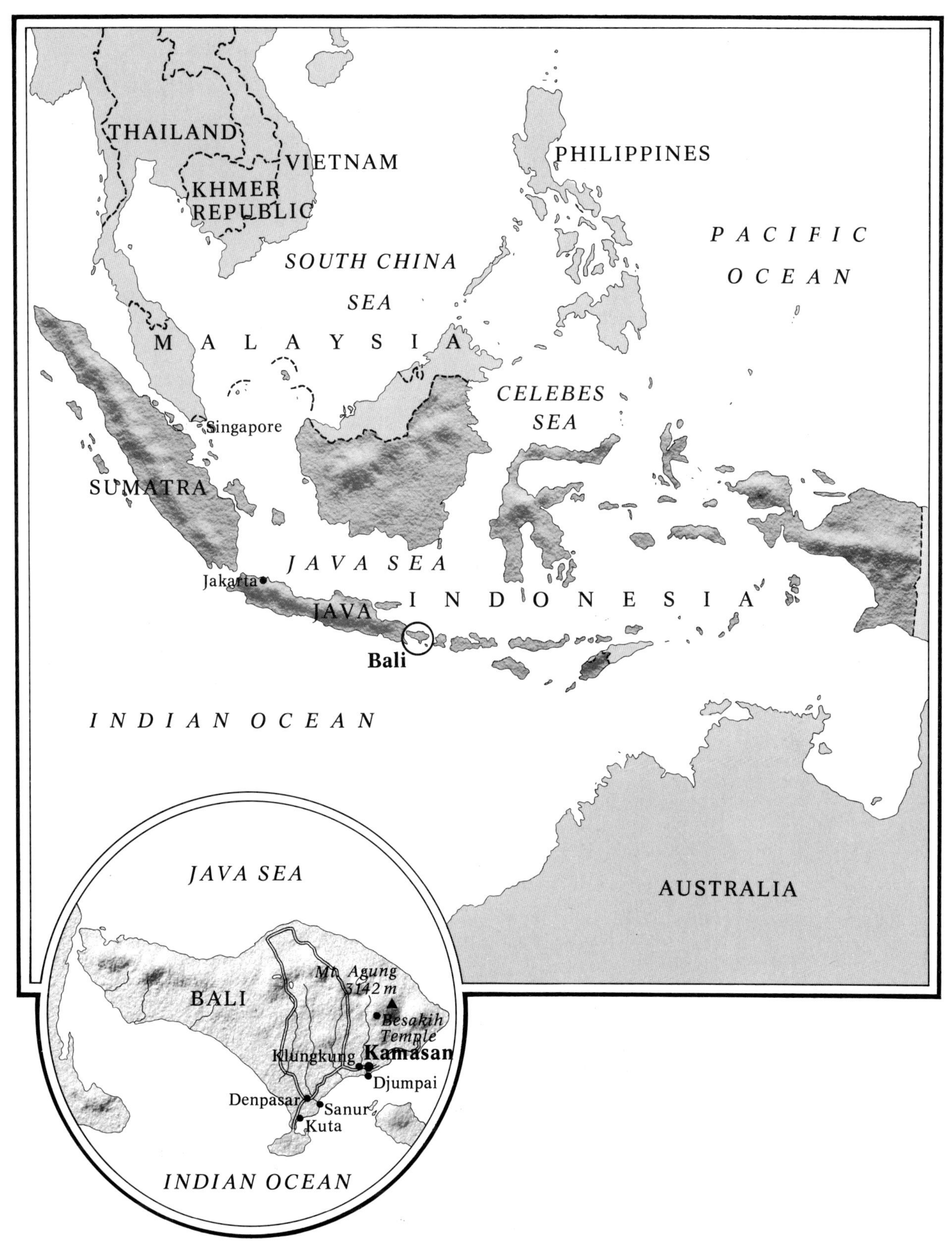
THAILAND
VIETNAM
KHMER REPUBLIC
PHILIPPINES
SOUTH CHINA SEA
PACIFIC OCEAN
MALAYSIA
CELEBES SEA
Singapore
SUMATRA
JAVA SEA
Jakarta
JAVA
INDONESIA
Bali
INDIAN OCEAN
AUSTRALIA
JAVA SEA
BALI
Mt. Agung 3142 m
Besakih Temple
Klungkung
Kamasan
Djumpai
Denpasar
Sanur
Kuta
INDIAN OCEAN

Balinese culture depends on the very effective exploitation of every square inch of soil. On the lower slopes of the mountains, where most of the population lives, elaborate and extensive terraces for the cultivation of rice cover the landscape. The control and distribution of water for these terrace systems are the responsibility of essentially egalitarian societies called *subak* in which all the users of the water have a voice. Above the level that the water can reach, on this spur, are houses surrounded by useful trees, coconut, breadfruit and betel nut – a mild narcotic very popular with the Balinese.

valued. The aristocrats, in particular, look for the justification for their high status outside Bali. Such descent is symbolised by the use of carved deer on the shrines in ancestral temples.

Initially, the Gelgel kingdom was one state. It soon became divided up through intrigue, revolt and war into nine separate states, each with its own Raja, only some of whom were linked by kinship to the *Dewa Agung* – literally 'highest God' – the Raja of Gelgel whose superiority was symbolically acknowledged. These ties of nominal fealty in no way inhibited wars and intrigues between the various rulers in the course of which the state of Mengwi was conquered and absorbed by its neighbours. There were also revolts within the states, and the result of a particularly successful one was the transfer of the court of the *Dewa Agung* from Gelgel to Klungkung a few miles to the north. But despite wars and revolts, the Rajas of the remaining eight states with their courts, their retainers, their tax-gatherers and armies, maintained a fairly genuine independence, in the case of the six southern states, right to the start of the twentieth century. During this period, the aristocratic Hindu–Javanese culture of the courts and pre-existing Balinese culture of the peasants, about which we know very little, interacted and influenced each other to produce the present distinct Balinese culture. The tide of Islam never penetrated Bali, and although emissaries from the Sultans came to try and persuade the *Dewa Agung* to convert, there never seems to have been any attempt at conquest. Indeed, the Balinese Rajas prospered and even conquered much of the neighbouring island of Lombok. The threat of Islam, however, was replaced, from the seventeenth century onwards, by the growing power of the Dutch who, setting out initially to monopolise the trade of the whole archipelago, gradually, directly or indirectly through puppets, ruled much of Java and all the other important trading centres of Indonesia. The Dutch merchants tried to gain influence in Bali with presents and offers of treaties, but although the presents were accepted, the Balinese princes refused to become part of the burgeoning Dutch empire. Throughout the nineteenth century, tension between the Balinese and Dutch continued. In 1846, the Dutch sent a military expedition to North Bali, and in 1882, they took over by force the two northern states of Djembrana and Buleleng. From then on, Dutch influence became more and more felt, and their tactics of intrigue and support for the enemies of the still independent states started to work. In 1894, a Dutch military expedition to Lombok was forced to withdraw, but they returned with reinforcements, and after a bitter campaign deposed the Raja and razed the city of Mataram to the ground. From then on, the end of Balinese independence was rapid; in 1900, the Dutch annexed Gianyar, which had asked for an alliance when it was being attacked by its neighbours, and in 1906, an expedition landed at Sanur and attacked the rulers of Badung. Realising that their cause was lost, the Raja led

A Dutchman with his drinking mug. A carving on the 'Floating House' at Klungkung, one of the few buildings of the palace area left after the destruction of 1908. This statue is now regarded as one of the guardians of the building and receives a small offering on important days.

out all his courtiers, wives and kin, dressed in their most superb silks and jewels, but carrying only *kris* and spears. Leaving the palace burning behind them, they confronted the Dutch Colonial troops. Despite entreaties to stop, they repeatedly charged the troops until all were shot down or had stabbed themselves to death. For days after, other members of the royal family were reported to have come to the Dutch demanding that they too should be shot, some stabbing themselves when this favour was refused. Similar incidents took place at the palace of Den Pasar, and shortly after, the Raja of Tabanan and his son killed themselves to avoid being exiled. The last remaining independent state, Klungkung, lasted two more years, before another suicidal 'fight to the end' completed the conquest of Bali.

The Dutch rule had none of the overt economic exploitation so characteristic of their rule in Java. The eight states were preserved, each with a regent who was a member of the traditional royal family, but with a Dutch adviser who held the real authority. Children of aristocrats were given a Dutch education and integrated to some extent into the colonial elite, but, on the whole, very little changed. The peasants were hardly affected by the change of masters since they still had to provide labour and pay taxes. In the 1920's, a tourist trade developed, and many Europeans who came to Bali spread word of the grace and beauty, not just of the people themselves, but of their temple ceremonies and dances, and of the richness of the whole culture. Some Europeans stayed, among them arists and musicians, who were not only to write about, photograph and paint Bali, but who have had a profound influence on the art, introducing new materials and techniques of painting and carving that have since become integrated into Balinese culture.

The Japanese occupation and the subsequent struggle to establish the Republic of Indonesia was a period of great trouble and revealed many of the tensions and hatreds that underlie the immaculate and delicate surface of Balinese society. Later the same tensions were revealed during the killings that went with the so-called 'cleansing' of Bali that followed the abortive communist coup in Jakarta in 1965. Under the Indonesian Republic, the old administrative structure has been more or less preserved, and the regents are still drawn in many cases from the old royal families. But there have been many other profound changes. Every village now has a school, medical services are much more widely spread, with the result that the population has doubled since the war, and the Indonesia-wide administrative services operate throughout the island. Even television has just arrived, while almost every household has long had a radio. The current tourist boom is on a scale completely different from that of the pre-war period. Recent projections are that by the 1980's, the number of tourists visiting the island in any one year will approach the size of the Balinese population. However, the present length of stay is only an average of four nights. The authorities have adopted a policy of providing the bulk of the accommodation in the south, where two villages with good beaches, Sanur and Kuta, and the capital Den Pasar, are swarming with tourists, who are taken by bus and car, or take themselves on motorcycles, to see special performances of dances and ritual dramas, put on for their benefit by villages in the densely populated areas on the slopes of the great volcanoes that dominate the island. Visitors also attend real Balinese ceremonials, for the tourist agencies run a very effective intelligence network on the dates and places of suitable performances, but apart from cremations, which take place in the open, there has recently been a tendency to restrict or refuse admission to unknown visitors to temple and other ceremonies. The impact of the new mass tourism can be surprisingly light. During the year my family spent in the village of Kamasan, about two miles from Klungkung on one of the major tour routes, only three tourists visited the village, apart from friends coming specifically to visit us.

In short, the Balinese seem to be coping with the tourist invasion as well as they have coped with others; that is, they are taking what they want, but they are not allowing themselves to be any the less Balinese. This appears to have been the story throughout Bali's history: outside cultures have come, perhaps as conquerors, perhaps only as visitors and traders, but Balinese society and culture have remained distinctive, accepting outward forms, but moulding them to their own different purposes.

Caste

This is nowhere more apparent than in the 'caste' system that came ultimately from India through the Hindu–Javanese kingdoms. In Bali there are four castes, each with impeccable Sanskrit names. The Brahmana is the highest caste in ritual terms and the caste that provides the *pedandas*, the high priests who alone can make *tirta* – holy water. Next are the Ksatriya, the caste of kings and princes from which many of the rulers come, and thirdly the Wesia, in theory merchants but in fact a caste with a military ideal, which has provided rulers in several of the states. These three top castes claim to have sprung ultimately from a god usually identified as Brahma. They are called collectively the *tri wangsa*, three races, and should marry only within their own caste. But the *tri wangsa* form only about seven to ten per cent of the population; the rest is classified as Sudra, the lowest caste which is considered to be of earthly origin. Unlike the Indian caste system, in Bali there are no sub-castes which classify all members of local groups into a complex hierarchy, defined in terms of beliefs and the pollution that the lower can inflict on the higher. The high priests do observe a set of restrictions, some of which are common to all, such as not eating meat (especially beef), but many of which are individual, for example not going under flowing water. These restrictions for high priests are basically to acquire and preserve their own *sakti* – supernatural power – and the purity necessary to use it. The same restrictions are often observed by members of other castes who wish to have *sakti*. The observance of these taboos is really a matter of individual preference rather than family or caste purity rules.

The observance of caste differences is more apparent in the rules of etiquette. Each caste has its own titles: Brahmana males are all addressed as Ida Bagus – Eminent and Beautiful, females as Ida Ayu with much the same meaning. There are a variety of honorific forms of address for each caste, down to the Sudras who all have the title *I*. When speaking to a member of a higher caste, members of a lower caste should use the high form of

A high priest – *pedanda* – of the Brahmana caste, being addressed by a Sudra in the correct most formal style. The difference in sitting heights and the gesture of the hands are very obvious indicators of different status. Nowadays such deferential behaviour is only seen in ritual contexts, such as this *Odalan* – temple festival – the high priest has come to make holy water and is being entertained by the temple priest, in white, and a leading member of the temple community while waiting for the congregation to gather.

the language, and the higher should respond in the low form. The linguistic situation on Bali is very complex, but there are basically two different languages. The common or low form is in origin an Austronesian language, one of the language family stretching from Madagascar to Hawaii deep in the Pacific Ocean. The high form comes from the Javanese court languages, is full of Sanskrit words, and is very elaborate and flowery in expression. There is also a middle language which can be used when people are not sure of their relative position and is now widely spoken in schools. In fact, few of the ordinary people speak the high form well, and usually only use a few standard phrases, either when addressing high priests or members of ruling families or on very formal occasions. Among the *tri wangsa*, the high form should be used when addressing parents as well as social superiors. The complexities of the system mean that very fine shades of respect or disrespect can be indicated by the choice of language and of words within it. There are special terms also for use to animals, and to use one of these to refer to a human is a deadly insult.

In general, all Balinese are concerned about correct or refined behaviour. Not to appear a crude fellow is of vital importance, and in public especially, smiling, gentle manners, with the correct use of titles and honorific forms, is absolutely necessary. For a man to lose his temper, or to be hasty or impolite, is not only crude, it means that he will be ignored, his influence and the attention paid to his words and actions will decline, and if this sort of behaviour persists, he will cease to be an effective member of his community.

The village

The formal structure of castes is really only a special form of the more general Balinese concern with hierarchy and is grafted on to indigenous rankings which are many and complex. Most Balinese live in villages that are divided into wards. The ward is the social focus of life for the majority of the population. If the village contains a *Puri*, a palace used by rich Ksatriya or Wesia families, or a *Geria*, the term for Brahmana courtyards, these will form separate units in the village, but there are many Ksatriya or Wesia families who have no political position or economic power and live as ordinary ward members, undifferentiated except in terms of polite address. It seems always to have been true of Bali that caste had no necessary relation to economic or political power. Friederich, who spent two years in Bali in the 1840's, speaking of the Brahmana, says: 'On account of their large number, a considerable portion of them live in extreme poverty, and they do not disdain to cultivate the rice-fields, to engage in the fisheries, and to do manual work for money.' Each ward runs its own affairs as a community of equals, each household has one vote, and all decisions are made or ratified by the entire group. The same sort of egalitarian organisation applies to all Balinese communal activities. All temples have associations, *seka*, which are basically of a democratic nature. So too are irrigation societies which control and maintain the canals and water on which wet rice cultivation

Planting rice seedlings in the rich mud of a *sawah* – rice terrace. The Balinese love of communal work and the tendency to form voluntary groups to perform almost every task are especially apparent in rice cultivation. Even the narrow walls between the terraces are used for bananas and other useful plants.

A temple gate, at Besakih, the mother temple of Bali. Such gates mark the entrance to the ritual areas, they are always approached by steps and protected by guardian figures and a ferocious head on the lintel.

Besakih. The three 'lotus thrones' on the right are dedicated to the Hindu trinity – Brahma, Siwa and Vishnu. In the background are shrines associated with rulers with nine and eleven roofs. The use of height to express both ritual and social status is clear. A small group from a distant village has brought offerings, possibly to intercede for a specific favour.

depends. *Seka* are formed for almost any purpose, from the organisation of orchestras and all sorts of performing arts, dance and drama right down to associations to hunt squirrels. Each *seka* owns property and has rights to subscription and work from all the households that belong to it. It elects officials, decides on the work to be given by the members, and controls its accounts. Some of the larger and richer temple *seka* own wet rice land – *sawah* – and receive income from the cultivation. The ward and *seka* organisations thus present a contrast to the formal hierarchy of castes and etiquette, being essentially egalitarian, both in form and practice, but providing positions, particularly the chairman and the other officials, that are of importance and carry prestige without any reference to caste, the old structure of the Raja's courts, or the modern administrative organisation of the Indonesian state.

Thus Balinese society as perceived from the village is very different from the view from the court and of the *tri-wangsa* generally. For the aristocrats, all is hierarchy with a great elaboration of shades of difference and their expression in very formal terms. For the villager most of his activities are dominated by egalitarian groups in which he has an equal voice to all other members. He will treat the elected officials with respect, but they are elected officials, and he may well become one. The incursions of powerful aristocrats into village life was part of a different social world. As with income tax in our

The central shrine of a *Pura Puseh* in Kamasan. This temple which belongs to a community of silversmiths and painters is used only during *Odalan*. The God images, which have nothing to do with the Hindu gods, are high up in the centre surrounded by offerings brought by the women each on a silver stand. In front are flags and other regalia belonging to the temple including solid silver state umbrellas.

own society, one can dream of a world without it and what could be achieved, but in fact one is accustomed to it and bears the burden. It doesn't alter the ordinary style of life. One may be a different person and behave in a different way when talking to an Inspector of Taxes, but such contacts are remote from real life. So in Bali, the demands and pressures of the wider system of the Raja's courts, or now the Indonesian administration, are occasions for great formality, pageants of hierarchy, but remote from the real life of the courtyard, the ward, the irrigation society and the temple, all of which are groups of conceptual equals. The tension between the extreme of formal hierarchy and its elaborate symbolic expression and the actual egalitarian organisations in which villagers spend most of their working life, radiates throughout Balinese life and is expressed in most of their activities.

Each ward has a meeting place (*bale banjar*) where decisions are made and feasts held. This *bale banjar* is sometimes very elaborate, depending on the prestige and wealth of the community, but it is basically a courtyard, with a large kitchen area, pavilions to provide shade, a shrine at which offerings are made, and usually a gate, which in some cases is so large and decorated that it may rival the gates of temples or princes' palaces.

The village is, then, essentially a collection of wards, but it also has an existence as a political unit. It is part of the state system with a 'chief', who used to be the Raja's representative, but is nowadays partly appointed and partly elected and who acts as the agent of the local administration. The traditional unity of the village is expressed in its common ownership and use of three temples that serve the whole village community. The *pura puseh* is the origin temple; *pura* is the Balinese word for temple, and *puseh* means navel. Here the gods, who go under a variety of names, are clearly the founders of the

Above
Offerings for a marriage. This display is for a small domestic ceremony. The major offerings are made from dyed rice paste, there are also elaborate mannikins made from cut and folded palm frond, piles of cloth and silver utensils. The making of these offerings, often of a bewildering diversity, is an occupation in which some women specialise. Their services are particularly important for such domestic rituals as marriage, tooth filing and cremations. In the background is a painting in traditional style showing scenes from a myth.

Left
For an elaborate cremation, the body is transferred at the burning ground from the tower into a sarcophagus of animal form. The animal must be one appropriate to the caste and status of the family. In the past disputes have arisen when families have used animals that their superiors considered were reserved for them.

For the member of a royal family of Ksatryia caste, the tower is very much larger and more elaborate. The nine roofs indicate the status of the dead man within the Ksatryia caste. The coffin is loaded on the tower from a large ramp built over the walls of the palace. For such magnificent cremations thousands of supporters of the royal family must be mobilised, there are hundreds of invited guests and all the rest of the population for miles around turn up to watch.

A *Pemanku* – temple priest – of the Sudra caste, gets ready to dedicate the offerings at the beginning of an *Odalan*. His equipment of bronze and silver is to his left. Some senior women of the temple community will assist him particularly with the ritual cleansing of the temple. *Pemanku* always operate from the ground while *Pedanda* – Brahmana high priests – always make holy water on an elevated platform.

village and the ancestors of the present population. The second temple is the *pura desa* – village temple – or the *pura bale agung*, literally the temple of the high council. Worship in this temple is concerned with the fertility of the wet rice fields and cultivation generally, and the congregation will include anyone who cultivates in the village area, whether they live in the village or not. Finally, outside the village, usually just by the cemetery, is the death temple – *pura dalem* – concerned with the gods as destroyers and with the recent dead who have been buried and whose spirits will be earthbound until they are dug up and given the proper cremation which will release them for entry into heaven. In addition to these three temples, most villages have many others. Often big *dadia*, extended kin groups united by both birth and residence either present or past, have their own temples for their own ancestors. Different castes or title groups among the Sudras may also have their own temples. These temples can be of every size and importance, some prosperous and enlarging, some deserted or with a handful of worshippers, but they all have their origin in the offering tables, *sanggah*, found in every courtyard, which become enlarged as the descendants of the original courtyard holders stay together and prosper. Many people's descendants fail, through poverty or lack of numbers, to remain as a coherent group and confine their worship to their own courtyard shrine and the large village-wide temple groups.

The Odalan

For each of these temples, there is a priest, the *pemanku*, drawn from the congregation, who is responsible for all the ritual and for dedicating the offerings to the gods of the temple. The most important ritual is the *Odalan*, a three-day festival that must take place on the anniversary of the temple's foundation. The Balinese year has thirty weeks of seven days and is still the

After the dedication of the offerings to them, the Gods are brought down from their high shrine to watch entertainments put on for their benefit. These God images are typical of many in the Klungkung area, they are made of old Chinese coins, with feet, hands and heads carved from sandalwood, they are dressed in rich cloth, with jewelled gold collars; their head-dresses are of fresh flowers topped by flowers made of gold leaf. This is a pair of gods, one male and one female, sharing a single name, the female is on the left but it is extremely difficult to see any differences in the images. This pairing of male and female aspects of a single divinity illustrates the Balinese idea of completeness which is only to be found in the conjunction of male and female.

ritual calendar for virtually the whole of Bali. Every 210 days, the god figures, made of old Chinese coins and sandal wood, are taken from their storage house, which should be high up, certainly above the heads of men, washed and re-dressed in fine garments, ornamented, often with special gold decorations and fresh flowers, and presented with their toilet set and betel chewing equipment which is often a beautifully worked set of silver miniatures. This is a re-enactment of the standard welcome of an honoured guest. They are then placed on the highest level of the central pavilion in the inner courtyard of the temple where they dominate for the next three days, while offerings are made to them and entertainments put on for them. As their initial welcome implies, the gods are basically treated as guests, invited into the temple, and honoured and amused by the congregation, who treat them with the greatest indulgence. But, like all guests, they are not encouraged to over-stay their welcome and, at the end of three days, it is indicated very clearly that it is time for the gods to return to their heaven and leave the mortals to get on with their daily life. In one *Odalan* we attended at a temple in Kamasan, on the evening of the third

Although many entertainments are provided for the gods, and the congregation, they start with a dance of welcome by the women. This performance is a considerable ritual duty. These old dances performed in temples by village women, are the basis from which developed the elaborate court dances performed by specially trained men and women.

In honour of the gods and also to show off their possessions, everyone wears their finest clothes and jewelry at *Odalan*. These girls have tiaras of gold leaf, the bare shouldered style is the traditional Balinese female formal dress, in less formal contexts the whole top of the body for both men and women was bare. The blouses are a Javanese style which is now much encouraged by the Indonesian government.

day, the god figures were taken out of the temple to receive worship and further dedication of offerings outside, and while they were thus distracted, the temple was stripped of all the paintings, decorations and offerings, so that when the gods were brought back, they found only a deserted temple with its grey stone, red brick buildings and pebbled courtyard in place of the magnificent and richly coloured spectacle they had just left. Such hints make the official farewells, which always take place, seem almost unnecessary, and the gods are put away for another 210 days.

The basic form of the *Odalan* is the entertainment of the gods and the dedication of offerings to them. But the entertainment is not only for the gods: the living, too, enjoy the visitors, the dances, the shadow plays and other performances that are staged. Every member of the temple community must come and, for the big temples with membership spread all over the island, as many as one hundred buses and trucks may arrive on any one day, loaded with families in their most beautiful clothes and finest jewelry, all coming to pray to their divine ancestors. The Balinese value a real crush not just as a symbol of success, but for itself; the word *rame* signifies a state in which it is almost impossible to move, and this condition induces direct feelings of pleasure and happiness, regardless of the occasion. I do not know what the Balinese reaction to the London underground in the rush hour would be, probably the purposelessness of the crush and the lack of ability to orientate oneself would be too disturbing for them, but the density of population gets near the Balinese ideal of *rame*.

Before an *Odalan* can take place, the men prepare the decorations of the temple, and the women prepare the offerings. These offerings, which figure in various forms in all rituals, both communal and domestic, are of enormous complexity. There are experts who know literally thousands of different offerings and the correct combinations of offerings for the correct purpose. Their services can be hired for rituals of the domestic life, such as marriage and deaths. For temple *Odalan*, the women of each household make one large offering consisting of a cone-shaped pile of fruit and rice cakes dyed with different colours, often three or more feet high, which they carry on their heads, sometimes in procession, into the temple, where they stay for the three days. In addition to these largest of offerings, there are myriads of smaller offerings, as well as cloth, barbecued chicken and ducks, elaborate forms of coloured fried rice paste that form part of the decorations, and hundreds of small baskets and trays made of palm frond containing usually a few grains of rice of different types, some flowers, and an egg or other sorts of food. Each group that visits during the *Odalan* brings offerings. The more substantial are put up at the feet of the gods and are taken away when the person making the offering goes, but there are also small offerings of cut palm frond and flowers which are left behind on the ground till the courtyard becomes carpeted with these symbols of devotion. The priest sits on mats on the ground in front of the major god house with his bronze bell, silver accoutrements, bowls, flasks containing *arak* (palm or rice spirit) and *berem* (rice wine), as well as the

The God images for a village temple are treated with the greatest respect; except when required for an *Odalan* they are stored in a specially built chamber high above normal village life. As they are removed they are carried on the head as a sign of reverence. They are then washed and dressed before being taken to the temple, where they are welcomed with a special ceremony.

minute posies of flowers which are used, held between the fingers, in all Balinese praying. As each group of offerings comes in, he dedicates them to the gods by chanting *mantras* and wafting the essence of the offerings towards the god house, while the bringers of the offerings kneel behind or beside him and pray, bringing the flowers between their fingers to the forehead and throwing them towards the shrine. People who do not live in the village may only stay an hour or so, the women dedicating the offerings, while the men straighten their accounts with the treasurer of the temple association, so that they can remain members in good standing. The members of the community who live round the temple are those on whom the main burden falls. Their offerings are the largest and most elaborate, and they stay throughout the *Odalan*. They must make all the arrangements and dance and stage all the entertainments, and they should also sleep in the temple at least on the first night.

The *Odalan* as outlined is perfectly adequate and correct, but involves no participation by anyone outside the temple community. A rich temple, however, will secure the services of a Brahmana high priest, a *pedanda*, to make holy water for them, especially on the first day, and also if possible on the third. It is important to realise that the *pedanda* and his holy water are not essential, but highly valued none the less, not only for the prestige that a *pedanda*'s services confers, but because the *tirta* – the holy water – made by a *pedanda* is in itself beneficial to the living and to the ceremony. The *pedanda* is received as befits one of his high status and is seated on a platform inside a pavilion, not as high as the gods, but higher than all the congregation. While he is waiting, senior members of the community engage him in polite conversation, sometimes even now using the most respectful form of address, while sitting at his feet with hands clasped and raised in a gesture of submission and supplication. This sort of exaggerated behaviour is nowadays only found in such ceremonial contexts, where the most refined behaviour and highest etiquette are suitable for the sight of the gods. It has no connection with the actual relationship between the two men: their behaviour is due to the context, not to their personalities.

When most of the congregation has arrived and had their offerings dedicated by the *pemanku* seated on the ground, the *pedanda* will begin making his holy water. The rituals of *pedanda* are many and involved, but basically the first step is to wash the feet, thus severing all contact with the profane earth. The rituals involve complex hand movements and passes with fire, incense, bell and water sprinkling brush. The instruments are of bronze and/or silver and are treated with considerable respect; they should only be carried on the head covered with a white dome. While the *pedanda* is preparing holy water, he is totally ignored by the congregation below him, and the *pemanku* continues his dedications with his bell and paraphernalia. The gestures and *mantras* of the two priests are clearly related in form, but those of the *pedanda* are integrated into a literate theology, ultimately the monotheistic worship of Siva and his manifestation as the sun, shared by many other *brahmana* priests on Bali, and containing many elements deriving from India. The *pemanku* on the other hand, has learnt his movements and dedications from

Offerings to the *butas* and *kalas* for the cleansing of the Klungkung area. The offerings are laid out in the eight directions, each with a minute offering table, with a ninth in the centre. The high priests are in the raised shelter to the left. The offerings are under police guard until the moment when they can be pillaged by the spectators.

his predecessor, is often illiterate, and has beliefs that are mainly polytheistic and concerned with ancestor worship. As the preparation of holy water nears its end, the congregation falls silent, and for the first time takes some notice of the *pedanda*. As the process is completed, everyone takes flowers and makes the gesture of worship three times to the ringing of the *pedanda*'s bell. Then the women and children crowd round him, as he sprinkles them with holy water and presses blessed rice on their foreheads.

Pedandas are always given some of the offerings, particularly flattened grilled ducks on skewers (ducks are the only meat that most *pedandas* may eat), together with fine fruit and sweet cakes; they will also be offered coffee and cakes before they go. *Pedandas* charge for their services, and indeed making holy water is their main source of income, but within a single village there may be traditional relationships of exchange, so that a *pedanda* comes to make holy water at one temple's *Odalan*, and the gong from that temple comes to play when the *pedanda* holds the *Odalan* at his own family temple. It is only at his own family temple that a *pedanda* ever prays on the ground, indicating his inferiority to his ancestors, although even then holy water is made on a raised platform.

Offerings are not only made to the gods, who embody goodness and health, but also to the evil spirits, *butas* and *kalas*, who bring misfortune, sickness and death. These offerings in fact are the first to be made, but far from being beautiful and objects of pride, they include morsels of food, sometimes even bad, that are put on the ground and are instantly eaten by dogs. The *butas* and *kalas* are satisfied by this early offering and keep their polluting presence away. Such cleansing offerings precede all ceremony; for some great occasions, a major cleansing of the whole state or town may take

Gunung Agung, the sacred mountain on whose slopes is Besakih, dominates the landscape, it is the source of holiness and the home of the gods is above it. In contrast the sea is the home of pollution. A village takes its god images and masks with all their regalia down to the sea to cleanse them by transferring any pollution they may have acquired to offerings which are then thrown into the sea. Such processions with their bands, flags, and spears as well as gods empty the village, they should take place once a year but will be more frequent if there is some special cause of pollution such as dissimilar twins.

place. These great ceremonies still occur, for instance before the Balinese New Year, sponsored and paid for by the members of the ruling family. In one such cleansing we saw at Klungkung, the offerings laid out on the ground consisted of substantial quantities of food and cloth, as well as baskets of offerings, many of which contained Chinese coins and other desirable objects. The offerings were arranged in eight clumps corresponding to the cardinal directions, N, NE, E, etc, and a ninth pile in the centre. The offerings in each pile were of the appropriate colour for each direction. Thus north was black, east white, south red, and west yellow. Cloths of the right colour are added to make the identification plain, and the intermediate points have intermediate colours: for instance, northeast has blue. In the centre, all the colours are combined, and a chicken with multicoloured feathers was sacrificed here. For such state occasions, many priests are present, and a raised platform with high priests in a row, all preparing their holy water and sacred fire, is quite usual. The ceremonies at Klungkung had four *pedanda siva* and one *pedanda buda*, but early reports suggest that there used to be eight *pedanda* of whom one was *buda* on such large ceremonies. The *pedanda buda*, who are presumably the remnants of a previous time of Buddhist religion in Bali, and only come from a small group of Brahmana families, have different *mantras* and some differences in the details of the making of holy water, but are not considered in any way in opposition to the *pedanda siva*, the more common type of high priest. For great occasions, particularly those staged by princes, both are essential, again illustrating the acceptance and integration of disparate elements, typical of Balinese culture. The rich and valuable offerings of such great ceremonies are, after dedication, pillaged by the spectators in one mad stampede.

Orientation

The concern with directions is very much an essential part of Balinese religion, but it is also important to every individual, who will become uncomfortable if he does not know his orientation at any particular moment. Although above I have spoken of the north and south, this translation of the Balinese *kaja* and *klod* applies only in south Bali. What the words really mean are 'toward the mountain' and 'towards the sea', so that in north Bali *kaja* is (to us) south, while in south Bali it is north. When moving about, Balinese constantly orientate themselves in relation to *kaja* and *klod*. When motor cars were first introduced, there were reports of Balinese who, unable to follow the twists of the roads at the speed of the car, became seriously distressed and quite ill, until they could again see Gunung Agung, the high and sacred mountain, and could find *kaja* again. So dominant are these fundamental orientations, that they are used not just for describing routes – even in towns nobody says turn left or right, always turn north, and so on – but for all occasions. If one asks of two men walking towards one: 'Which is your brother?', the answer will be: 'the one to the east.' The temples and their various component buildings and pavilions are similarly orientated towards the mountain, and there will always be a special high shrine dedicated to Gunung Agung in the northeast corner of the inner courtyard of every temple. In general, *kaja* is good, holy and beautiful, while *klod* is bad, evil and ugly. The sea is dangerous and the place that receives all the impurity, both physical and spiritual, that the Balinese produce. The ashes of the dead after cremation, all that remains of the mortal flesh, must be thrown into the sea, and when any event has affected a whole area, the gods must be taken to the sea to be cleansed of their impurity. Lesser forms of spiritually dangerous material are merely thrown into running water which conducts it to the sea.

In 1972, soon after we arrived in Kamasan, the whole area was polluted by the birth of opposite sex twins. This disaster is considered to create pollution because of the incestuous proximity of the brother and sister in the womb. Opposite sex twin births only cause pollution among Sudras; it is said that it is welcomed as an auspicious event among the three higher castes, presumably because it reflects their divine origin, incest being a virtually universal practice among gods. For example, one famous line of pre-Madjapait kings was the issue of repeated brother and sister marriages. In the old days, the house of the parents was taken apart and carried outside the village boundaries, where the parents lived miserably till the pollution was cleansed, and where the children always died. Nowadays, the parents continue to live in their house, but in a state of great shame and withdrawal, and in the three cases which occurred while we were there, at least one child died out of every pair. The calamity of different-sex twins creates a state of pollution that suspends all ceremonies and any sort of religious activity for at least six weeks. In 1972, there were three such births in the area covered by the three temples of which Kamasan village was a part, and many *Odalan* had to be postponed and marriages delayed, until the cleansing could be performed. Two of the births were very close together and could be cleansed at the same time, but the disruption of ritual life and forebodings produced by such a spate of twins created a pronounced period of pessimism and distress. For the cleansing, all the god figures from every temple have to be taken down and carried in procession to the sea shore. Each procession has its own gong, and the gods travel on the heads of their bearers, shaded by umbrellas and followed by offerings, till they are all drawn up on the sea shore and the rituals take place. It is important to realise that there is no idea of cleansing by water; on the contrary, the pollution with which they are tainted is transferred by the rituals to the sea which is its natural place, using the medium of offerings, which are thrown into the sea. The gods themselves would be polluted afresh by any contact with sea water. These occasions were genuinely joyous. People's spirits visibly lifted at the disposal of the pollution and the recommencement of that incessant ritual life which seems to occupy every Balinese village.

The cleansing of dissimilar twins on the beach. The offerings are laid out in the cardinal directions – mountain, sea, rising and setting sun, and centre. The *Pedanda* seated on a specially made platform with a white cloth 'roof' is preparing holy water to be applied to the twins and their family. The 'pollution' will be mystically concentrated on the offerings on the ground which will be thrown into the sea. This cleansing must take place six weeks after the birth. At the same time, but on a different part of the beach, the gods of the village are also cleansed and ritual life can then resume.

This dislike of the sea and of close contact with it has had one useful effect in modern times. Even fishing villages build their houseyards at least a few hundred yards from the beach; the intervening space is dry fields, often planted with coconuts. This has suited the tourist industry very well, since the tourists wanted precisely the beachside locations that the Balinese disliked, so that in Sanur or Kuta one now finds a dense tourist belt along the beach, and behind it the Balinese village almost untouched, except for taxis, buses and the ubiquitous motorcycles roaring down the main street. The Balinese believe in reincarnation for the souls of those who have been cremated and reached heaven. In fact, their idea of heaven is rather like an inferior

Bali – they cannot imagine a state that would be preferable to being a live Balinese. The peculiar sequence of births of dissimilar twins in 1972 was explained by one of my friends, the chairman of an important temple community, as follows: 'It's all this birth control, it is cutting down on the number of souls who can get back, so that when one is told it is his or her turn to go and be reincarnated, their friend says "please take me along with you, I am so tired of waiting", so that's why we have all these twin births.' This explanation not only illustrates the idea of reincarnation and the value that Balinese place on their own life and culture, but also is a fine example of their ability to cope with anything new and make it thoroughly Balinese.

Human qualities

It has been said that the Balinese treat their gods, princes and babies all in the same way, that is, with a tolerant indulgence. This is certainly true of the newborn who are ceremonially hailed at birth in the high form of the language, but they are, after all, reincarnated ancestors. The baby receives a great deal of ritual attention, some of which should involve a priest at various stages. At six weeks, the baby and mother are freed from the impurity of birth, the baby's ears are pierced, and he should receive anklets and bracelets of metal. Further ceremonies follow at 105 days and 210 days. These occasions, like all other domestic rituals, must be accompanied by offerings, but the size and number of them, the number of guests and the status of the priest and the ceremonies he performs, are all matters which reflect the aspirations of the family and their ability to pay. Fathers seem almost universally indulgent towards their young children, but mothers often tease their babies after they are a year or so old. They push them away and borrow other women's babies to nurse and cuddle, apparently trying, and certainly succeeding, in driving their own baby into a howling, sobbing tantrum at which they then laugh. This sort of behaviour, which seems less common than when Margaret Mead reported it in the thirties, presumably has something to do with the detachment and control that adult Balinese manifest to such an extraordinary degree.

Babies are not allowed to crawl. There is a horror of appearing to be in any way animal-like, and babies are in no way exempt. When a baby shows signs of wanting to crawl, an older child is assigned to watch it and lift it to its feet when it tries to move: if the baby crawls, the child gets into trouble. Fathers often build little sets of hand rails at baby height in their courtyards, so that the infant can hang on as it sways precariously around. Some babies use a sitting bottom shuffle for a time, which seems to be allowed, but most simply develop walking skills quickly. Every extra 210 days of age after the first can be celebrated, but this is only done on any scale in very prestigious households.

The next major ceremony is the puberty rite of girls. This cleanses the girl from the pollution of first menstruation, and at the same time makes all aware that she is now a woman of marriageable age. She appears superbly dressed and decorated as an adult woman and has to make a suitable change in her general behaviour. Shortly after puberty, both boys and girls should have their teeth filed. Teeth filing is widely reported throughout the world and in other parts of Indonesia: in Bali it seems linked again to the suppression of animality. The Balinese in their art seem obsessed with fangs, not only animals such as pigs, which do actually have tusks, but all animals, for instance deer and even fish are portrayed with sharp curving fangs. Similarly all the evil spirits, the *butas* and *kalas*, the women who transform themselves into witches, *leyak*, the *raksasas*, who are coarse and dangerous, but may serve as guardians of temples, are all shown with huge fangs, and some have extra fangs growing through their cheeks and from their foreheads. Pointed, long and irregular teeth are thus associated with animals and evil spirits, and the filing of teeth is an essential duty. The object is to produce flat, even teeth, the opposite of the curved pointed fang. Teeth filing should be performed at puberty for both sexes. If it has been omitted, it is often combined with the marriage ceremony, so that the young couple have their teeth filed together before they are married, thus combining two ceremonies into one to save on offerings and the feeding of guests. In a family that has had recent good luck, a tooth filing with invited guests may be arranged for a group of adolescents and young adults, but when the expert turns up (nowadays some use flexi-drive carborundum wheels), various middle-aged or old men and women will suddenly remember that they have never had it done and hop up on the elaborate public bed to present their teeth for attention. If by any chance the teeth have not been filed before death, it is the duty of the descendants to ensure that it is done before burial or cremation, since otherwise the deceased, having never been really human, can have no chance of attaining heaven and reincarnation as a human being.

The Balinese view the body as essentially a set of limbs, trunk and head that are only loosely articulated and almost capable of independent life, certainly of independent movement. They imagine graveyards as being inhabited, among other horrors, by disembodied arms and legs, each with their own face. Balinese dance and particularly the developed courtly dances, such as the *legong*, involve gestures and movements which exemplify this view of the body to the highest degree: sometimes, watching such a dance, it is difficult to believe that the arms are really firmly attached to the body. This suppleness is not only the prerequisite of professional dancers, it is part of everybody's life, and the movements are valued by all Balinese. Our daughter, for instance, was taught every time she washed to press her fingers back and perform other exercises to increase flexibility and maintain the ability to move each finger separately. Similar drills are encouraged in children of both sexes and are essential if they are to perform the dances necessary to honour the gods in the *Odalan*.

Skill in movement is not confined to dance: it is important and valued at every level and in every activity. Men and women must walk, move and make gestures in the correct and graceful way for their sex, but they should also be able to imitate the other sex's movements. Manual skills in Bali are similarly very highly developed and of a high order, but they are not considered exceptional. The man who lays the bricks for a new gateway should also be capable of carving the soft grey stone into fantastic faces to serve as the guardian of the gate. More recently, the introduction of the European style concept of 'fine art' has led to some distinction between artists and craftsmen, and many aristocrats and some Sudras now earn their living by the production of art in our sense. In most of Bali however, craft activities, based on the household, continue to produce not only a very wide variety of useful objects, but also many things of real beauty and distinction, without involving the idea of individual creativity at all. The possession of high skills is not considered surprising. They are developed within the family and passed on from generation to generation, and there is a very high degree of family specialisation. Some families are blacksmiths or silversmiths and such obvious specialisations, but there are an enormous number of other specialisations that are more surprising: weavers of hats or even of conical rice strainers. Each family jealously guards its skills, which may form its only source of cash, except for paid labouring, and takes its specialised product to the markets which proliferate at every level from village up. Where girls have special skills, such as in colouring traditional paintings, there is a great deal of care taken about their marriages, since not only is there a danger of losing their skills, but even greater danger of someone else acquiring them, and thus breaking into the trade of painting. Under these circumstances, the already general tendency of Balinese to marry with close kin becomes even more exaggerated, and in Kamasan, for instance, the two wards of Sanaging and Pande Mas have cores of families of painters and silversmiths where marriage with an outsider cannot be remembered. Such highly cohesive groups, if they remain commercially successful, often become a dominant force in village politics, and influential in the whole area. In this case the group expresses their position not by any individual ostentation, but in a very Balinese way through the magnificence of the *Odalan* at their temple *Bale Batur*, the quality of the performers they hire for the occasion, the extensions they undertake on the temples and the value of the temple property, which includes two solid silver umbrellas.

Balinese religion is inseparable from being Balinese: if one is not attached to the right temples, where one performs one's rituals and labour duties, one is not Balinese. When under Dutch rule, some converts were made by Christian missions, they were declared dead by their families and considered to have forfeited all rights in the family property. After lengthy court cases and much bitterness, the Dutch finally forbade mission work on the island. Although there are some Christian missions on the island now, they have had little success. Nor has Islam made any inroads. Although there are a few established Moslem communities on the island, they are not regarded by the Balinese as Balinese, even though Balinese is their mother tongue, and their ancestors have lived there for generations. Since they do not worship at temples, they cannot be Balinese. In this sense, the Balinese community is completely closed – only those born and bred Balinese can be Balinese, and this, of course, fits well with the dogma of reincarnation. But if all the ancestors are reincarnated and there is, so to speak, a limited stock of Balinese souls, which is constantly recycled to provide the present population, who are the ancestors that are worshipped in the temples? The actual figures that are treated with such indulgence and are the focus of the *Odalan* ceremonies have

names, but these names are not those of any gods. Although Brahmana often identify the gods of the temples with gods of the Hindu pantheon, even they admit that these identifications are meaningless to the worshippers. There is little doubt that these god figures stand for the deified ancestors of the community, but for generalised and not specific ancestors. The god figures always occur in pairs, one male and one female, who share a single name. The figures themselves are often so alike in form and costume, that it is very difficult to know which is male and which female. In fact, the only reliable way of differentiating them is by their earrings: women have a round plug earring and men one that decorates the whole outer edge of the ear. This pairing of the sexes represents the two aspects of humanity that are united in divinity, but also emphasises the ancestral aspect of these gods. In most temples, along with the fully developed god figures, are sets of smaller images, often simply a face in beaten gold or painted in black on a shaped piece of gilded wood. These may not be named, but are, or were once, images of actual ancestors used as substitutes for them in one of the elaborate series of ceremonies involving cremation, and later added to the figures which serve as the focus of worship.

Facing page
Burial of an old Sudra woman. The grave having been filled and returfed is covered with one of the major body symbols, made of palm frond. A close relative leaves some offerings by the head of the grave. On the third day further offerings will be made and thereafter at the annual *Galungan* festival offerings will be renewed until the bones are dug up and cremated.

Cremation

The cremation of the dead is a religious duty, for only when people are cremated can their souls be released to heaven. The body of a *pedanda* must not touch the profane earth and must be cremated without burial. Most people are buried, as a temporary expedient only, and their relatives must disinter their bones and cremate them. In the old days, the bodies of princes and their families were sometimes kept above ground for years before they were cremated, thus avoiding the odium of being buried, and giving time to raise the necessary resources to stage a suitably lavish cremation. At even the simplest burial by the poorest family, two features are apparent. First, that the corpse,

Galungan occurs once every Balinese year – 210 days – at which ancestors are invited to revisit their households and are entertained by their descendants. The uncremated dead are also remembered by offerings made at their graves.

If a dead person is to be cremated straight away without burial it is usual for the party carrying the corpse to the cremation tower to be intercepted by other members of the ward. The fight over the body that follows is an occasion for behaviour by men that is the opposite of their normal refined polite behaviour. The struggling and shoving mass of men is kept cool by water thrown over them by bystanders but trance states are frequent. This is one of the few occasions when men can relax from the rigid code of correct behaviour that otherwise dominates their lives. Eventually the corpse, carefully protected by bamboo lathes, is got aboard the cremation tower, the fighting stops and the fighters unite to carry the tower to the place of cremation.

The towers used in *Mukur* are all white, yellow and gold. They are used to carry the ashes down to the sea. They are however not burnt but thrown into the sea or left to disintegrate on the beach.

Above
Although all the physical body has been cremated and the ashes thrown into the sea, religious duty requires that dead relatives should be cremated a second time at the *Mukur* ceremony. *Mukur* often involves a whole village and thousands of ancestors. Small body symbols are made and burnt in pottery vessels, and the ashes treated in much the same way as those of real cremations.

Right
The final act of cremation, a man throws the ashes of his grandmother into the breaking surf. In the background is Nusa Penida a dry island traditionally used as a place of exile, and believed to be infested by many demons.

even newly dead, is given offerings of food and drink: sometimes a hole is dug by the head of the corpse three days after it has been buried, into which drink is poured. Second, symbols of the body start to be given ritual attention. An image of the body, made with strips of palm frond with decorations of flower at the joints, is laid on the body and later over the grave. It is merely the first of a long series of symbols of the deceased that are made for all the following rituals. As cremation of either an unburied corpse or disinterred bones is by far the most expensive of all the domestic rituals, in poor villages, communal cremations of hundreds of recently dead may be organised with each family sharing in some of the expenses. The duty of burning the bones is inescapable and must be performed by the individual family members for their own ancestors. Offerings are made to the corpse or bones at every stage, and many of these consist of symbols of the body of the dead.

Basically, cremations have three parts: the proper treatment of the body and the dedication of symbols of it at the death temple. Then the placing of the remains in a cremation tower and transporting it to the cemetery, where the remains are transferred to a sarcophagus of animal form and burnt. Finally the ashes are collected, there are further rituals of purification and creation of further body symbols before the ashes are thrown into the sea. Every aspect of these ceremonies can be immensely elaborate or very simple. There can be many *pedandas* or none: in fact, cremations are a real measure of a family's wealth and cohesiveness and of the justification for its claims to high prestige. But there are certain minimal elements in all cremations. The treatment of the remains and the creation of symbols of the body and the soul already have elements of worship, and each member of the family takes a farewell in an attitude of prayer. At the origin temple one of the principal body symbols, a container of a coconut, which will later hold the ashes, and other symbolic objects, all wrapped in white cloth, are carried by a young close relative in a baby sling exactly as if it were a real baby. This and other body symbols are blessed and purified by the *pemanku* and later lead the procession with the cremation tower to the burning ground. The carrying of the corpse from its house to the tower is started by the family, but as they emerge from the houseyard, they are attacked by men from the ward, and an extraordinary fight over the corpse ensues. The corpse, done up with strong bamboo laths to a cigar shaped package, tosses and sways as men charge one way and the other, sometimes losing complete control of themselves as this extraordinary ritualised fight continues. Eventually the party trying to get the corpse to the tower wins, and the fight stops. The fight is said to confuse the corpse and prevent its soul finding its way back home to haunt the family, but it is also said that the men of the ward try to prevent the corpse leaving as an expression of their sorrow at the death. Whatever the explanation, it is certainly a time when the normal rules of polite behaviour vanish and, in both gestures and action, men express that aggression which has no outlet in ordinary life.

With the remains in position on the tower, the men who fought now pick it up and carry it away: when there is no corpse, only bones, there is no fighting, but the tower is twirled and whirled around on its way to the

A small cremation tower on its way to be burnt crosses a river. The body is on the platform just under the roof.

As the body in its sarcophagus is set alight, so are the tower and all the other constructions made for the cremation, all the offerings and symbols of the body are also thrown on to the pyre.

cemetery to confuse the remains. It is the carrying of the tower that demands resources beyond the family. For even the poorest cremation, several dozen men are necessary, and help from the men of the ward, if not the whole village, is essential. The helpers must be provided with at least food and drink, and this forms the major part of the cost of the simplest cremation. For a large cremation, the tower can become immense, with hundreds of men needed to carry it, while the sarcophagus and other paraphernalia require dozens more. At the place of burning, the corpse is moved to the sarcophagus, if there is one, otherwise it is burnt with the tower. Final rites are performed, and the remains are drenched in holy water, before being burnt. The ashes and incompletely burnt pieces are collected and ground with a sugar cane pestle before being put into the coconut, remade into a body image, and given further ritual treatment before being carried, again in a baby sling, down to the shore, where a close relative throws them as far as he can into the waves.

Cremations are joyous affairs, the proper launching of the soul on its journey is a cause for celebration. The towers are in the brightest colours, and the animal sarcophagi often amusing as well as beautiful. But the duty of descendants is still not over, although nothing remains of the actual corpse. Fresh sets of body symbols should be made, and the whole cremation process repeated in a ritual known as *mukur*. This time it is only the symbols that are burnt and thrown into the sea. These second cremations are much rarer and usually only take place if a group of families decide that the time is ripe and pool their resources. All their retainers, tenants and traditional associates seize the opportunity and add their relatives to the ceremony. At one we attended,

The full burning of the body takes some hours, the ashes are carefully collected and any bone fragments ground up so that all that is left of the body is a fine powder. At this stage the process of making new symbols of the body starts again. They also make, of cloth and branches, a symbolic house for the spirit of the deceased – on the extreme right. With the family gathered round, a final series of ceremonies takes place, in this case with a *Pedanda* on his elevated platform preparing holy water. Gunung Agung, the holy mountain, associated with the heaven to which it is hoped the soul will gain admittance, is the pure direction. The ceremony is however within a few yards of the sea in the opposite direction for which the physical remains are destined.

well over a thousand souls received their second cremation. The *mukur* towers are slimmer than those for cremations, and the colours are only white, yellow, and gold, creating a stunning effect, especially in mass. It is from the images recreated for *mukur* that come the gold faces, that eventually reach the family shrines to be worshipped as gods.

Men and women

As we have seen, Balinese god figures come in pairs, the male and female barely distinguishable from each other, and, as with the gods, so it is in life. There are clearly defined costumes for each sex; there are sets of roles considered suitable for each sex, and a division of labour considered normal in domestic and agricultural work, but these are not rigid boundaries. There are virtually no roles that only men can play, and vice-versa. Men and women work on the roads or do portering jobs together and develop the same muscles doing so, although men carry on their shoulders and women on their heads. Women learn and perform men's dances in men's costumes, and this is taken perfectly seriously. Men do perform women's dances, except the *legong*, but these tend to be comic performances. There are women *pemanku*, and many women are mediums and healers. When a new Brahmana high priest is consecrated, his wife and/or sister is consecrated as well. These women, known as *pedanda istri*, usually help the *pedanda*, but they can perform all the rituals themselves and may do so after the death of the man. There are also *pedanda istri* who have their own practice and were consecrated in their own right. In the work of the various associations, it is households that are members and provide the labour, and a woman is as good as a man for discharging the labour obligations. The list could go on, but the point is simple. There are virtually no roles that are totally restricted, in theory or fact, to one sex to the exclusion of the other. This does not mean that there are no sex differences; men and women habitually choose to display different styles of behaviour and engage in different activities. This is perhaps most noticeable in the area of refined behaviour. For men to be refined, withdrawn, imperturbable is a continuous obligation. Except for moments of special licence, such as fighting over the corpse, men must be gentle, non-aggressive and unfailingly polite. Women, too, on important social and ceremonial occasions appear in the same way, moving with incredible grace and flicking langorous glances as well, but the constraint on them is not so absolute. Women in their ordinary clothes on the way to market, for instance, shout, laugh, get angry and hurl the most breathtaking abuse at each other and at men. Many women, too, appear as domestic tyrants, shouting and bullying their husbands and children, while the men only mumble or try to take no notice. The markets, which are dominated by women, present a totally different atmosphere and sort of behaviour, jolly, argumentative and noisy, to the ceremoniousness and low conversation typical of meetings of men. The strain of continual refinement must be heavy for the men. Although some rituals provide short periods of violent release, it goes some way to explaining the sudden outbursts of insane violence, both for individuals who may suddenly run amok, and for whole communities, such as the terrible killings that took place in many parts of Bali after the abortive communist coup in 1965.

Facing page
Beside the symbolic house of cloth a close relative nurses the coconut swathed in cloth which contains the ashes. The ashes are treated like a baby often being carried in a baby sling, thus indicating very clearly the expectation that the dead person will be reincarnated soon as a member of the same family.

Similarly the 'fight to the death' which so surprised the Dutch troops in 1906, but which appears to have always been the correct behaviour for defeated Balinese armies.

In public and in ceremonial, the Balinese are in one sense continually acting in a beautiful, gracious and never-ending play, a play that covers all life and the after-life as well; the episodes may be serious, comic or tragic, but they are always beautiful, always graceful, always well staged. Their whole culture is a communal work of art; the effect to the outsider is entrancing. The Balinese, too, seem in love with the perfection of their own performances and the beauty of their culture, which is probably more threatened by the rationality of the modern Indonesian nation state than by the millions of tourists who come to glimpse briefly fragments of a superb performance.

Further reading

BATESON, G. and MEAD, M. *Balinese character: a photographic analysis* New York: Lyceum of Natural History now Academy of Sciences, 1942.

BELO, J. ed. *Traditional Balinese culture* Columbia University Press, 1970.

COVARRUBIAS, M. *The Island of Bali* New York: Knopf; London: Cassell, 1937.

DE ZOETE, B. and SPIES, W. *Dance and drama in Bali* OUP (East Asia) 1938; n.e. 1974.

FRIEDERICH, R. H. T. *The civilisation and culture of Bali* edited by E. R. Rost. Calcutta: S. Gupta, 1959. (Originally published in Batavia, 1849–50, in Dutch).

GEERTZ, C. *Deep play: notes on the Balinese cockfight* in *Daedalus* Winter 1972.

GEERTZ, H. and C. *Kinship in Bali* University of Chicago Press, 1975.

The Kayapó of Central Brazil

Chapter Nine

by Terence S. Turner

Location, ecology settlement pattern and population

The Kayapó Indians inhabit a large area of Central Brazil, lying south of the Amazon between the Araguaya and Tapajós rivers and extending south to the headwaters of the Xingú. Their territory was one of the last areas of Brazil to be penetrated by elements of Brazilian national society: the western Kayapó groups were peacefully contacted only in 1958, and one small group remained uncontacted until 1971.

Brazilian ranchers seeking new land exert continual pressure on Indian land.

In common with many other Amazonian Indian societies, the Kayapó suffered considerable losses of land and population before and since the establishment of peaceful relations with the Brazilians. Encroachments by ranchers and wild rubber- and nut-gatherers, occasional massacres (in which the Kayapó sometimes gave as good as they got), several disastrous epidemics, and the forced removal of some groups from their traditional lands all played their part. Over the last decade, however, the population has again been on the increase (thanks in part to improved medical assistance from the Brazilian government and missionary groups to some villages) and most communities appear to have held their own economically.

Barring further expropriations or thefts of land by private or governmental agencies, or new epidemics without adequate medical assistance, the Kayapó give every indication of being on the road to survival and successful adaptation to coexistence with Brazilian society. This is in large part the result of the spirit of the Kayapó themselves and the resilience of their institutions, which have enabled them to maintain the integrity of their communities and preserve their social and ritual organisation. The reader should understand that the institutions and practices described in this essay are not mere relics of a crumbling cultural past, but integral parts of a living contemporary society which has retained its vigour and integrity under formidably adverse conditions.

There are today nine Kayapó villages, varying in population between eighty and over four hundred (at the time of first contact, two villages were reported to have around 1,500 each). The overall population is about 2,000.

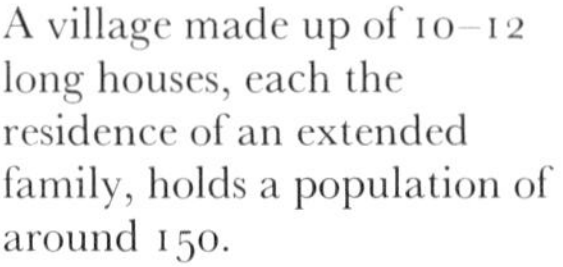

A village made up of 10–12 long houses, each the residence of an extended family, holds a population of around 150.

PANAMA
VENEZUELA
ATLANTIC OCEAN
GUIANA
SURINAM
GUYANA
COLOMBIA
EQUADOR
BRAZIL
PERU
Xingu National Park
Brasilia
BOLIVIA
PACIFIC OCEAN
PARAGUAY
CHILE
ARGENTINA
URUGUAY
River Xingu
River Mancava-Micu
Xingu National Park
River Suia-Micu
Zachary Guedes

Each village is an autonomous social, political, and ceremonial unit; there is no inter-village or tribal political or ritual structure, such as is possessed by a number of other tribes of the same region. The villages are situated on watercourses in mixed forest and savannah or open grassland country. The environment is rich in fish, game and wild plant products. The Kayapó exploit these aspects of their natural environment by fairly intensive hunting, fishing and gathering. Part of every year, the whole village goes off on prolonged hunting-and-gathering treks lasting one or two months. There may be two or three such treks in a single year. The rest of the time is spent in the base village, where the main economic activity is agriculture of the 'slash-and-burn' variety common among primitive societies inhabiting forested areas.

In the slash-and-burn method, a patch of forest is cut down, and the felled trees and brush, after being allowed to dry for several months in the sun, are burned. Crops are planted directly in the clearing thus created without prior tillage of the soil, by means of a digging stick. After three years, the growth of weeds and the diminution of the fertility of the soil make it more

Kayapo villages are built near rivers, which are used for daily bathing and children's play as well as for fishing, transportation, and as sources of water.

Felled trees are left to dry before burning off to clear the garden for planting.

profitable to clear and burn off a new plot than to continue cultivating the old. In this way, families continually shift the location of their gardens. Land is in plentiful supply, and is not held as property. Whoever clears and plants the garden has the use of its crops while it is in production, but afterwards it simply reverts to the common pool of potential garden land. After twenty years or so, when it has grown back to forest, anyone can clear it again for a new garden.

As the use of the slash-and-burn agricultural technique implies, there is a large amount of land in proportion to population. Villages are on the average 150 miles apart, with the land between them almost entirely uninhabited by other tribes. Population density is thus extremely low. The pattern of population distribution is one of moderately large, socially self-contained settlements, each surrounded by a vast area of wild country, which is periodically exploited through the collective hunting-and-gathering treks made by each community. There are no territorial boundaries, in the sense of

A Kayapo mother spends much time grooming and painting her children ('dressing them up' as it were). Here one of the children returns the favour.

delineated hunting-and-gathering territories belonging to a single community, but the distance between villages makes them unnecessary. There is plenty of land to go around, and no one needs to poach on anyone else's home grounds.

The structure of Kayapó society

The family: basic set of roles

Kayapó villages consist of an open circle of houses surrounding a wide central plaza. There is normally one men's house, or sometimes, in large villages, two men's houses, in the middle of the plaza. The houses around the periphery of the village circle are often called, in contrast, the 'women's houses'. They are family houses, or, more precisely, *extended family* households, and are thought of as 'belonging' to the women who dwell in them.

The organisational principle of these extended family households is simple. A woman remains for her whole life a resident of the house into which she was born (her mother's house), while a man must move out of his mother's house and into his wife's house upon marriage. This means that all of a woman's daughters, and all of her daughters' daughters, should remain under the same roof, together with their husbands and children (that is, their respective *restricted* families). After three or four generations, the household tends to split, with the more closely related groups of sisters setting up household together next door to one another. The whole set of *restricted* families formed by the marriages of such a related group of women in a single household comprises the *extended* family.

The restricted families that go to make up an extended family household remain distinct social and economic units within it. Each family has its own sleeping and eating area. Each mother has her own gardens (all gardens are said to 'belong', during their productive life, to the woman of the family that clears, plants and harvests them), and she harvests and cooks food from them for her own immediate family. In this she is assisted by her unmarried daughters. Her husband brings his game or fish to her for distribution to kinfolk (both hers and her husband's), some of whom live within and some outside the household. She always keeps a portion for her own restricted family and cooks only that portion (the rest is distributed raw).

Aside from the daily care and harvesting of the gardens and the gathering of wild products in the immediate vicinity of the village, the main activity of women is the care and socialisation of young children. Women's economic tasks of gardening and gathering are, not by coincidence, the main economic activities capable of being performed by someone simultaneously charged with looking after a child. Men's tasks (hunting, fishing, and long-distance gathering expeditions, not to mention raiding) are by contrast, those that are the least compatible with child care. The female occupations of gardening and gathering are also the most plentiful and reliable in terms of output, and are therefore the most easily manageable in terms of the organisation of production, distribution and consumption. This manageability is socially exploited to channel women's economic activites at the simplest or lowest level of social organisation, the individual restricted family. This is also the level within which women's socialisation (child care) activities are concentrated. I use the terms 'simplest' or 'lowest level' in the sense of the simplest,

Young children accompany their mothers during 'working hours'. Boys soon learn to play with one another in separate groups, but little girls stay with their mothers and play at imitating them. In this way their play merges into training for adult women's work.

most restricted grouping. This is, in Kayapó society, the individual restricted family, consisting of a single monogamous couple and their children. The extended family or the collective village institutions to be discussed below constitute *higher* levels of social organisation in these terms. It is at these higher levels that male economic activities, such as the distribution of hunting, fishing, and gathering produce, as well as male-dominated socialisation functions such as initiation and other transitions in the post-childhood adolescent and adult phases of the life cycle, are focused.

In terms of sheer volume, e.g. the proportion of total food consumption or total time spent on socialisation, women's economic and socialisation contributions far outweigh men's. This quantitative preponderance of female production in both modes, however, is not reflected in the social position of women *vis-à-vis* men. Men dominate Kayapó society as a whole, not because they contribute more to it in quantitative terms, but because their contributions are associated with the higher levels of social structure, while women's contributions are, as we have seen, associated with the lowest level: the restricted family unit organised primarily around the care and socialisation of young children. In any complex organisation, the higher levels of organisation exercise control over the lower levels: men therefore exercise control over women.

Manioc is split and left to dry in the sun.

Women hand spin cotton onto wooden spindle spools.

The basis of the dominance and control of men over women in the social organisation of productive activities, and particularly in the organisation of family and extended family roles, is an important point for the understanding of Kayapó social organisation as a whole. The reason for this is that the structure of the extended family, which as we shall see is the basic point of reference for the structure of Kayapó society as a whole, is based squarely on the exploitation of men's control over women in order to control other (younger) men. Specifically, this means the exploitation of the control over young women exercised by their fathers, and to a more limited degree, their mothers, as a basis for getting control over their husbands, who are forced to move in with the parents of the young women. In the absence of property in land, livestock, or other resources that might serve as extrinsic bases of social control, Kayapó society has resorted to the exploitation of a class of its own members (young women) as the basis for developing a relatively complex, stratified society based on the domination of young men (and women) by older men (and, to a lesser extent, older women).

The extended family household

The members of an extended family household can be divided into three broad generational categories. First come children, who are still members of their first, or *natal family*, that is, the restricted family into which they were born. Second come parents, that is, mothers and fathers with dependent children. They are members of their second family, their *family of procreation*, that is, the restricted family in which they have children. Third and last come the grandparents, who stand in the relation of parents-in-law to the father and no longer have a restricted family of their own in the sense of a procreative unit consisting of parents and young children. They have, however, something which counts

Boys are left to play on their own from an early age. Girls, on the other hand, remain close to their mothers and play by imitating their work.

Children are elaborately painted and decorated. Red is used on the face, and black designs frequently used for the body.

Above
Men gather for dancing in the men's hut.

Right
Ropni, one of the leaders, speaks Portuguese and runs most of the contact diplomacy with the Brazilians.

for far more in terms of social prestige among the Kayapó: the status of heads of *extended* families and, therefore, of households.

This status may be thought of as having both a positive and a negative aspect, both of which are equally valued. On the positive side, as parents-in-law, the grandparental couple receive the deference of the in-marrying sons-in-law. The basis of this deference is the simple fact that the parents-in-law still exercise residual control over their daughters. This control is sufficient to prevent the removal of the daughters from the extended family by their husbands, and thus to compel the husbands to join the household of the daughters' parents. In their capacity as new, subordinate household members, sons-in-law must render various economic services to the parents-in-law such as helping to slash and plant their gardens, helping repair the house, and

Kukrut, a grandfather, works at basketry, an exclusively male speciality; his daughter and grandchildren work behind him.

contributing fish, game, and certain manufactured articles like baskets and mats. This relationship is accompanied by an attitude of extreme respectful inhibition on the part of the sons-in-law, who during the first few years of courtship and marriage avoid as far as possible speaking or eating in the presence of their parents-in-law (if they do speak, it is very softly and with downcast eyes). This behaviour is reciprocated, but to a much weaker degree, by the parents-in-law, who may and do speak directly to the sons-in-law and eat freely in front of them.

The other, negative aspect of the prestige of the parents-in-law is that, as household heads, they are no longer, in the man's case, subject to the constraints of being the subordinate son-in-law, or, in the woman's case, to the constraints implicit in her role as the instrument of the control exercised by her parents over her husband. Both grandfather and grandmother, in their roles as parents-in-law rather than as parents, are, in short, 'free' in terms of the constraints upon which the structure of the Kayapó extended family household rests. Both are, by the same token, able to exercise a measure of pre-eminence or dominance over the junior members of that structure. That is why both men and women of this senior age category are far more assertive and expressive in their social behaviour than younger people of either sex. This age-grade hierarchy, as we shall also see, serves as the basic structure of the political system of the community as a whole.

Facing page
Kumàyt is a member of the older sub-division of the mature men's or father's age set and has sons-in-law of his own.

Foot of page
The men's hut stands at the centre of the village, in spatial and social contrast to the women's houses (the extended family dwellings) around the periphery of the village plaza.

The men's house and the women's communal society

In the centre of the village plaza, as we have already noted, stands a men's house, or in large villages two men's houses. The number of men's houses makes no difference to the internal structure of the men's house as such; I shall describe the structure of a single men's house, but the same description would apply to both men's houses in a double men's house community.

Boys are taken from their maternal households to live in the men's house when they are still very young, usually around the age of eight.

They remain residents of the men's house until they make themselves fathers by impregnating a girl to whom they are 'engaged' or who, at least, is willing and able to marry them as a result. Upon becoming fathers in their own right, and therefore, in Kayapó terms, husbands in the full sense (for the Kayapó regard pregnancy, rather than mere sexual intercourse, as the consummation of marriage), they move out of the men's house and take up residence in their wives' households.

Removal to the household of his wife does not, however, terminate a young man's association with the men's house: rather, it marks the beginning of its most important, adult phase. The men's house is in effect divided into two halves corresponding to the two broad age categories of unmarried youths and mature men or 'fathers' (the literal meaning of the Kayapó term for the adult male age category). Men of the 'fathers'' age grade, although they no longer live in the men's house, organise themselves into one or more societies, each headed by one or more chiefs. The members of these societies use the men's house as a club house, where they can pass the time of day together or separately, talking, making artifacts, or merely sitting, smoking and watching the passing scene. The most characteristic men's house activity for men of this age grade, however, are collective gatherings, when the whole 'fathers' society sits together at the front of the house (the open side facing the centre of the plaza) and listens to oratory by its senior members and leaders (chiefs). These gatherings, which usually happen several times a week in the afternoon or evening, constitute the political assemblies and tribunals of the community. The 'fathers' men's societies and their chiefs are, in short, the *de facto* and *de jure* political entities of Kayapó society. Oratory and the articulation of collective decisions by the chiefs, who are primarily defined as the leaders of the 'fathers' societies, are the main public forms of the political process. It should be clear that by 'political' I mean all of the conventionally distinguished aspects of political activity: legislative, executive and judicial functions, and the exercise of leadership, authority, influence and power.

Closer observation of the meetings of the 'fathers' societies reveals significant differences in the degree and type of participation of their members of different ages. These differences appear above all in oratory and the organisation and performance of collective rituals and hunting-and-gathering treks. A new member of a 'fathers' society (say, a young husband with one or two young children, of the sub-age grade the Kayapó call 'fathers of few children', or alternatively 'young fathers') rarely takes an active role in any of the activities of his society. His role is rather that of the passive listener, whose consent is important in the overall concensus that ideally forms the basis of all collective acts of the society, but who plays no active part in shaping that concensus through speaking or personal leadership. These more dynamic aspects of the adult male role are exemplified by the behaviour of the older sub-age grade which the Kayapó call 'fathers of many children'. The members of this sub-grade are men whose children have begun to come of age. Their older sons will already have moved to the men's house, and their older daughters will already have begun to be courted by potential husbands. They are, in short,

Ropni works on a feather headress in the men's hut.

men either on the threshold of father-in-law-hood and grandfather-hood, or who have already actually achieved these statuses (which are, as we have seen, merely two sides of the same coin, given the Kayapó principle that marriage is only consummated by childbirth).

A third sub-age grade composed of the oldest men, those aged enough to have become semi-dependants in their own households upon their own daughters and sons-in-law (who, as a rule will by this time have already attained the dominant adult status of fathers-of-many-children), may often be observed sitting a little apart from the other men, taking little active part in the ordinary activities of their society. These elders, however, are apt to give orations at key points in public controversies, or during ceremonies, when it is thought most important and beneficial to have the wisdom and judgement of those whose fund of experience and social detachment places them above the level of particular conflicts, and best qualifies them to direct the performance of collective ceremony.

Just as the adult men of the 'fathers'' age grade are divided into a series of sub-grades with distinctive modes of public behaviour, so the

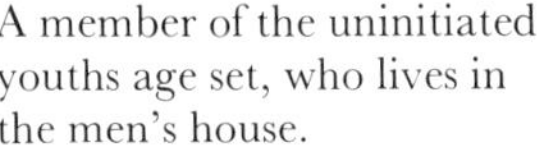

A member of the uninitiated youths age set, who lives in the men's house.

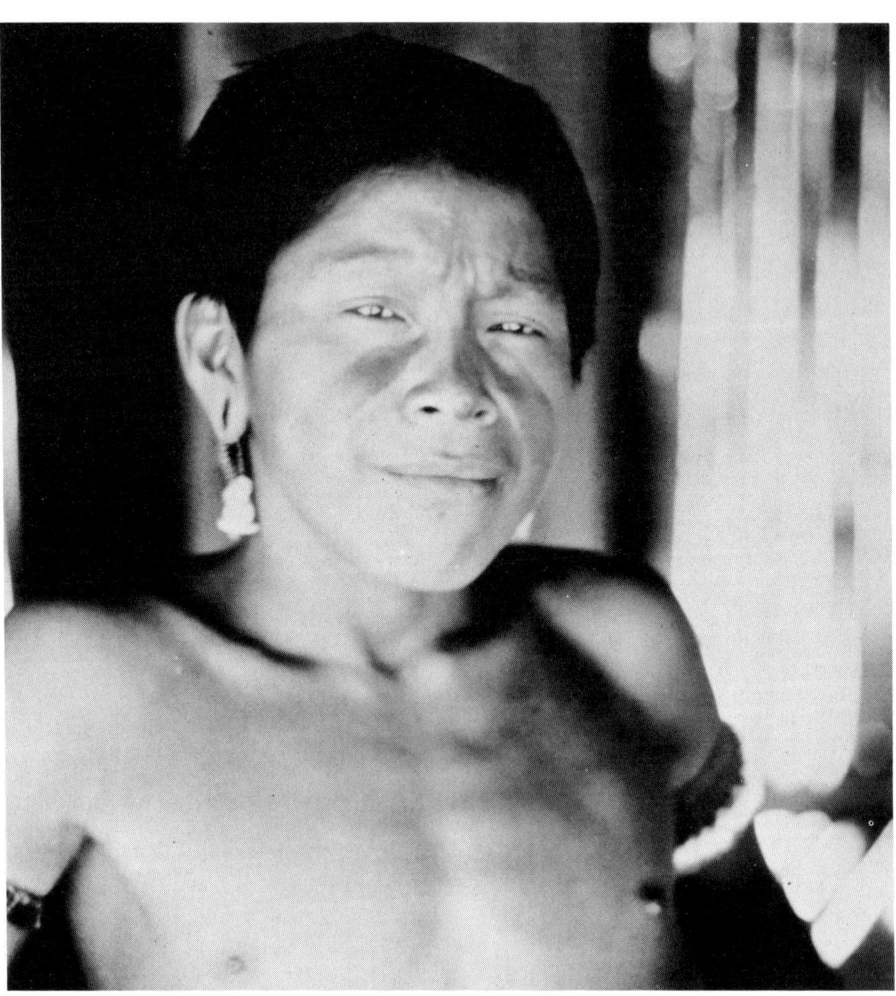

youths and older boys residing in the men's house are divided into the sub-grades of uninitiated and initiated youths. The former category consists of boys from the time of their first induction into the men's house until their initiation, which occurs perhaps half-a-dozen years later, about the age of fourteen. Initiation consists, above all, in a symbolic marriage ceremony. I say 'symbolic' because it is not expected that the initiates will actually marry and set up housekeeping with the girls with whom they go through the ceremony. Rather, the ceremony consists of a public recognition of the youths' general marriageability, or in concrete terms, their ability to begin their own courtships and affairs, leading ultimately to a real marriage with the wife of their choice. Youths of this age grade may be characterised as 'bachelors', that is, marriageable men who are not yet married, in contrast to the younger, as yet unmarriageable uninitiated boys with whom they share the men's house as a residence.

The courtships and sexual liaisons of the 'bachelors' follow a strict social form, which has as its main point to render them socially 'invisible', that is, to avoid public recognition and forestall the readjustments of social relations that would be required by full-scale marriage. 'Bachelors' are supposed to creep to their sweethearts' or fiancées' houses only in the dead of night, and after sleeping with them, to creep back again to the men's house before the crack of dawn, 'so that they won't be seen by their prospective mothers-in-law'. The prospective mothers-in-law, of course, know perfectly well what is going on. The point of the arrangement is that is provides a social channel for experiments in mutual compatibility (for both the girl's and the youth's consent are necessary for a marriage), free from the pressures and responsibilities that attend the formal recognition of affinal relations between a young husband and his parents- and siblings-in-law.

Young boys are recruited into the men's house by a ritual sponsor called a 'false' or 'substitute father'. This personage leads the (approximately) eight-year-old boy out of his parental household (while his parents and relatives sit wailing 'for dead fathers', among other deceased relatives) and paints him black in the middle of the village plaza. After this the 'substitute father' leads the boy into the men's house. The wife of the 'substitute father', also called the boy's 'substitute mother', then brings him a meal and a load of firewood in his new domicile, which he shares out among his age-mates (usually several boys are inducted together, and there are normally some previously inducted but still uninitiated boys who thus form part of the same age set as the new boys). A boy's true mother and sisters assume these logistical functions after the first symbolic contribution by the 'substitute mother'.

The effect of adoption by the 'substitute' father and mother is not to sever the boy's practical ties of economic dependence on his natal family, but to end his further social ties with his parents and household for purposes of his further social development. In more specific terms, it transfers the formal social setting of his status as an older boy and adolescent from his natal household and family to the men's house. In this new setting, the boy's previous social identity, based on his individual membership in his restricted family and his personal relationship to his parents, is submerged in the egalitarian, homogeneous group of age-mates, and their subordination in turn, on a collective basis, to the older age sets and sub-sets of initiated youths and 'fathers' within the hierarchical structure of the men's house.

In the men's house, in other words, a boy first loses (for all public purposes) the individual identity that goes with membership in a particular family, and acquires the qualities of adult male identity at a collective level of social existence in which his own individual identity counts for little as such. Only after intitiation and a period of experimental relations with the opposite sex, of which society takes no formal notice, is he regarded as ready to take on a socially meaningful individual identity again, as a 'father', that is, as the head of a particular family. Even this relatively 'individualised' status is, as we have seen, of a subordinate and limited nature. The full development of socially sanctioned autonomous individuality and self-expression only occurs at the *end* of a man's term as a father of young children, that is, at the dispersal of his restricted or 'nuclear' family. It is then, the transcendence of the relatively low level of social organisation represented by the restricted family, with its subordinate position within the extended family household, and the resulting accession to the linked statuses of grandfather, father-in-law and head of the extended family household, that lays the social foundation for the full development and assertion of 'individuality' as defined in Kayapó culture.

The male age grade (category) and age set (group) structure of the Kayapó as I have described it may be summarised in the following table, in which each age grade and sub-grade is followed by its distinctive social characteristic or recruitment relation in parentheses.

1 *Childhood* (approximately 0 – 8 years. Residence in natal household)

2 *Adolescence: Unmarried youths* (Residence in men's house)
a 'Painted ones' (induction into collective age set and men's house by 'false' father and mother)
b 'Bachelors' (initiation, a *pro forma* marriage establishing general marriageability)

3 *Adulthood: 'Fathers'* (Residence in wife's household)
a 'Young fathers' (consummation of marriage by becoming *true* father; a son-in-law)
b 'Fathers of many children' (dispersal of nuclear family, becoming a father-in-law and head of household)
c 'Elders' (aged men retired from active role of household head and participant in men's collective activities)

Women are also grouped into a series of collective age grade categories and age set groupings based on them. At around eight years of age, when boys are inducted into the men's house, girls are recognised as moving into an age grade whose Kayapó name can be most directly translated as 'big little girls'. The name emphasises the continuity of the social status of the adolescent girl with that of the 'little girl', as female infants are called. The social basis of this continuity is, of course, that girls, in contrast to boys, do not leave their natal families or households as this point in their life cycle. There is no 'women's house' analogous to the men's house.

'Big little girls', however, do take part as a group in communal rituals, and thus comprise a collective age set, although it lacks any formal organisation. Girls of this and the following age sub-grade are classified within a more general age grade of unmarried girls, which effectively corresponds to adolescence. At the time girls are judged ready for motherhood, that is, for marriage in the fully consummated sense (this is usually in the later 'teens, when they are full-grown), they go through a rite of passage almost identical with the boys' ceremony of induction into the men's house. The girl is ritually adopted by a 'false' or 'substitute mother' (whose husband also becomes the girl's 'substitute father'). The 'false mother' leads her out of her parents' household and paints her thighs, breasts and upper arms with broad stripes of black paint. This rite establishes her general marriageability and readiness to start a family, in a way analogous to the broadly contemporaneous boys' initiation.

With this public painting, the girl becomes a member of a new age grade called 'black-thighed ones' (much as the boys of the youngest men's house age grade are called 'painted ones', after their similar rite of passage, which involves an all-over paint job). With membership in this age category, the young woman becomes a member of a collective women's society, composed of the wives of the younger men of a given men's house. In a village with two men's houses, she joins the wives of the men's house to which her 'substitute mother' is attached; if the man she marries belongs to the opposite men's house, however, she shifts her membership to the women's society attached to his men's house.

The younger women's society consists of the newly inducted 'black thighed ones' plus young women who are still in their active childbearing phase. The latter form a distinct age sub-grade, designated 'mothers of few children'. This category corresponds exactly in conceptual terms to the men's sub-grade of 'young-fathers'. After a woman's children have begun to grow up and her family begins to break up (her sons moving to the men's house and her daughters beginning to have suitors), that is, when she approaches the status of grandmother/mother-in-law, she moves up to a senior age grade called 'mothers of many children'. This age grade corresponds to the men's 'fathers of many children', but is the basis among the women of a separate age set, the senior women's society. The chief activities of the two women's societies are to organise an annual women's ritual and to meet every ten days to a fortnight to paint one another. As among men, the oldest women may withdraw from active participation in the collective activities of their society to the status of 'elders', an equally honorific status for women as for men.

Women of the senior women's age set of 'mothers of many children', who are nearing or fulfilling the status of female household-head, grandmother and mother-in-law, are as self-assured, assertive, and inde-

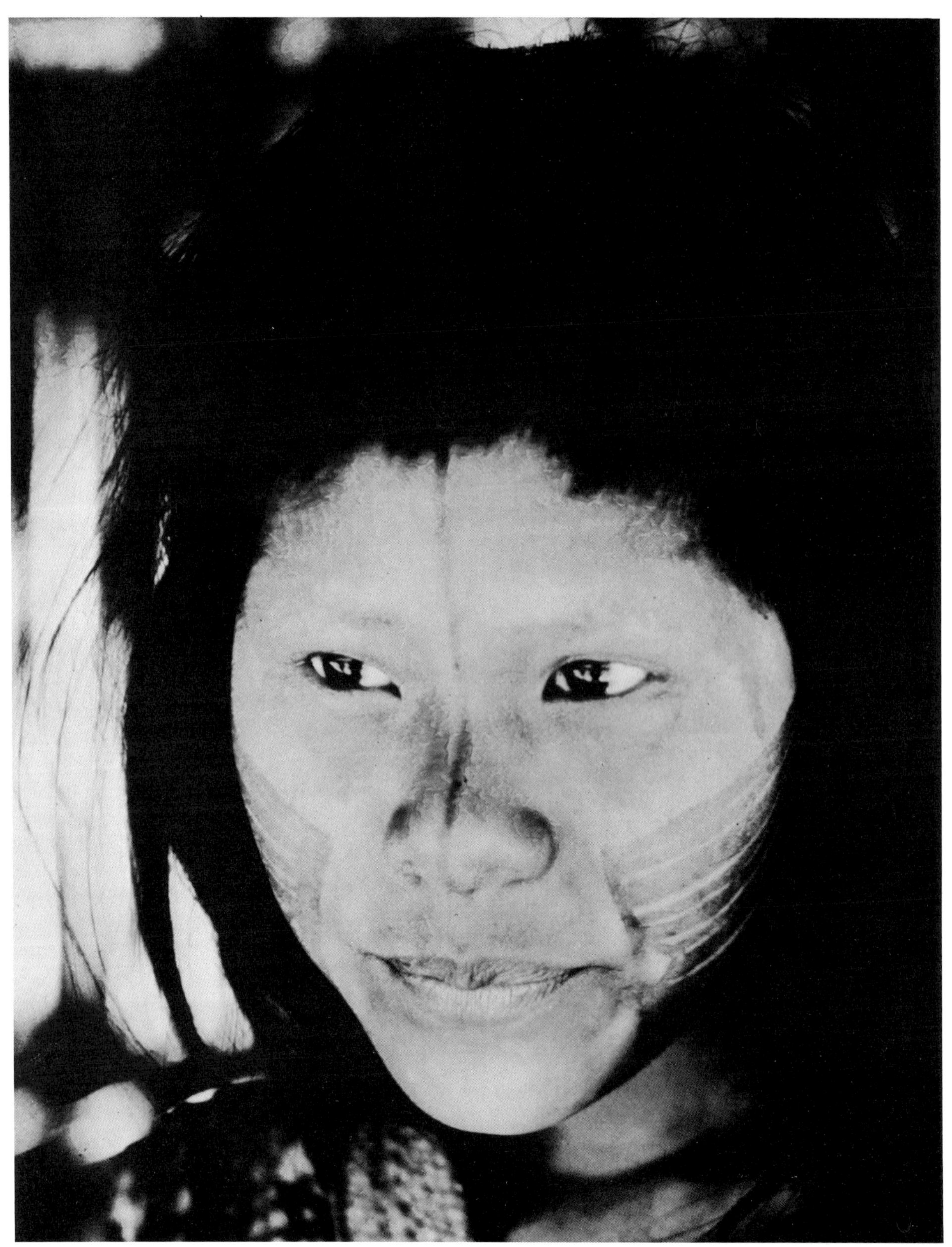

pendent in their comportment in their own social domains, to wit, their own households and the collective activities of their age set, as are men of the corresponding male age sub-grade. The difference between them lies in the nature and scope of the socially prescribed settings of male and female activities, rather than in the degree of socially sanctioned self-assertiveness and prestige within the domains allotted to each.

Opposite page
A black thighed one remains in this age set until the birth of her first child.

The women's age grade and age set structure as described above can be summarised in the following chart:

1 *Childhood* (approximately through 8 years)

2 *Adolescence: Unmarried Girls*

a 'Big little girls' (unorganised as age set)
b 'Black-thighed ones' (adoption by 'false' mother and father; generalised marriageability; induction into younger women's age set society)

3 *Adulthood: 'Mothers' of 'few' and 'many' children*

a 'Mothers of few children' (wives of 'young fathers')
b 'Mothers of many children' (wives of 'fathers of many children', mothers-in-law, heads of households; induction into senior women's age set society)
c 'Elders'

The formal structure of society as a programme for its own reproduction

The abbreviated description of Kayapó communal institutions that has been provided up to this point suffices to show that the men's house is only a part, albeit the focal part, of a more complex set of collective categories and groupings based upon 'age' or 'generational' criteria (age grades and age sets, respectively) which comprehensively include the adolescent and adult population of both sexes. I have placed the words 'age' and 'generation' in quotation marks because although the age grade and age set groupings of Kayapó society constitute a 'ladder' of socially defined age categories, it is clear that these categories are not defined in terms of abstract age, for example, in numbers of years, but rather in terms of positions in the structure of family and household relations. The communal structure of Kayapó society, in short, can be seen as a generalised projection of the life cycle of Kayapó men and women, as defined in terms of the successive 'moves' made by each sex through the structure of the extended family household. For a man, this would mean moving from son to son-in-law, to becoming a father and then a father-in-law. By this I do not mean to imply that Kayapó communal institutions are merely reflections of family and household organisation, considered as more basic, pre-existing, or independent realities. On the contrary: from the opposite (top-down) point of view, the organisation of Kayapó society at the communal level can be understood as a kind of collective mechanism or programme for guiding the process of forming and dispersing families in such a way as to reproduce the structure of the Kayapó extended family household.

This can most easily be grasped by considering the most puzzling aspect of the communal groupings we have examined so far: the role of the 'false parents' as the sponsors of both boys' and girls' membership in organised age sets. The effect of adoption by the 'false' or 'substitute parent' in both cases is not to sever or destroy the relationship between parent and child. It obviously continues the parental relationship both in its terminology and in the relation of tutelage or sponsorship between the 'substitute parent' and the adopted 'son' or 'daughter'. The effect is rather to separate this relationship from its previous focus (the family) and to transfer it to a new social setting. The fulcrum of the shift is the men's house for both sexes, but the nature of the shift involved has the opposite character, in terms of household and family structure, for boys and young women, respectively.

The adoption of a boy by his 'substitute parents' links his separation from his parental family with his separation from his parental *household* during the balance of his 'natural' period of childhood/adolescence (i.e. the period *before* he is ready to become attached through marriage to another family and household). The tutelage of the 'false' father, together with the separation from his natal family and household entailed by residence in the men's house under the 'false' father's aegis, comes to an end at the point when the boy becomes a 'true' father in his own right, and moves from the men's house into his wife's household. The adoption of a girl, or rather, a young woman (since it is through the rite of adoption that she moves from the social category of girlhood to that of young womanhood) links her separation from her parental family with her marriage and consequent attachment to her family of procreation within the *same household.* The rite establishes her general marriageability, in a way analogous to the initiation ceremony for boys. The age set into which it inducts her, the younger women's society, is continuous with that of young wives and mothers, and is formally tied to marriage to the younger male category of 'fathers' in the men's house.

The symbolic tutelage of the women of the junior women's society by their 'substitute' mothers, established by the induction rite, is only terminated when the women pass on to the senior women's society at the *dispersal* of their families of procreation (i.e. as they approach grandmother/mother-in-law status). Women, in other words, are defined for purposes of household and family structure by the symbolic structure of the age set system as 'children' (or perhaps our category of legally dependent 'minors' would be a more accurate gloss) during their years as active mothers of families. The basic principle of the structure of the Kayapó extended family is, as we have seen, that men must move away from the households into which they are born and move into the households in which they marry. The Kayapó place great emphasis on the separation of men from their parental households and their integration into the households of their wives. This arrangement, left to itself, might be expected to give rise to an insoluble 'contradiction'; the more the attachment of the husband, in his capacity as father, to the wife's household is emphasised, the more completely must sons be separated from their fathers' households and families to repeat the pattern of attachment to *their* wives' households in the next generation. The more strongly fatherhood is emphasised, in other words, the more strongly must the ties of sons to their fathers be severed in order to perpetuate the pattern.

This 'contradiction', of course, never arises in the Kayapó system because of the removal of sons, under the aegis of the 'substitute father' from their fathers' households during the crucial period in which their fathers are emerging to dominance within those households, following their initial period of subordination to their parents-in-law. This removal is, in turn, the precondition for the emphatic integration of young husbands, in their capacity as 'fathers', into their wives' households. The male age set system, operating through the institutions of the men's house and the 'substitute' parent, thus makes possible the pattern of male relationships required by the Kayapó family and household.

The female pattern of relations inculcated by the women's age set system represents the necessary complement to the male pattern that has just been described, given the structural requirements of the extended family. An extended family is based upon ties *between* the minimal family units that go to make it up. Kayapó extended families, as we have seen, are based upon the emphatic severance of the family ties of the male offspring to their parents and the corresponding emphasis upon the attachment of sons-in-law to their wives' parents. This places a premium upon the *continuity* of the attachment of female offspring to their parental families after their marriages. Since this attachment is the connecting link between a woman's husband and her parents, it becomes the inter-family tie that is the basis of the structure of the extended family. This is the reason for the extension of the woman's status as 'child' or 'minor' (in effect, the extension of her family bond to her parents) beyond the boundaries

Kukrut as a senior member of the father's age-set wears a relatively large lip disc.

of her parental family into her own family of procreation: by this means, she is transformed into the inter-family link through which her family of procreation is subordinated to the control of her parents. This link is the foundation of the structure of the extended family household. The men's and women's collective age grades and sets, for all their apparent differences in structure, thus appear to be different combinations of the same set of elements. This set of elements consists, in turn, of the basic relationships that make up the structure of the Kayapó family and extended family. The different combinations of relational elements in the collective male and female age organisations correspond exactly to the different combinations of these elements in the roles of males and females within the extended family system.

Taken together, the male and female age set organisation, as embodied in the men's house and women's age societies, may thus be considered a kind of collective programme for the replication of the Kayapó extended family structure. The communal structure of Kayapó society can thus be understood as an extrapolation of the structure of its basic 'segmentary' unit, the extended family household. This structural relation can in turn be understood as the product of the functional relation between the two, wherein the communal institutions serve as the social mechanism for reproducing and regulating the extended family household.

One of the general inferences that can be drawn from this analysis is that a society's notions of 'generation' and 'age grade' ('child', 'adolescent', 'adult', etc.), sex roles, and other general social categories arise from and reflect the key social processes in which people of the categories in question are involved. Another is that the collective institutions and structures of a society derive their structure from their functions of creating and reproducing certain fundamental patterns of relations at the most basic levels of social organisation.

Kayapó society as a political system of prestige. *Values or what is at stake for the Kayapó*

The foregoing account of Kayapó family and social institutions is not offered merely as an exercise in formal analysis. The formal structure of systems of social relations and cultural categories is the expression of the organisation and co-ordination of processes, relations, and forces at a deeper level, and is thus the surest guide to the nature and identity of those forces. These underlying forces and relations must in turn be understood before it becomes possible to explain what is really at stake in the acts and behavioural patterns through which men and women sustain and recreate (or occasionally transform) their social order. Why, we want to know, do the Kayapó bother with extended families and the elaborate superstructure of age sets and men's houses that goes with them? What values are at stake for the actors on the social stage? This general question may now be addressed by examining the relationship between the formal structure of social relations discussed in the previous section and what can, in the largest sense, be called the political aspect of Kayapó society. I use the term 'politics' to denote the processes through which access to socially valued attributes and possessions is regulated, and the organisation of prestige, authority, dominance and subordination that results from different degrees of control of these valued attributes by different persons and groups in the society as a whole. Some degree of competitive struggle, tension, conflict, and resulting instability is an inevitable result of such processes and the unequal distribution of values to which they lead. The Kayapó are certainly no exception to this rule.

The process of reproducing the structure of the extended family household is the most complex, and therefore the most demanding in terms of its organisational requirements, in Kayapó social life. No process of economic production, distribution or consumption, for example, even approaches it in this respect. This is the reason for its central importance, as the predominant focus of the formal structure of Kayapó society as a whole. For the same reason, the various forms of constraint and subordination, and their complements, freedom from constraint, autonomy and dominance, defined within the framework of extended family structure, both at its individual household and communal levels of projection, are the most highly valued attributes of Kayapó social identity.

This argument can, with equal merit, be stated the other way round: the process of reproducing the extended family household, and the concomitant process of recruiting and thus reproducing the whole hierarchy of age sets that make up the social structure of the community as a whole, can be regarded as a mechanism for generating certain social values and producing differential access to them. The essence of the 'values' in question lies in the contrast between the social restraint or subordination imposed upon those at the lower levels of household and age set structure, and the social autonomy, assertiveness, and dominance of those at the highest level.

The structure of the Kayapó extended family forces young sons-in-law and young wives and mothers (i.e. those actually engaged in the production of new families) to surrender a significant degree of their autonomy as social actors in exchange for membership in an organisation (the extended family) controlled by those no longer actively engaged in such production. Control of this organisation, vested in the roles of father- and mother-in-law is the only means of acquiring full social autonomy and escaping the subordination and constraint imposed upon those forced to join the extended family in junior capacities. What I have called the process of the reproduction of the structure of the extended family household is a gradual process of exchange of the key values of dominance and subordination, whereby the senior generation of the household gradually yields its monopoly of the dominant position in exchange for a prolonged period of deference and subordination on the part of their married daughters and sons-in-law.

This pattern of subordination and domination, and the gradual process of exchange of one for the other accompanying the ascent of the generational ladder, is also present, as I have already briefly described, in the communal age set system focused upon the organisation of the men's house. Just as the structure of the age set system can be seen as a generalised expression of the key steps in the reproduction of the extended family household, so the social relations and values of subordination and dominance at the communal level can be seen as generalised counterparts of the concrete relations of deference and leadership at the household level. Politics at the communal level (which means, in effect, men's house politics) is essentially a business of manipulating and exchanging these generalised relational values of subordination and dominance. I shall now attempt to illustrate these propositions with a brief account of the political aspects of the Kayapó age set system.

The political aspects of the age set organisation

'Bachelors' play a prominent and distinctive role in village affairs. Barred from direct participation in the councils and activities of the adult men's or 'fathers'' societies, they nevertheless compete with the older men in the vigour, style and assertiveness with which they carry out whatever collective activities are determined by the latter, whether these be of a ceremonial, labouring, military or merely sporting nature. In activities of all of these categories, the bachelor youths and the adult men or 'fathers' tend to be opposed to each other as the complementary halves of the total society, or, more specifically, of the collective social undertaking or activity at hand. In collective work projects such as garden-clearing or some types of hunting and gathering expeditions, the bachelors usually work together as a separate team, in competition with the older men. In indigenous sports such as Kayapó field hockey or ceremonial wrestling, the 'bachelors' form one of the two competing teams, and the 'fathers' the other. In collective ceremonies, the 'bachelors' and 'fathers' make up distinct segments of the dancing line.

The competitive rivalry of 'bachelors' and 'fathers' is thus the most prominent single feature of the age set system. This rivalry is grounded in the positions of the men of each set in the process of dispersing and forming families within the framework of the extended family household. The life of the 'bachelor' youths is highly valued by the Kayapó for its qualities of freedom

In ritual the men often split up in age sets, both in preparation and during ceremonies.

and vigorous social assertiveness. The 'bachelors' are not only free of domestic responsibilities but have the socially sanctioned freedom to carry on affairs with whatever girls please them. They are not, however, autonomous, free and assertive as individuals, but only as a collective social group.

The strongly collective, virtually homogenised character of the activities of the bachelors' age set reflects their lack of particular attachments to individual households and families. It is, on the other hand, this very lack of ties to particular families and households that leads to their exclusion from the perquisites of full social responsibility, which remain the prerogative of those counted capable of acting as autonomous social *individuals* (i.e. mature men). This means, above all, participation in the councils and decisions of the adult men's ('fathers') age set.

Adulthood, or what in our society would be called 'legal responsibility' is thus contingent in Kayapó society upon the assumption of marital responsibilities and affinal attachments to a family and the household in which it is embedded. The acquisition of such attachments and responsibilities, as we have seen, is an onerous business at first; the young husband must serve a long probationary period of relatively intense deference and self-restraint in the household of his in-laws (precisely the opposite of the carefree, if collectively conformist, assertiveness of the bachelor youth). The step from bachelor-hood to marriage is thus surrounded with reluctance and ambivalence for a bachelor; it represents the indispensable step towards freedom from the constraints and subordination imposed upon the socially immature, and thus towards the full, individualistically assertive manhood of the senior men of the 'fathers' age grade, the 'fathers-of-many-children'. In the short run, however, it leads to a relative loss of social freedom and autonomy, in the form of the subordination of the 'young father' to his parents-in-law.

Often the front group in the dancing line will be older men and the back younger men.

The 'bachelors' and the 'fathers' thus face each other across the great social divide of marriage and the relatively onerous subordination this entails (at first, at least) for a young husband in his wife's parents' household. From the standpoint of the 'fathers', young girls engaged in tentative liaisons (as yet unconsummated by childbirth) with the bachelors are fair game for extra-marital sexual relations. Bachelors, whose feelings for their fiancées may be decidedly untentative, typically resent such incursions, but ordinarily find it difficult to do anything about them.

There are a number of culturally sanctioned forms of extra-marital sexual relations among the Kayapó. Some of these involve the collective intercourse of a whole age set or men's society with one or more women. Usually, the latter are drawn from the ranks of 'unmarried' girls and women, that is, primarily, the fiancées of the young men of the 'bachelors' age set (with a smattering of widows and unengaged single women). The 'fathers' not infrequently send the 'bachelors' off on a long gathering expedition and in their absence appropriate their fiancées for their own sexual purposes. Occasions of this kind, in spite of their cultural sanction, give rise to considerable bitterness and resentment on the part of the 'bachelors'. Duels with war-clubs (for which a formal code of rules exists, calculated to prevent disabling or fatal blows to parts of the body such as the head and genitals, and based on a strict blow-for-blow format in which the adversaries take turns bashing each other until a 'technical knock-out' is achieved by one of the parties), some of them between 'bachelors' and 'fathers', are a recognised part of communal life. Sometimes these reach collective proportions, and the Kayapó tell of occasions when such collective battles between 'bachelors' and 'fathers', motivated by sexual jealousy, actually led to the splitting of whole villages and the founding of separate communities by the two embittered age sets.

The collective solidarity of the 'bachelors' age set, or in other words, the strength of their common attachment to the men's house, is based upon the stringency of their separation from their natal households. The structure of Kayapó society, both at the household and the communal level, as we have seen above, is based upon the balance between the separation of sons from their parents' household and the attachment of fathers to the households in which they become parents. The solidarity of the 'fathers'' age set is the direct concomitant of the strength of this attachment. There is, in short, ideally a balance between 'bachelors' and 'fathers' age sets in so far as the strength of their collective solidarity is concerned. This solidarity, however, is expressed in opposite ways that reflect the opposite characteristics of the social bases of solidarity of each group: negative separation from the household in the one case and positive attachment in the other.

The age set status of the senior members of the 'fathers' age set is based on their position as the heads of individual households. They have arrived, as individuals, by a process of progressive exchange of subordinate attachment to their wives' households for dominance within them. As household heads they have gained freedom from the subordinating constraints of extended family and household structure analogous in important respects to the freedom the 'bachelors' have acquired through the simpler, collectively-based process of separation from their particular natal households. The stereotypic comportment of the senior men of the 'fathers' age grade (as exemplified, for instance, in their most characteristic public activity, oratory) is one of aggressive self-assertion as *socially autonomous individuals*, analogous in many respects to the aggressive self-assertiveness of the bachelors as members of a *socially undifferentiated collectively*, except, of course, that the 'fathers' also dispose of the instruments of publicly sanctioned political dominance and authority.

The senior men of the 'fathers' age set owe their position of political dominance as well as their social recognition as individuals capable of independent political action to their status as heads of households. At the most basic level of political organisation, Kayapó society is an egalitarian coalition of extended family households. The problem of the political integration of the society as a whole is, then, a problem of integrating the heads of these segmentary household units into a unified political structure strong enough to offset the centrifugal tendencies inherent in any coalition of egalitarian and potentially autonomous social units.

Returning to the tension between the 'bachelors' and 'fathers', we can now see that the latent conflict between them has firm roots in the structure of the social system. The very complementarity of structural positions (e.g. separation and attachment to households) that renders the 'fathers' dominant over the 'bachelors', and thus able to abuse their dominance, also renders the 'bachelors' the equals of the fathers in the crucial matter of effective age set solidarity, and thus provides them with the basis for effective resistance. It is not only the forms of solidarity and integration at the household level that are incorporated into the structure of communal institutions, but the forms of tension and conflict associated with them. This, too, is part of the problem of communal integration that must be overcome by a viable political structure.

Kayapó communal institutions provide such a viable focus of communal political integration because they provide an arena in which the male heads of particular households can compete for generalised forms of the values of prestige, authority and dominance associated with the leading position in the household, elevated to the more potent level of attributes of communal leadership and authority.

These attributes of household leadership become 'generalised' and 'raised to the communal level' through the organisation of the communal men's house institutions. The top position in the hierarchy of age sets and sub-sets within the men's house is in a precise structural sense a counterpart of the top position in the individual household, but with all of the additional prestige and authority inherent in a communal institution. The fact that at the communal level this position can be occupied by an entire sub-set of the 'fathers' age set makes possible a degree of egalitarian competition for marginal increments of public prestige (e.g. through oratorical prowess) without threatening the basic perquisites of individual autonomy and dominance that are the inherent attributes of membership in the sub-set of 'fathers of many children'. Kayapó communities tend to stay together in large part because the communal life of the men's house is simply more interesting, as the source of more highly valued attributes of social identity, than the life of the individual households for their politically crucial members: their male heads.

There may be more than one society of 'fathers' found among the members of the 'fathers' age set within a single men's house, and as indicated earlier, there can be two men's houses in a single village, each with its own 'fathers' society or societies. The relationship among plural men's societies of the same community is egalitarian; each forms an autonomous political unit in its own right, with its own chief (or chiefs; a society may have more than one such leader).

The members of each men's society are bound by custom to behave respectfully and with restraint towards members of other men's societies in contexts where society membership is important (for instance, during collective meetings and debates). Individuals of any age or sex, but particularly senior men, also run the risk of becoming the butts of communal satire for seeming overly assertive, conceited or otherwise self-centered. Kayapó has a rich vocabulary of mocking expressions to put in their place individuals who overstep the fine line between acceptable self-assertion and self-aggrandisement at the expense of the bonds of reciprocity and interdependence that tie a person to others and to the community as a whole: 'the one who walks like a duck' (i.e., so heavy with self-importance that he or she waddles rather than walks); 'the one who is always crying about him (or her-) self'; 'the one who always chooses the best things for him (or her-) self', etc. Such informal sanctions are very effective in constraining public behaviour within acceptable limits. At the highest level of social organisation, where the co-ordination of the 'segmentary' or structurally equal households making up the community must be achieved, strong anti-hierarchical values like the condemnation of undue self-assertiveness, pride or selfishness, and the emphasis upon positive generosity, interdependence and reciprocity thus operate to restrain and contain the competition for prestige and dominance within limits compatible with the basic structural equality of the household heads actively engaged in it.

There is no paramount authority above the level of the chiefs of the particular 'fathers' societies. Within a single society with more than one chief, moreover, each in principle stands on an equal footing with the others. All chiefs of the 'fathers' societies, on the other hand, are invested with a rather vague and diffuse authority over the community as a whole. The Kayapó title for 'chief' means literally 'he who delivers the ritual chant'. This refers to the role that must be performed by a chief, in certain *communal* rituals, of chanting in a special falsetto manner. Aside from his ritual functions, the chief also performs other functions on behalf of the whole community; he articulates, as orders for the village as a whole, the decisions reached by the men of the 'fathers' society or societies in council; he leads communal labour projects and distributes trade goods brought into the community by Brazilians; and his oratorical exhortations carry a moral *cachet* for the entire community. Each chief nonetheless owes his position to his role as the leader of his own 'fathers' society. In his public functions he must therefore strive to reconcile the particular interests of his men's society with those of the community at large, since to fall into the position of advocating either against the other must undermine either his base of political support or the communal legitimacy and authority of his office.

Chiefs attain their position, and afterwards retain it, through the support and willingness of men of a 'fathers' society to follow their leadership. There is no principle of inheritance of office in one family or descent-line. A chief thus embodies in the highest degree the competitive egalitarian individualism that characterises the 'fathers' age set as a whole. Chiefs are the winners, as individuals, of the competition for prestige and leadership within their societies. By virtue of their triumph, however, they become identified, through the duties and attributes of their office, with the solidarity of the community as a whole, and thus become the functional links between the interests of communal integration and the competitive individualism of their own societies. The chieftaincy is thus both the highest expression and reconciliation of individualistic dominance and automony, on the one hand, and collective egalitarian interdependence on the other that are the fundamental values of the Kayapó political system.

Further reading

TURNER, T. S. *Tchikrin: a central Brazilian tribe and its symbolic language of bodily adornment* in *Natural History* vol. LXXVIII, no. 8. October 1969. pp. 50–59.

TURNER, T. S. *The Gê and Bororo societies as dialectical systems* in *Dialectical societies* edited by D. Maybury-Lewis. Harvard University Press, due Autumn 1978.

TURNER, T. S. *Kinship, household and community structure among the Kayapó* in *Dialectical societies* edited by D. Maybury-Lewis. Harvard University Press, due Autumn 1978.

Further general reading part two

BATESON, G and MEAD, M. *Balinese character: a photographic analysis* New York: Lyceum and Natural History now the Academy of Sciences, 1942.

BELO, J. *The Balinese temper* in *Character and Personality* vol. 4, 1935, pp. 120–46.

BELO, J. ed. *Traditional-Balinese culture* Columbia University Press, 1970.

BOISSEVAIN, J. *Some notes on the position of women in Maltese society* in *Nord Nytt* vol. 3, 1972, pp. 196–213.

BOISSEVAIN, J. *Saints and fireworks* (London School of Economics, Monographs on social anthropology, no. 30) Athlone Press, 1965.

BOISSEVAIN, J. *Hal-Farrug: a village in Malta* Holt, Rinehart and Winston, 1969.

CAPLAN, A. P. *Choice and constraint in a Swahili community: property, hierarchy and cognatie descent on the East African coast* OUP for the International African Institute, 1975.

CAPLAN, A. P. *Boys' circumcision and girls' puberty rites among the Swahili of Mafia Island, Tanzania* in *Africa* vol. 46, no. 1, 1976, pp. 21–23.

GEERTZ, C. *Peddlars and princes: social change and economic modernization in two Indonesian towns* University of Chicago Press, 1963.

GEERTZ, C. *Deep play: notes on the Balinese cockfight* in *Daedalus* Winter 1972.

GEERTZ, C., and H. *Kinship in Bali* University of Chicago Press, 1975.

LEVI-STRAUSS, C. *Tristes tropiques* Cape, 1973; Penguin Books, 1976.

SUTHERLAND, A. *Gypsies: the hidden Americans* Tavistock Publications, 1975.

SUTHERLAND, A. *The body as a social symbol among the Rom* in Anthropology of the body Seminar Press, 1977.

TURNER, T. S. *Tchikrin: a central Brazilian tribe and its symbolic language of bodily adornment* in *Natural History*, New York vol. LXXVIII, no. 8 October 1969, pp. 50–59.

TURNER, T. S. *The Ge and Bororo societies as dialectical systems* in *Dialectic societies* edited by Harvard University Press, due Autumn 1978.

TURNER, T. S. *Kinship, household and community structure among the Kayapo* in *Dialectical societies* edited by D. Maybury-Lewis ibid.

Glossary

Category — A class or division in a scheme of classification examples. Humans and animals are two categories of living organisms.

Class — see *Category*.

Culture — 'That complex whole which include knowledge, belief, art, morals, laws, customs, and any other capabilities and habits acquired by man as a member of society.' (TYLER, *Primitive Culture*, 1871, 3rd ed, vol 2, London: Murray.)

This definition is still current in anthropology. Modern definitions refer to the 'organisation of experience shared by members of a community', including 'their standards for perceiving, predicting, judging and acting'. Anthropologists never use this word in its popular sense of education and the arts. To anthropologists culture is a characteristic feature of all human societies; each people can be said to have a distinctive culture.

Group — A number of persons who share some social relationship. A group implies some form of organisation.

Examples: 'woman' is a category; the Women's Institute is a group of women.

Metaphor — Relates two ideas, categories or other references by associated implication. The meaning of two thoughts supported by a single word or phrase, will be a result of their interaction. Metaphor has a dynamic aspect. It engenders thought by bringing together two ideas.

Examples: the poor are the Negroes of Europe; There is a wind of change in society; The growth of the village (social relations are likened to plant or animal growth).

Role — The socially prescribed behaviour appropriate to a particular status.

Example: the role of the woman in Britain has changed from that of her predecessors.

Status

1 A socially defined position which implies rights and duties.

Examples: teacher, mother, trade-unionist, bachelor, grandfather.

2 Relative prestige.

Example: 'The status of teachers has declined.' 'He has high status in the community.'

Anthropologists tend to use status in its first meaning and use prestige or rank for the second idea.

Structure

Form as opposed to content. Structure is used in social anthropology with several levels of meaning.

Harris: 'Structure is the order in a system'. The more stable aspects of roles action and interrelationships.

Structure is also used to refer to an *ideal model* of the society.

Examples: The structure of a village refers both to its layout and the organisation of villagers.

The structure of a university is formed of its constituent parts, the roles of different teachers, administrators and students. The structure of ideas implies the interrelation of ideas in a (more or less) coherent whole.

Symbol

An arbitrary but conventional association between two or more references.

'A material object or quality taken to represent something immaterial or abstract.' *Shorter OED*.

Symbols typically condense many related meanings in a single powerful image.

Examples: The serpent is a symbol of evil. White is a symbol of purity. The national flag is a patriotic symbol.

Ritual

Sometimes called social dramas, rites, ceremonies. A patterned sequence of events with symbolic meaning. Ritual may be private or public, secular or religious.

Index

Italic figures indicate illustrations

Acknowledgements

Acknowledgement is due to the following for permission to reproduce photographs:

AGENCE HOA-QUI page 91; BARNABY'S PICTURE LIBRARY pages 31 (bottom), 39, 42, 44; BAYERISCHE STAATSBIBLIOTHEK, MUNICH page 79; BIBLIOTHEQUE NATIONALE, PARIS page 85; JEREMY BOISSEVAIN pages 52, 57, 110, 111, 112, 114, 115, 116, 118, 121, 122, 126, 129, 132, 134, 137 (both), 138 (top); CAMERA PRESS LTD pages 38 (Bob Snyder), 40 (bottom), 46 (Chris Smith), 47 (A. G. Hutchinson), 48 (Charlotte March), 49 (In/Bild), 50 (Bill Coward), 58 (Edward Leahy), 72 (top left – R. B. Bedi), 72 (centre left – Tom Hanley), 72 (right – Terry O'Neill), 77 (top – Brian Weeks), 77 (bottom – Gary Freedman), 78 (John Kelly), 86 (David Channer), 88 (Sam Waagenaar), 89 (Horace Bristol), 102 (David Channer); PATRICIA CAPLAN pages 31 (top), 53, 54, 104 (top), 140 (both), 142, 144, 145, 148, 149, 150, 151, 152, 154, 166 (both), 169, 170, 171; DAVID EVANS front cover (bottom left) and pages 61, 62; MARY EVANS PICTURE LIBRARY page 32; ANTHONY FORGE pages 66, 210, 211, 214, 215, 216, 217, 218, 219 (both), 220, 221, 222, 223, 224, 225, 227, 228, 230, 234, 235, 236 (both), 237, 238 (both), 241, 242; R. GOULD front cover (top left) and pages 93, 94, 146, 156, 158, 162, 163, 164, 165; KEYSTONE PRESS AGENCY LTD page 36; THE MANSELL COLLECTION pages 18, 34, 35, 80; FRANCIS MORGAN front cover (top and bottom right) and page 189; AXEL POIGNANT pages 21, 103; RADIO TIMES HULTON PICTURE LIBRARY pages 19, 33, 40 (top), 69, 81, 82 (left), 87 (both), 95; PETER RAMSDEN pages 41, 51, 55, 60, 64 (top), 135, 138 (bottom), 139, 245, 246, 249, 254, 256 (top), 259, 261, 269, 273; IAN STONE pages 59, 73, 97, 98, 248, 250, 252, 253, 255 (both), 256 (bottom), 258, 262, 266, 272; STELLA STONE front cover (centre); ANNE SUTHERLAND pages 64 (bottom), 71, 74, 101, 104 (both), 178, 183 (top and bottom left), 184 (top), 185, 186, 188, 202 (top), 204, 205, 206; THE TRUSTEES OF THE BRITISH MUSEUM page 14; VICTORIA AND ALBERT MUSEUM (CROWN COPYRIGHT) pages 20, 100; WALLRAF-RICHARTZ MUSEUM, COLOGNE page 82 (right).

Acknowledgement is also due to:
GERALD DUCKWORTH & CO. LTD. for the drawings by Nicolas Bentley on page 37, reproduced from *Cautionary verses for children* by Hilaire Belloc.

The five societies